S.H.E.
Share • Heal • Empower.

Ava—
All Stories Matter,
including yours.

Shannon Hagan Cohen

COLLECTED JOURNEYS
Paired with Artwork

~VOLUME TWO~

Compiled and Composed by:
SHANNON HOGAN COHEN

DECKLE WAY PRESS
Del Mar, California

S.H.E. Share Heal Empower

Copyright © 2023 by Shannon Hogan Cohen

All rights reserved. No part of this publication may be reproduced, distributed, or transmitted in any form or by any means, including photocopying, recording, or other electronic or mechanical methods, without the prior written permission of the publisher, except in the case of brief quotations embodied in critical reviews and certain other noncommercial uses permitted by copyright law.

For permission requests:

DECKLE WAY PRESS

Attention: Permissions Coordinator
1155 Camino Del Mar, Suite 116
Del Mar, California, USA 92014

"Sharing stories — one uneven page at a time."

www.DeckleWayPress.com

Ordering Information:
Special discounts are available on quantity purchases by corporations, associations, and others. For details, contact the publisher.

Orders by U.S. trade bookstores and wholesalers:
Please visit www.ShareHealEmpower.com

Library of Congress Cataloging in Publication Data:
ISBN (paperback): 978-1-7320335-6-6
ISBN (eBook): 978-1-7320335-5-9
Library of Congress Control Number: 2018902026
1. Women's Non-Fiction 2. Inspiration and Motivation 3. Personal Growth

First Edition, Volume Two, 2023
Printed in the United States of America

10 9 8 7 6 5 4 3 2 1

Interior Design and Editing: Lorie Hopcus
S.H.E. Logo: Shelby Hogan
Front Cover Design: Aaftab Sheikh
Back Cover Artwork: Gretchen Belcher

This book is dedicated to all women worldwide—
there is no triumph without vulnerability and grit.

&

To my sons, Cole and Cody—
who enrich and enhance my life's purpose.

CONTENTS

Foreword ... ix
A Note From The Author ... xv
Chapters
- 01— Olivia and Danielle ... 1
- 02— Linda ... 19
- 03— Yuliya ... 40
- 04— Brittany ... 52
- 05— Alix ... 64
- 06— Bailey ... 78
- 07— Sharon ... 91
- 08— Dr. Debby ... 105
- 09— Izza ... 118
- 10— Mia ... 127
- 11— Tomoko ... 140
- 12— Monay ... 154
- 13— Ania ... 168
- 14— Jamie ... 184
- 15— Asha ... 199
- 16— Siri ... 213
- 17— Jen ... 227
- 18— Marina ... 244
- 19— Jane ... 257
- 20— Virginia ... 271
- 21— Charline ... 283
- 22— Ohafian Women Warriors ... 299

Artist Gallery Introduction ... 321
Artist Gallery ... 323
Artist Biographies ... 347
Acknowledgments ... 367
S.H.E. Foundation ... 370
About The Author ... 371

FOREWORD
~The Alchemist~

I met her not by chance, I believe, but by divine design. Imagine me walking down the main street that winds through the beautiful coastal enclave of Del Mar, California, on vacation back in September of 2021. Strolling with my husband, I was amazed to see a coffee shop called the Bohemian Alchemist. When I saw the décor—exotic Turkish rug-wrapped pillows, a cozy loveseat on the floor, and art objects from all parts of the world—there was no stopping me. The place felt just like the website describes it: like being part of an ancient caravan.

When the owner demonstrated her ceremonial process of preparing coffee in the time-honored Turkish tradition of warming the cup in a tray of sand to bring out the mellow flavors, I had to hang out for a while. It seemed to be just my kind of headquarters for creative thinking. No rushed cups of cappuccino here. This was a place to settle in, slow down, and enjoy the aesthetic.

As my husband and I waited for our order to be prepared, in walked a beautiful younger woman and her vibrant husband. I was immediately drawn to her. I believe it was a moment of soul recognition, one of those moments not to be ignored. The four of us started chatting, and soon my husband and hers were deep in conversation, and so were she and I. Given that human connection and exchange are deeply woven into the tradition of Turkish coffee consumption and enjoyment, I believe our meeting was meant to be. I've been blessed to call her a friend ever since.

I learned that lovely Shannon lived right there in Del Mar, and that she was an accomplished businesswoman, author, and seeker. Dedicated to the journey of knowing herself deeply and helping other women to know and appreciate themselves, I discovered that she had published a book and formed a foundation—both of them titled S.H.E. And, that she was already planning the second volume of collected S.H.E. stories.

Shannon has a deep interest in connecting with unsung "SHEROs," shedding light on the stories of incredible women from all corners of the world—stories of despair and discovery, struggle and salvation, hardship and healing. She recognizes these women, perhaps in the same way I recognized her—there is a kismet that occurs, a connection that sparks conversation and sharing. And through that sharing, Shannon weaves a magical mosaic that honors the art of storytelling, healing, and empowerment.

Like an actual mosaic, this complex creation requires discipline, perseverance, vision, and commitment to put together. It is far more involved than just a good idea. And so, I asked Shannon, "Why do you do all this? Why do you travel the world looking for women and their stories? Why the search for the right artist to pair with each storyteller?" "Connection," she replied. "I love connecting deeply with other women, particularly those who are vulnerable and brave enough to keep on trying to make themselves and their lives better, not only for themselves, but for their loved ones. I love casting a light on these women, as we all long to be seen."

In this collection, you'll meet Danielle and Olivia, a mother and daughter who are working to heal old wounds and to create change in themselves and their relationship. I think this

FOREWORD

story will speak to everyone with a mother, and to every mother with a daughter. And also resonate with anyone struggling for more intimacy and authenticity.

You'll meet Linda, a survivor of a very serious case of COVID-19. This is a woman who not only survived, but chose to thrive, and was motivated by the love for and from her family. For me, her story is food for thought about the role of familial love in the process of healing.

Yuliya is a testament to courage and to putting one's child first. She fled Ukraine with her young son. Facing the enormous trauma of war, she had to make a quick decision to put the lives of her son and herself ahead of being able to stay in her homeland, where her husband had to remain. Again, you'll see how strong the role of familial love and connection is in this poignant story.

I knew nothing about the Ohafia people from an Igbo town in Abia State, Nigeria—until I read the powerful story of the Umu Olugu clan of women and their matriarch, Chief Miennaya, her daughters, and her granddaughters. The matrilineal tradition and the fierce, loving values that has held this lineage together are inspirational.

The process of collecting and sharing these stories, and all the other ones you'll find in this book, is inspiring. Shannon has gathered these remarkable narratives—illuminating stories of courage, of discovery, of fortitude, of perseverance, of strength, of love and loss—to honor the journeys of these SHEROs. In so doing, she enlightens us with a greater understanding and empathy for the many roads that women are traveling. It is a remarkable caravan of connection.

S.H.E. SHARE HEAL EMPOWER

There is an irony and poignancy to my meeting Shannon that summer day at Bohemian Alchemist, as I believe she is a storytelling alchemist—weaving impactful narratives from the magical connections she fosters with women from all walks of life and circumstance.

I invite you to join me in exploring this collection of journeys. And as you explore, you might wonder: What story might you tell about your own journey? How might sharing your story offer you greater healing and empowerment?

One last comment about my fortuitous meeting of Shannon. When she asked me to write this foreword, she instantly began an alchemical process within me. I will be 80 by the time you read this, and my life is full of blessings. Yet, at the same time, I am still on the lifelong journey of transformation and discovery. Shannon drew me in, as she effortlessly draws in the women in her books, at such a pivotal point in life. Her invitation to contribute to S.H.E. came as I was feeling burdened by double vision and a parade of physical problems that had plagued my family—bringing my own writing and artistry to a halt. I thought maybe I was through contributing. But my younger friend lit a spark in me. I thought, *if I could write this foreword for Shannon, then could I also find ways to keep on creating?* As I pondered this thought, I immediately sensed something transformational happening. I felt seen—not unlike the many SHEROs in Shannon's books. And feeling seen allowed me to again see myself, my worth, and my continued potential. Meeting Shannon was a gift in a multitude of ways. And now in my 80s, I find this incredibly inspiring. Thank you, Shannon, for being you and for bringing all of these amazing and inspiring SHEROs' stories to our attention.

~ By Pamela Hale

FOREWORD

Pamela Hale, MA, has been a spiritual director, energy healer, life coach, and photographic artist. She is the author of the award-winning book, <u>Flying Lessons: How to Be the Pilot of Your Own Life</u>, creator of the <u>Sand Spirits Insight Cards</u>, workbook and trainings, and creator of the photographic fabric creations called Earthskin Designs™. Pam lives outside Tucson, Arizona, with her husband. She is the mother of two daughters, grandmother of five, and is looking forward to the birth of her first great-grandchild.

Website: Pamelahale.net
Email: pam@ThroughADifferentLens.com
Instagram: @pamhaletrachta

A NOTE FROM THE AUTHOR

Life is always nudging me to explore. I wake up with curiosity and go to bed wanting more from living. I have always been interested in what I don't know—confident that our vast universe will continually impart greater knowledge and personal growth. I am a seeker and, as such, feel my openness to learn and be inspired has enriched me with a "magnetic field," for lack of a better term, that seems to draw in stories and narratives that are both healing and empowering.

On a personal level, the power of storylines has been profound in my own healing from an early childhood trauma. I lost my father at the tender age of eleven and never truly grieved or understood the impact of his death—apart from having developed a very early insight on the fragility of life. Then, well into my thirties, I learned of my mother's silent suffering at the hands of my beloved father.

It is my mother's story that has really been the impetus to what I do today—serving as the conduit of others' stories—to share, heal, and empower. Witnessing her strength in finally sharing her own story, undeterred by the backlash she experienced from some members of our family, was so personally profound. In allowing herself to be vulnerable and exposed, she shed years of fear, anguish, and insecurity. Sharing her story has empowered her to live life more fully and more joyfully. It has been a gift to experience and a gift to receive—answering so many unanswered questions I had as a child. My mother's story not only freed her from her past, it also provided such a meaningful narrative to so many other women who have experienced different forms of abuse.

Storytelling is one of the most ancient, soul-retrieving arts—a powerful means of communicating, inspiring, connecting, and sharing. This art, together with the narratives of a select number of women who intersected with my life, is how *S.H.E. Share Heal Empower, Volume One* was birthed in 2018. The collected journeys of these women—including that of my mother—taught me new ways to look at the world. Their personal stories of resilience, empowerment, persistence, and victory, challenged me to discover things about myself that I never really knew—motivating me to grow and evolve in my own life.

The S.H.E. community is founded on the belief that storytelling can be magically impactful, life-changing, and meaningful. The stories we share enlighten, empower, and illuminate. Sharing through storytelling builds community, shared experience, and unity in thought that we are not alone. It confirms that what we experience in life is often shared by others and, therefore, a possible beacon of insight—allowing us that nugget of inspiration or strength that will move us forward in life more joyful and untethered to the physical and emotional barriers that can hold us back.

Following a short respite after the publication of *S.H.E. Share Heal Empower, Volume One*, and 558 days into a doctoral program studying the transmission of trauma within intergenerational identity, I felt an unmistakable need to pivot back to the S.H.E. community. I had been traveling through Europe and parts of Asia—for both business and pleasure—continuing, as always, to gather and be inspired by the stories of women that crossed my path.

A NOTE FROM THE AUTHOR

During my travels, I had the opportunity to visit Paris and meet with a remarkable woman we featured in Volume One, Chapter Four, named Lauren. At the time, Lauren was a YouTube-vlogging teenager struggling with anxiety and an eating disorder. Her story theme was "I can do hard things." Three years later, she followed her advice and moved to the City of Light—not knowing the language or anyone—to be an au pair for a family living in Versailles. This gritty girl now attends the International Fashion Academy (IFA) in Paris and has landed an internship with a Parisian perfume house, handling their marketing and social media. She has no plans to return to the States. Celebrating Lauren's steadfast perseverance to overcome the hurdles that challenged her—to effectively manage her anxiety and eating disorder—and seeing the excitement and joy she felt living in Paris and pursuing her dreams was so rewarding... and inspiring! Hearing her "new" story relit my S.H.E. spark. Serendipity always finds a way, even at a cabaret show 4,900 nautical miles away from home.

I relish the opportunity to sit down anywhere and have intriguing conversations with people from all walks of life. It has helped me personally in my own journey to heal and grow, but most importantly it has shown me that the experiences of others can be profoundly impactful—to both the ones who share their stories *and* to those they share them with.

Something deep within me drives my desire to tell tales of insight, triumph, and breakthrough—and to offer hope to others through those narratives. In *S.H.E. Share Heal Empower*, *Volume Two*, you will meet twenty-two amazing women from all over the world—from a twelve-year-old influencer to an eighty-year-old Moroccan filmmaker. I want everyone I meet to recognize that they are never alone. I know what it feels like to be abandoned in dark times, to long for encouragement. We all need to be seen, but most of all, we need each other.

Each of us has a story. One single story can affect people differently, but an untold story is ineffective. The impetus for my desire to empower and educate comes from the perseverance and pain my mother endured for more than thirty-plus years. Her rock-solid resilience and unimaginable human spirit inspired me to showcase other women who, through their storylines, can teach us to adeptly overcome our innermost chaos and confusion while navigating the labyrinth we call life. And these stories will again inspire other stories, from other women, from all walks of life and parts of the world, to also come forward and share their own personal adversities and triumphs—a varied and ongoing chorus of women helping women by sharing their own vulnerabilities and resilience.

No story is ever too small to make a difference.

CHAPTER ONE

Danielle & Olivia

*E*very family has a story. For some, the family of origin is a solid foundation that feeds confidence in navigating life's challenges. For others, it can be a source of pain, hurt, and conflict. And then, there is the intricate interplay between these bookends—the muddle in the middle—that envelopes the lot of us, myself included. True to all our stories is the fact that what we experience, what we see, what we endure, and what we entrust shapes us and, in turn, influences how we shape others—whether intentionally or inadvertently.

There is no road map for understanding and moving past familial dynamics; no manual for how not to have your trials and tribulations seep into the life you craft and the children you raise. Only our awareness and the desire for positive growth can *forge a path that heals old wounds and ways. It requires being vulnerable, and that can feel risky. The reward is that it can lead to greater connectivity and better communication—both keys to breaking free of unhealthy dynamics and achieving long-lasting, healthy relationships. I experienced this on my own journey through pain and loss. When I meet others who are open and vulnerable enough to admit their own shortcomings (we all have them)—and their desire for positive change—I feel an immediate connection. There is something beautifully raw and pure in this honesty; a purity of heart that can build bridges, strengthen connectivity, and free us from repeating past transgressions.*

Meet Danielle and Olivia, a mother and daughter duo that immediately captured my heart and exemplify all that is possible in redirecting our course in life.

Olivia was home on holiday when I connected with her and her mother in late 2022. The two women had wrapped up their girls' lunch at Lourdes Mexican—a favorite spot from their surf-session days—so we huddled up with our colas and coffee, nestled in a booth with the Pacific Ocean as our backdrop. Sensitive to developing a rapport that would ensure that both Danielle and Olivia would feel comfortable in being honest and open with me, I gently engaged Danielle to share her story first. I could sense a smidgen of fear in both Danielle's and Olivia's eyes and in their somewhat guarded posture. When they looked at one another, however, that seemed to immediately evaporate, as if they had channeled a fortitude of strength and approval between them—safe passage to share their story, to disrupt the cycle of misery they had perpetuated, to break free from the identities they had each submerged themselves in for years.

DANIELLE & OLIVIA

In a nutshell, Danielle is a mother who has always wanted stability and security for her daughter. Yet, the constant crush of past experiences from her own youth only emboldened the negative chatter that lived within her, making it difficult to grab hold of that elusive stability. As a young girl, Olivia could sense her mother's sensitivity to conflict or change of plan. She could see her edges of fragility. In Danielle's efforts to protect, Olivia felt there was little room for expression or disagreement. Going with the flow was the safer option, until it was no longer serving or sustainable. Olivia had finally reached a stage of maturity that demanded change; a stage that would allow her and her mother to embrace their vulnerabilities, to be honest and open about who they are as individual people, what they want out of life, and what they want in their relationship with each other.

Danielle and Olivia are here to remind us that our relationships are never perfect. We mask our true feelings, erasing ourselves a little bit more each and every time we deny ourselves authenticity; we look for ways to fill the emotional voids we feel, dodging real solutions for temporary and often damaging fixes; and we put blinders on to the facades we create in our efforts to protect ourselves or prevent having to do the hard work required to be our best and most authentic selves.

Relationships can be beautiful spaces of restoration, freedom, and mutual evolution if we're willing to do the hard work of really connecting with ourselves—and with each other. My desire to empower myself—and other women as a part of my efforts with S.H.E.—was undoubtedly rooted in watching my mother live her life from what I assumed was a position of weakness. However, when I started asking my mother tough questions, her authentic answers brought insight and information to the hurt child within me. From that moment forward, our time together offered a window of freedom from our tangled past. Ultimately, I realized I could have grace for my mother and her past experiences—that both of our narratives can be equally valid, and equally forgiving. How we reflect upon and handle the hard and sometimes uncomfortable conversations we need to have in order to heal is really what truly matters.

 Curating intimacy is a daily practice, as is sharing our struggles. When that intimacy is between a parent and child, there are so many other factors that play into the mix. As parents, I think we all have dreams and hopes for our children. And, it's not uncommon for us to sometimes become so intent on the vision we create in our own minds, that we forget to allow nature to take its course, to move away from guiding (or controlling) and toward supporting and encouraging. Danielle and Olivia's story is about helping each other answer an essential question: how can we successfully forge more meaningful and fulfilling relationships? In the following exchange, journaled during their road trip along the California coast, from Southern California to Oregon, Danielle and Olivia share some of their inner-most feelings about the journey they are on (both literally and figuratively) to begin answering this pivotal question as it applies to them—one of the most important relationships in each of their lives.

DANIELLE

Less inner chatter and more inner peace are where I want to be as a mother. While I have enlisted many ways to achieve this over the years—some healthy, and others unhealthy—I am finally at a place where I feel committed to the effort.

As I reflect on my life today—as a mother of a twenty-year-old girl and an eighteen-year-old boy—I realize that I am not in control of their happiness. We are at a point in life where I have to let go and allow their growth to occur. As a mother, I want to protect my babies from pain. While I feel this is a fairly universal desire among parents, I have learned from my experiences that there is a fine line between supporting them when they fall and protecting them from falling. The former, for me, has come from faith, courage, and understanding of my past—an altruistic and empowering approach, but not always easy to put into practice. The latter is borne from a place of fear, control, and a self-seeking desire to protect me—not an especially flattering approach, but one I feel is not uncommon in parenting.

As I head north up the coast to Oregon, with the car loaded full of Olivia's belongings, I look over with pride at my smart and strong daughter sitting beside me. Her curly, chestnut brown hair glistens with sun-kissed highlights—a tangible imprint of the years she devoted to surfing and surf competition. As my mind returns to those times spent together, tears well up in my eyes.

OLIVIA

I am obsessed with excitement, thinking about this next chapter in my life. Eugene, Oregon, was never a place I felt I would be moving to. My whole life I lived in Southern California near the beach. Since I was eight years old I have surfed with my

Brazilian father. Mom is an excellent surfer, too. I guess it was bound to happen—me becoming a California surfer girl.

Now, however, I'm embarking on a new path away from the surf, sand, and sun of my youth. While that side of Olivia will never leave me, it now serves a new purpose in guiding me on the next steps in my journey of self-discovery. I am learning, for probably the first time in my life, what it is that I don't want to do anymore and finding that letting go of what no longer serves you (however wonderful at the time) feels incredibly freeing.

DANIELLE

When Olivia was fifteen, her life looked very different than mine. I was a junior in high school and had been uprooted from all my family and friends. My mom and stepdad moved us to Michigan, hoping this geographic shift would have a positive impact on my behavior and deter my younger sisters from growing up "too fast" (as I had). I felt comforted by the fact that my mom was nurturing and tried hard to help me fit into my new surroundings. She always had a special way of making me feel loved. This sense of security, however, was cut short when my mom was killed by a drunk driver on her way to pick me up from a Halloween party. I was fifteen.

I want to say I felt a sense of peace with my mom's passing. I strangely believed it was the plan of the universe, but I was sad. I had lost my one and only constant. Not knowing how to process what I was feeling, I shoved most of my emotions down. Smoking weed and eventually turning to the bottle were my anesthetizing agents. After years of watching my father's struggle with alcohol, one would think, *why do the same*? And given how my mother's life was cut short, the thought of turning to alcohol should have appalled me. But, I don't question life. There are no answers for what we do in moments of despair.

I told Olivia about my growing up in the '80s during the new-wave dance scene, partying and going to dance clubs on Hollywood Boulevard. Living in a suburb of Los Angeles, I was in the heart of the party scene. At fifteen, I was getting into clubs. I was already familiar with drinking, as my dad allowed me to consume gin and tonics when I was only twelve years of age. And at eight, I had already found relief by smoking pot with my uncle. My relationship with drugs and alcohol was very intertwined in my life. Once I became a mother, however, I knew I needed a type of cognitive restructuring to help change how I viewed drinking and drugs. Looking back now, I am thankful to be part of a program for the last eighteen years that has guided me toward staying sober. Prior to getting sober, I dealt with disappointment by numbing out. I finally realized that this was not a sustainable approach.

At fifteen, Olivia was already heavily immersed in competitive surfing. She had used her body in sport, cognizant of the need to be fit and healthy. She steered clear of all extraneous activities and unhealthy deterrents that could impede her performance—a focus that I admire her for.

Since recovery, I now turn to my spirituality, service, and community of like-minded people who see me. Coming from a neglectful home life after my mom died, I became preoccupied with the need for control. I never realized how it manifested in micromanaging people, perfectionism, and addiction. Experiencing a web of trauma as a child, control became my attempt to feel safe. All my controlling behaviors with Olivia were safety-seeking—attempts to circumvent her from experiencing any degree of the pain or insecurity I felt. In assuming this approach, I inadvertently entered both myself and Olivia into a state of chronic hypervigilance.

Rewiring the way we operate, and why we operate that way, takes time and concerted effort. It's not a simple flip of a switch. The voices in my head still create mental turbulence. Working to control everything around me is how I conditioned myself to stay safe. Internally, I have little Danielle hiding and feeling a bit helpless. I want to protect her and, in turn, have overcompensated toward Olivia. I recognize the damage in this. It is what has forced me to work on changing the dynamic. I am open to change and no longer resist it.

OLIVIA

I am grateful for this road trip with Mom, taking in the best sights and scenic routes from California to Oregon—along my favorite coastline. It feels nice to have time to bond.

I never really heard Mom's full story. I think we are both in better places to understand each other now. Plus, we are captive, just the two of us processing our past in her black Prius packed with all my worldly belongings. No distractions. These moments in life—sequestered in the car with no roadblocks in our way except, perhaps, ourselves— allow Mom and I to connect on a different, deeper level. We have always struggled with communication. I get it. As a teenager, it seemed like there was always some type of trouble or challenge to address. Not only with my mom, but with my dad as well. Their divorce often put me in the middle of them—a no-win situation. And given that I have always been pretty shy, I am prone to internalize my feelings. At some point, this isn't the best. I do recognize

Mom has been muddling in misery for some time. I know that life has a lot of change. I am learning that these new moments we are experiencing—as I move away, live on my own, make my own decisions, become more independent—are all points of transition. They alter our relationships to different degrees, requiring us to evolve and adapt as we move forward. I want to be more open with my mom; to share my feelings with her without them being interpreted as an attack on her.

  This roadtrip was the first time Mom shared greater detail on how messed up my grandpa was. I never knew the whole story. I knew my grandmother had passed away and grandpa was an alcoholic, but I didn't fully know the extent of his actions. I know she has a bunch of sisters—half, step, and full—but some of her past is still blurry to me. She lived in Michigan for a brief stint, then ended up back in Los Angeles and graduated high school in 1986. She then went on to attend a college I thought about attending—University of California, Santa Barbara (UCSB).

  I remember a story Mom shared about something her girlfriend said about being a chameleon and making friends with whoever would satisfy her needs. Mom was offended by the comment and told me that while she felt she was just being friendly and open-minded, she later learned (with guidance from her spiritual program) that she was a people pleaser—which is different from being a friend. I like to think I am a pretty good friend, I don't have many of them, but I check in often, even if they don't respond. I am eager to meet new friends in Eugene. Maybe I am more cautious and still learning to be a friend. I definitely know how to set boundaries and will not be taken advantage of.

For most of my teens, I hung out with the guy friends I surfed with. I knew I was gay in middle school, but coming out at that time was not an option. I already struggled with fitting in, as I did not have the typical, tanned, blonde-haired, California-surf-girl look. I did not want it to affect my competition outcomes. I felt a great deal of pressure to perform well and believed that coming out would only add to that pressure—the homophobic vibes in and around the surfing community are real and I did not want this mindset to negatively affect my scores.

When I met my first girlfriend online a couple of years ago, I was excited and wanted to share my excitement. Telling my friend, also named Olivia, that I had a crush on someone of the same sex felt natural. I felt I was finally being true to myself, where I have always belonged. Every time I was in the water surfing, my new love was all I could think about and I knew I needed to tell someone. Olivia was excited for me. I knew she could keep my secret safe. I did not tell my mom right away. I waited a couple of weeks after telling Olivia. My dad took longer to tell. Though my mom did question me years ago, I was not ready to have that conversation with her.

It has been hard to shed the image of what people thought I was or, instead, what they wanted me to be. There is so much assumption made in trying to define people, as if we can all fit into neat little boxes—what we should be in life, how we should live, how we should look, who we should love, etc. I think this says more about the insecurities of others; their inability to accept anything different than their own way or viewpoint.

DANIELLE & OLIVIA

Danielle

I am a survivor. I have endured numerous traumas in my life, many during my youth, a time considered to be the most impressionable. I have faced death, divorce, abandonment, abuse, and addiction. Finding my roots in rocky water and rediscovering my relationships has been empowering. It has broadened my periphery, not only in better understanding myself, but how I want to relate to others. I am still learning to mother myself, to be gentle with myself as I work on healing the scars of my youth. I have learned to listen and give voice to the echoes of my past—the many challenges and circumstances I faced—as this allows me to take back my power and to be victorious, and not a victim. This, in turn, helps me be a better mom. I had a hunch Olivia was gay and asked her several times, but as I told her after she came out, maybe my timing and approach could have been better. I know now that the words you use and the approach you take are critical to truly connecting.

I know so much of my parenting of Olivia (and Kai) stems back to my father's rejection, neglect, and domestic and substance abuse. The fact that he never admitted to or atoned for his behavior only added to the void I felt. Sitting with my mom on the couch when I was four or five and having a beer bottle thrown in our direction, the loud noise of it shattering behind us, is something you never forget. I recently told a girlfriend that we all share a form of "human fuckedupness." She laughed and looked at me, wanting a definition. All I could muster up was how each of us is not that different or unique. We all suffer from some form of trauma, even someone who has had a privileged, cushy life. And while the magnitude surely differs from one person to another, knowing we all deal with something is what can allow us to have greater empathy for one another.

I like to wear my heart on my sleeve. I have one friend who never shares anything personal; it kind of trips me out. Perhaps that is her safety mechanism. I know that when and if she is ever wanting to share more, I will be there for her. My chant, however, continues to those around me, especially now as I keep learning and growing. I keep reminding myself to be cognizant of my own needs, as well as the work I need to do to disengage from what I know is wrong to feel. I want to help others release pain's control over us when we share. As a mother and adult, learning to create these new boundaries—regulate my emotions and calm the voices in my head—is a daily effort.

OLIVIA

As I was growing up, Mom was definitely sensitive. As a teenager, I could not be candid with her about certain things. When I would try to share something with her about how I felt, she would often act offended, as if what I was saying was directed at her in some personal way. She has recently mentioned how her sensitivity was a defense mechanism on her end, which makes sense to me now. Emotionally she had to be tired. She had a lot on her plate. She was a single mother, working three jobs as a teacher and tutor—she even trained teachers—to foot the cost of my surfing career and make life easier for my brother and me. Thinking back to all the meals she made makes me smile. She is a fantastic cook. She never follows a recipe, which frustrates me now that I will be my own. Making a meal for Violet, my girlfriend, will not be easy, but I'm excited for the opportunity. Maybe I will try to make chicken tacos. They are my favorite.

Now that I am twenty, and moving out, there is an added element of maturity and independence I feel. I think this will help in forging a stronger relationship with my mom. I have a better understanding of her and all she has gone through in life. And, in turn, she is open to truly listening and hearing what I say, which allows us both to be present with one another and connect at a deeper level.

I will miss Kai now that I will be living in Oregon, but our many memories together keep me smiling—like remembering all the fun we had on the giant tire swing in the big tree at my dad's house. My all-time favorite memory with Kai was scaring people with this toy snake we got from the fair. I don't remember whose idea it was to tie a string around that plastic reptile and slither it through the grass as people approached, but it was hilarious. We loved playing outside together. He will have to visit me in Oregon—a giant outdoor playground of trees, and the same beautiful coast of water we grew up on.

I am thankful for my friends. They were a sounding board when I quit school and work simultaneously, before deciding to move away. Both Mom and Dad were pretty pissed. I remember telling my dad that I needed a break. I didn't have time to be myself and I longed for this. I was done and over with the ocean and surfing competitively. Leaving my sales job at Surf Ride after four years also felt empowering. I want to explore life and myself more. I am ready for this next wave.

DANIELLE

This past year and a half has given me space and time to think. When Olivia opted out of surfing competitively, I was crushed. Undoubtedly, I was wrapped up in her success and the focus her competition brought to our lives. I realized that I had made her achievements a part of my own identity. She was my "surf daughter," and this was my life. I kept thinking of all the time and commitment she put in—the ten years we dedicated time, money, and energy to her future. All that effort suddenly felt like a loss. It might seem selfish to say it (but I am being honest with myself), I feel like I sacrificed my time and myself for everyone all those years, especially Olivia, and I wanted to be appreciated more. The financial side for me was heavy. There were alliances between our divorced family, which was detrimental. I know that now. I cannot take back those tumultuous teen years, but we can learn together from them.

I didn't realize all that Olivia was going through in her teens. I am grateful that she was open with me—sharing that she was unhappy and dealing with depression. I know she felt a good deal of pressure to perform and this weighed heavily on her. She started surfing at such a young age. Her surfing and the success she achieved just took on a life of its own—a literal wave that consumed us. She was also at a point in her life where I think she wanted to have a bit more breathing room to discover herself and make her own decisions. She had experienced her first heartbreak in a relationship and was dealing with the emotions of that loss, as well. She needed time to regroup in order to rebound and find greater clarity of purpose and path. I think we both needed some time to process this shift in our lives, each of us in our own way.

For me, I was grieving the loss of a large focus of my life and the void I suddenly felt in my own purpose—the loss of that identity I had assumed. For Olivia, I think she needed time to adapt to a new cadence in her life; one that would allow her to spread her wings a bit more and discover what she really wants out of life. Though I was shocked with her decision to quit surfing, school, and her job, she took the bold step to just course-correct her life and I'm proud of her. I believe her decision to move to Eugene was wise, even though I will miss her dearly. I want my daughter to feel seen and accepted by me. If that means I need to work harder and be more aware, I am willing to do the difficult work.

I am proud of Olivia for knowing how to set boundaries. My lack of them stems from the apparent turmoil in my life and the rejection I felt growing up. I struggled with self-esteem and loving myself. I have compassion for people and tend to be a people pleaser—using it as a protective barrier to gain appreciation. I am learning through awareness and self-compassion that I don't need to have affirmation of myself or my opinions, and that is empowering.

Being in the spiritual program for eighteen years with only two relapses has allowed me to be real and raw. Three years ago, I relapsed and never really talked about it to the kids. The void in my soul opened up. There was tension. Navigating this road to recovery for myself is not easy. Still, these new freedoms both Olivia and I now share allow us to chart a new path forward, a wide-open road like the one we are traveling, to make better decisions and choices that will benefit our relationship.

OLIVIA

This move to Eugene in January 2022 was the best decision I could have made for myself. I am both excited and scared. I think about the book, *The Alchemist,* by Paulo Coelho, about how the universe conspires to help you (even though I have not finished the whole thing) and take comfort in this thinking.

I am happy to spend more time with Violet. She is just the best—hardworking, hardheaded, extremely smart, and sweet, just to name a few of her many attributes. I met her online and commented on one of her TikTok videos. Within ten minutes, she direct messaged me, and we instantly connected and started communicating. We are opposites. I am quieter and shyer, but learning a lot from her. I like the classes I am taking at the local community college. Violet works and goes to school full-time, too. I am hopeful our schedules will allow time for us to see more of each other.

I am renting a place with five other girls. I think this will be a riot of fun, and a significant change from my life in California. It's weird how I reconnected with a former friend from high school, Halle, and through her ended up securing a space in this house with these girls. Halle and I had initially rebonded over our similar experiences—breakups we each went through and common struggles with our moms. It felt great at the time to have someone who understood the emotions I was dealing with, and really great now that she will be a roommate. It feels like this was all meant to be; that I am exactly where I am supposed to be at this time in my life (the universe conspiring!). Some things I don't question because the answer doesn't always present itself. It just is what it is.

DANIELLE

Looking at the ocean passing by on my left, sipping my steamy cup of Starbucks coffee, I feel like the voids in my life are beginning to fill in. I look at the guardrails along the coast and feel my parenting style was similar to this fixed-wall protection system—designed to prevent my children from going over the edge, myself included.

Connecting with my childhood pain has been vital in my personal development and in improving my relationship with Olivia and Kai. It has served as a roadmap to charting a better path forward. It's blurry at times, but in weaving together the bits and pieces of what I experienced and how it affected me, I feel I can start to discard the shame and doubt I've carried all these years, making room for greater clarity in my journey to heal. I recognized that feeling of not belonging and being different when I was five. And all that ensued after that point in time—the loss of my mother, the instability and poor influence of my father, and the unhealthy relationships I entered—just kind of reinforced that mindset. I no longer want to be stuck in the overwhelming confusion of my past.

All my relationships have been tricky to navigate and incredibly humbling. Sometimes I think our lives must be completely shaken up, changed, and rearranged to relocate us to the place we are all meant to be. It's easy to get lost in our worlds. Digging deeper into who we are takes courage. And overcoming obstacles takes time, and sometimes therapeutic help.

For myself, my spiritual program has been incredibly helpful. There are spiritual programs and guides available to us if we choose to pay attention. Our past, and the myriad of childhood commotion that can swirl within us, can overflow into our present lives in destructive ways if we aren't mindful. Adulthood teaches us that no one is coming to save us. Personal accountability is our path to freedom, which means creating new habits for a different way of interacting with ourselves and others. We all struggle with guilt and grief over losing time and opportunities. Making our hearts and heads listen is an opportunity for another story to be written.

I realize that I no longer have to be that human guardrail for Olivia, or myself for that matter. Though I will always be here for her, I know it is time for her to spread her wings. I know that this is that point of transition all parents face—that process of letting go and adapting to a new normal. I am happy that my daughter can finally embrace her independence. I feel grateful that she opened up to me about her sexuality. I want her to feel confident and secure in who she is and where she is heading. I have great faith in her ability to navigate life.

The emptiness I have felt from my past is disappearing slowly. Surrounding myself with a community of like-minded people with shared experiences has benefited me, and the transition with Olivia has brought me peace and calm. I strongly feel that the tension that bubbled between us during those teenage years is dissolving, allowing us to connect on a more intimate level. Despite the fact that we are all a product of our upbringing—in some form or fashion—I am encouraged to rewrite the script. Olivia and I are feeling our way into a brighter future—one that lets go of the parts of our past that no longer serve us; one that will forge a path of greater understanding and connectivity. Whether near or far, life's road is much better when we don't have to travel it alone.

CHAPTER TWO

Linda

*S*urvival. *This is a word that assumed greater clarity in 2020. I think for most people, survival is something we may have witnessed from afar or, on some level, from within the confines of our own lives. And I think for many people who have experienced upheavals or downfalls, sadness or loss, it can feel like a solitary experience—the masses move on.*

COVID-19 changed this landscape. Survival was suddenly at the forefront of humankind—the masses were in this together. Borders, age, religion, ethnicity, prosperity, politics— none of that mattered. COVID-19 brought a relentless surge of sickness, struggle, fear, and death into full view; a universal lens that made all of us acutely aware of our desire to survive—to not fall victim to this illness.

This is the story of Linda. She, unfortunately, was not one of the lucky ones who skirted the grips of COVID-19. Thankfully, however, she was one of the lucky ones that lived.

Linda's story illuminated something quite significant. Science books will tell you that all living things are highly organized and coordinated into many living organisms or cells, which are considered the fundamental units of life. Linda's story will prove that "the fundamental units of life" extend well beyond our cells; that we require far more to flourish, to overcome…to survive. What if we added mutual care, community, and a feeling of being valued as necessities for the continuity of life; for durability, endurance, and continuance? And modern medicine and its advancements, and approved therapeutic and diagnostic methodologies?

We are more than cells. Linda's story illustrates the power of connection. We need each other, we need community, we need to feel loved. While we certainly cannot downplay the significance and importance of medical intervention, there is much written about the "will to live" and what drives this will. Positive attitude and/or mindset are often touted as being critical in our drive to survive. While having a will to live does not guarantee survival, its potential should never be underrated.

Prior to the onset of COVID-19, Linda's life was full and rewarding. She was just shy of her 50th wedding anniversary (49 years in December 2022), having married her high school sweetheart and best friend in life, Mike, shortly after graduating from college. Together they raised three children: Michael (Mikey), Maureen (Mo), and Mark. They've always been a close-knit family, involved in their community and activities, gathering numerous friends along the way. And, Linda is quite

LINDA

a social butterfly. She is on two ladies' golf leagues, one in Oakbrook, Illinois, where she has played with the same group of women for twenty years, and the other just a little over an hour away in Michigan City, Indiana. When she wasn't swinging her 5 wood, she played a weekly game of Mah-Jongg and attended a monthly book club with her retired teacher friends from Riverside Brookfield High School—where she taught Physical Education and Dance for almost twenty years. Linda was also a PTA volunteer, serving in the roles of President and Secretary at various schools her children attended; a Girl Scout and Brownie leader of her daughter Mo's troops; and, a member of her Junior Women's Club and Newcomers gatherings. I was exhausted just hearing about her many activities. Linda definitely didn't let grass grow under her feet. She was one very active, engaged, and involved woman, wife, mother, and friend. That was until COVID-19 entered her life.

Linda and her husband had just returned from a long vacation in March of 2020 when they started to feel ill—feverish, achy, fatigued. They convalesced at home for several days before finally seeking medical attention. Both tested positive for COVID-19 and were immediately admitted to the hospital. While Mike eventually improved and was released, Linda's condition quickly escalated and she was placed on a ventilator while in a medically induced coma. She remembers little of what transpired during this time.

Linda was one of the fortunate victims of COVID-19—she returned home to her family. Her journey to recovery is an excellent testament to her vigor and to her "Team Linda" community of collaborators, which included the devotion of her family, and her medical and rehabilitation teams. She has regained her ability to function independently, making progress each and every day since her return home.

When Linda and I finally connected in the fall of 2022 via Zoom, the medical tables had turned. She had assumed the role of caregiver for her husband, Mike, a retired lawyer and former Mayor of their hometown, who had just undergone a lumbar laminectomy surgery for spinal stenosis—making more space for his compressed spinal cord and nerve roots. Despite this turn of the table, both Mike and Linda were grateful to again be reunited with each other, and with their family—including Henry, the cutest little dachshund. It was clearly evident that their bond as a couple, and as a family, was something they cherished and nurtured. And given Linda's story, that connectivity no doubt played a role in her recovery. As did the close relationships she has with each of her three adult children.

Between Linda's caregiving of Mike late in 2022, and the holidays approaching, we continued to collaborate via text and email, piecing together her story with the assistance of her family. Unlike all the stories I've shared to date—getting first-person accounts of unique S.H.E. journeys—Linda was not conscious or aware of the unfolding of her story in real time. The details of her story are woven together in bits and pieces—the fragments of memory that she recalls, along with the real-time experiences that her loved ones endured from afar, as the hospital was quarantined from visitors during the entirety of Linda's hospital stay. As such, her story is a collaborative effort, and presented here in a kind of diary format, with Linda and her daughter, Mo, sharing insights of what was taking place— from Linda's perspective and from the perspective of Mo and her family.

COVID-19 was a tragedy few could have imagined in their lifetime. As Linda's husband, Mike, recounted "We did not *think Linda would live." Millions of people perished worldwide at the hands of this virus and Linda came frighteningly close to being counted among them. Her story is one of survival, yes, but also an amazing story of how love and connection may have intervened at just the right moment.*

LINDA

In February 2020, my husband, Mike, and I drove to Charlotte, North Carolina, to visit our oldest son. We enjoyed the time we spent with Michael, our daughter-in-law, Lindsay, and two grandsons, Issac, who was six at that time, and Caleb, who was three. After visiting in Charlotte, we continued on our way to various stops in Florida before ending our whirlwind vacation with a seven-day stay on Sanibel Island.

We returned home to Riverside, Illinois, just outside of Chicago, on Sunday, March 15, 2020. Driving from Florida back to Illinois is a long trip, over 1,300 miles and twenty-plus hours if one was to go straight through. I had a headache the whole drive home but didn't think much of it because I typically get car sick, so I attributed my headache to that.

On Monday, March 16, I was really tired. Again, I didn't think it was a big deal because we had been traveling and I just assumed it was normal to feel exhausted. I took some Tylenol and just rested.

By Tuesday, March 17, I had started running a temperature. My standard temperature is always 97.6 degrees Fahrenheit, but it was climbing to over 102.4.

After that Tuesday, things get a bit blurry. My youngest son, Mark, showed me a text thread a few months ago, that chronicles how Mike and I were feeling at that time, days before we were admitted to the hospital. In the thread, Mark asks "How are you guys doing?" My first response was "Terrible!" In subsequent texts I shared that my temperature had spiked, but that his dad's was normal; that we both were achy and lethargic. I ended the text thread with "We are doing all we can to cope," and "I would not wish this on anyone."

Lindsay, Mikey's wife several states away, was looking up urgent care locations and urged Mike and me not to wait for our doctor to find an appointment time. At that point, Mike had similar symptoms, but not as bad. Remember, this was the first month of the COVID-19 outbreak and everyone, including the medical community, was dealing with an unprecedented time and the global reaction was fear of the unknown.

Mike drove us both to the doctor's office on Tuesday or Wednesday. We called ahead, and they met us in the parking lot. They administered a flu test on both of us—which was negative. I just thought we had a common virus that needed to run its course. COVID-19 was just beginning to break in the news. It didn't register with either of us that this might be what we had. By Thursday, we were both running a fever and could not break it. Mine was much higher.

On Saturday, March 21, we were both advised to go to MacNeal Hospital. We went to the back door of the emergency room, where they did a COVID-19 test on each of us. We both tested positive. I was informed that I also had COVID-19 pneumonia. Mike and I were immediately admitted into isolation. I remember being there at first. I recall asking one of the nurses

LINDA

to take a message to Mike, who was next door to me. That's the last thing I remember doing.

MO

When my brothers and I learned that both Mom and Dad had been admitted to the hospital with COVID-19, we were really concerned as we knew so little at that point about this virus and what to expect. Further compounding our worry was the fact that we could not see them.

A few days after they were both admitted, Dad was released. He returned home on Monday, March 23, 2020, but was still sick for an additional three weeks—suffering with fatigue, weakness, and a cough.

I was nominated to support Dad when he returned home because I lived the closest. Mikey was several states away and Mark lived an hour away. Mom and Dad had been married for nearly 47 years at that point (and together for far longer than that), so Dad had never really been without Mom for an extended period of time. We didn't want him to be alone. Those first days, the neighbors sent soup, and Mark's friend's family sent pizza.

On March 24, we learned that Mom had been placed on a ventilator, just one day after Dad came home.

LINDA

I was put on a ventilator on March 24, 2020, just three days after being admitted to the hospital. I don't remember it. All I remember is that something was put into my mouth, and I couldn't talk. I didn't like that feeling. I was put into a medically-induced coma sometime during this procedure. At one point, maybe two days before the ventilator was inserted, a kind nurse told me my husband was okay and not to worry. When Mike was discharged from the hospital, he was not even allowed to say goodbye to me.

MO

Until Dad fully recovered, my brothers and I took charge of monitoring Mom's care. Both Mark and I lived locally so we set up a spreadsheet to record information about Mom—the doctors and nurses we spoke to, the time of day, her status, oxygen reports, the medicines that were administered, etc. Mikey took up the task of gathering names of all our relatives and friends and sending out many emails. We kept everyone aware of how Mom was doing, as her family and many friends were concerned for her. Many friends we talked to connected us to other friends that were doctors and could help explain what was happening. While this was helpful, it didn't lessen how much we missed and worried about our mom. Mikey and his thoughtful wife, Lindsay, sent pizzas to the hospital to thank the medical teams. We appreciated all they were doing, especially in our absence—as we could not visit our mom—and wanted them to know that. In the meantime, I kept Dad company.

I quickly established a routine that Dad could count on. At least once a week, we'd make dinner together. He cooked the meat and I made the sides. We even made Mom's Mexican steak recipe with a can of Rotel, tip steak, cumin, and chili powder—just like she makes it. We kept each other company, and sometimes just cried together.

At times, dad and I focused on our telephone conversations with Mom's doctors, and what questions we wanted to ask her medical team the following day. Other times we just distracted ourselves with a sense of normalcy. We watched our favorite TV shows and took Henry, their beloved dog, for walks around the neighborhood. During our strolls, neighbors and community members would stop us and ask for an update on Mom. Every conversation ended with positive vibes being sent Mom's way.

We took a trip to our beach house on Easter Sunday just to get away. It had already been almost three weeks and Mom was still on a ventilator, with little change in her condition. We took Henry on long walks and, just like at home, we were approached by neighbors asking for an update on Mom.

Shortly before the Easter holiday, Mom's doctors informed us that there wasn't anything else they could do for her. She had been in the same state, with no improvements for several days. The doctors discussed the option of putting a trach in Mom's throat—which is a long-term solution as people aren't meant to be on ventilators for as long as she had been up to that point. The trach would keep her stable while allowing us, as her family, to make decisions about hospice, etc. We were also informed that Mom would need to be transferred to Loyola University Medical Center, as they needed to free up beds at MacNeal. This was when Dad decided to contact a priest. The situation was so dire, and Dad was struggling, so I think he just needed someone to talk to. And, because Mom was showing little signs of improvement and had been on a ventilator for so long, Dad wanted last rites to be administered. We weren't giving up, but we all felt this was important to do—for all of us and for our mom.

Dad knew a chaplain from our community who was able to coordinate with the chaplain at Loyola, who suggested that he could arrange a FaceTime call. This felt HUGE. Due to this being the very beginning of the pandemic, we had not been able to see or communicate with Mom the whole time she was in the hospital. As we coordinated the date and time for the call, we were informed that Mom's transfer to Loyola had been arranged. She was transferred on April 8, 2020. At this point, she had been on a ventilator for 16 days.

Once Mom was at Loyola, we learned that the only time the chaplain would be available was during the middle of the workday and Mikey and Mark were not going to be able to join us. So, I researched how to record a FaceTime call to send it to Mikey and Mark afterward. You can record the call, I learned upon research, but there would be no audio component, only visual. Mikey and Mark said that was better than nothing, so I configured my iPad to record the call.

I remember it so clearly. Dad, Henry, and I gathered in my apartment. Since the chaplain was not allowed to enter Mom's room, he put his phone in a plastic Ziploc bag and handed it to the nurse, who was in so much protective gear it looked like she was entering a war zone (I remember thinking that I had never seen anything like that before). She walked the phone to Mom and held it up so we could see her. I remember Dad and me just saying "Hi, Mom" over and over and over again. The nurse said, "Linda, your family is on the phone." I was expecting Mom to basically look dead, based on the state the doctors had told us she was in during my previous communications with them. I truly didn't believe she would acknowledge or respond to us. We were just hoping that somewhere deep down she'd know we were there. So, you can imagine our surprise when she opened her eyes!!!!! Like literally opened her eyes! I distinctly remember that it seemed like she wanted to talk to us. I could see it in her eyes and a few facial movements. I held up Henry and told her he was here and let Henry have some FaceTime—LOL! I told her that Mikey and Mark were at work, but that we were recording the call for them, and that they were both with us in spirit. I needed to tell her that Mikey and Mark were thinking of her. I wanted her to know that her whole family was here. It was just amazing, and totally unexpected that Mom, who was still in a medically induced coma, reacted to our voices. It was the best gift we could have received. It just told us that she was still there; still with us.

After a bit of time, the nurse took the phone back outside the room to the chaplain. He then handed the nurse some holy oils, and she went back into the room while the chaplain held the phone to record through the window. The chaplain read Mom her last rites as the nurse put the holy oils on my mom's head. Dad and I just listened. We thanked the chaplain and told him that this meant everything to us. Afterward, I sent the video to Mark and Mikey and told them what we had said to Mom since there was no audio. They said they could tell when Mom heard our voices, and when she saw Henry, because they saw the expression in her eyes on the video. I remember them both crying.

We all fully believe that Mom needed to hear from and see her family because she miraculously started getting better from that day on. The doctors say it was quite the medical miracle (they may not have used those exact words, but they did express that there wasn't any other way to describe her incredible turnaround).

On April 13, 2020, Mom was removed from her ventilator. And, on April 15, she was transferred out of the

Intensive Care Unit (ICU) to a regular patient room at Loyola. It was miraculous! Up to the moment of our FaceTime call, she had shown little to no improvement. We have to believe that the love and devotion we all have for her—that all her friends and extended family have for her—made a difference. While she may not have heard us consciously, I believe that our voices resonated somewhere deep within her, giving her the strength to keep fighting.

LINDA

I know in my heart of hearts I must have unconsciously heard Mike and Mo speaking to me. They couldn't talk directly to me, but their voices were played over a phone so that I might hear them. In later viewing the video they recorded, I seemed to know they were watching me. The chaplain gave me my last rites. The doctors didn't think I was going to make it. Then, suddenly, I moved my eyes and slightly turned my head. I don't remember this, but I was amazed when I saw the video! That was the first time during my hospitalization that I indicated that I knew what was happening. While I'm unsure if it was actually medically possible to have heard Mike and Mo that day, I do believe that God let me *feel* their love. From that moment on, things began to improve. I continued to fight. I never gave up, nor did my medical team or family.

On Monday, April 13, I was taken off the ventilator after 21 days. I have no conscious recollection of what was happening in my life until I was finally placed into a general hospital room at Loyola University Medical Center on April 15, 2020—nearly four weeks after being admitted to MacNeal. At one point, I do remember a nurse telling me that I had been the second person admitted to MacNeal with COVID-19 weeks prior, and my husband had been the third.

LINDA

Once I was transferred out of ICU, all I remember is that I wanted to eat. My first request was coffee. When the nurse arrived, a spoon was sticking straight up in the cup, and I asked, "What is that, is that ice cream?" It was not. The nurses had to feed me, as I could not yet swallow properly and a lot of care needed to be taken to prevent me from choking. For six days, the only "food" I could be fed was applesauce, with my medication tucked inside. I told them to put me back on an IV. Not being able to eat was upsetting. It all felt humiliating. I could not swallow, get out of bed, or go to the bathroom.

I recall ringing for the nurse and asking to talk to my husband. I missed him and my family. No one could visit me. This was the absolute worst. Maybe I was even depressed. Staying positive was all I had, but it was challenging. I knew if I worked hard, I could get out of there.

Though I was finally conscious and aware of my surroundings, I was having numerous dreams and hallucinations when I slept. I don't know if they happened prior to this time—when I was in a coma and on a ventilator. I do know that they upset me. One time I believed I saw spiders dropping down in front of me and asked the nurse to get rid of them. Another time, I thought I heard Mo's voice in the hall outside my room. I kept asking the nurses if it was her (no, it wasn't). "Remember Linda, no visitors are allowed," they told me. But I still felt like I could see Mo and her friends hanging out in my inner doorway, laughing and having a good time. One dream had me searching for Henry. I had lost him at an outdoor concert but no one could see me or help me find him. I finally went home, and Mike had him.

The most concerning one I remember was being at a cemetery near my mom's and dad's graves. I was lying on the ground and a skeleton rose up near me saying, "You're not ready for me. You need to go back." Each hallucination and dream I had was vivid. I am unsure when they all transpired, but I felt lucid, and there were many of them. I wish I knew what happened when I was on that ventilator in the ICU for an extended period of time. It may be worth exploring, or maybe not.

On Monday, April 20th, I was transferred to Marianjoy Rehabilitation Hospital for inpatient acute care. I remember the ambulance that took me to Marianjoy hitting bumps in the road. It was hurting my back. I asked them to go slower. At one point, I told them to pull over, put something under my hips, or I would call an Uber! I had never used an Uber before, and secondly, I didn't even have my phone! They put a folded blanket under me and the rest of the ride was doable.

MO

Even when Mom was finally transferred to Marianjoy Rehabilitation Hospital, Dad and I kept the tradition of our get togethers going, adding laundry duty to our routine. As Dad had to pick up Mom's laundry every couple of days, we made it something we looked forward to doing together. He'd come to my apartment and we'd grab lunch while the clothes were being washed. We'd walk Henry, get the clothes dried and folded, and then he'd be on his way to drop Mom's clothes off. Dad was not allowed in the hospital.

LINDA

Once I got to rehab, I was taken off some medications and the hallucinations stopped. I had a multidisciplinary team comprised of speech therapists, occupational therapists, physical therapists, psychiatrists, and chaplains to address any deficits left behind from having COVID-19 and being on a ventilator for such a long time. I had to relearn how to stand, walk, get out of bed, use the toilet, dress, and shower without assistance. Since the virus attacks the lungs, the oxygen levels in my blood would drop with any activity, which meant my heart rate would quickly elevate. The first time I walked with the walker, I was only able to take four steps with the therapist. Relearning and remembering how to lean back when walking, and not forward, still boggles my mind.

I recall watching an interview from ABC7 news, where I was interviewed the day before I left to go home, thinking *wow, pushing myself really paid off.* One of the doctors from Marianjoy Rehabilitation Hospital said, in that same segment, "Many COVID-19 patients become severely deconditioned." I can attest to this as tasks like brushing my teeth, getting dressed, and going to the bathroom had to be relearned. Though my recovery started slowly, my mind was always moving faster. I wanted to increase my physical and occupational regime so that I could go home to Mike, Henry, and my family. I started getting feisty. Occupational, physical, and speech therapies were scheduled five days a week, for three hours each day. A psychologist came in several times to check on my mental wellbeing. The chaplain called me but couldn't come into the room. He sent me some aromatherapy oils to try to get my smell activated again. Lemon was the winner. I still couldn't eat or drink yet. My throat was irritated, and they didn't want me to choke. I kept asking for water, but could only have a few ice chips at a time. At first, I couldn't do much, but the therapists were very encouraging.

I had a daily schedule that became very rigorous. If the therapist told me to do something five times, I would try to do it more. I wanted to get my strength back. As time went on, the gym was opened for COVID-19 patients. There, we worked on climbing stairs, setting the table, using a walker to go up a curb, and playing games that made us reach and stretch—things that I never thought twice about before COVID-19. After about two weeks, I ordered and ate food. The food there was good. At first, it was a soft diet and then it moved to a regular one. The doctors, nurses, and therapists gave me excellent care. They were patient and kind.

MO

I remember the day before Mom finally came home. Dad and I sat at the same kitchen table in my home that we had lunched at for all those weeks Mom was in rehabilitation, only this time we sat with markers—like giddy school children—coloring a sign that said, "Linda's Home."

LINDA

It was two days after Mother's Day when I was released from Marianjoy. My six-year-old grandson, Isaac, made a song and had his mom, Lindsay, videotape him singing it. His brother, Caleb, who was too young at the time to really sing along with his brother, did chime in with "I miss you, get better." To watch this tape felt so extraordinary. Again, family love—this was always my sole motivation to getting better.

Mo and Mike had made a "Linda's Home" sign and put it on our porch window. When I saw it, I was utterly overwhelmed. Lindsay, Mikey, and the boys made a sign in front of their house in Charlotte, as well. On the street in different chalk colors, it said, "She Did It! Grandma (Mom) Beat Covid-19! Welcome Home!" Mark and his fiancé, Brittany, brought me my favorite flowers – pink tulips. There was a beaded accent on the vase that Brittany had created herself, depicting the word "Bigs," which is their nickname for me. (I'm not sure why, though. Maybe I should ask them.) I remember telling Brittany, before she and Mark were engaged, that we are a "close-knit family." Well, she fits right in! The whole clan called me the night I returned. The ability to see each other and be together was a moment of pure joy. My family is my rock! I couldn't be prouder of them or love them more. I had to show them I could do it. They knew I could. I had the best team supporting me both at the hospital and at home.

A few days after getting home, one of our neighbors called Mike to arrange a time that would work for all our neighbors to gather outside our home to welcome me back. I had beat COVID-19 and they wanted to celebrate my return! Though I was still in a wheelchair, Mike pushed me out to our front yard so I could see everyone that had assembled there. They all cheered for me, which felt so great. I told them about my journey and I even kicked up one of my legs for them! I was a dancer, after all!

Once home, though still relegated to a wheelchair, I continued my rehabilitation. For the first month, nurses came to our home two times each week to oversee my therapy. Then I went to outpatient rehabilitation for six months. During this time, I underwent both Occupational Therapy (OT) and Physical Therapy (PT). My right hand/arm had shooting pains going down it. The left arm wasn't affected, but my hand was. The OT mainly worked with my hands. I wore braces on them for weeks to help relieve the pain. My doctor then sent me to a neurologist for Electromyography (EMG) tests. These are diagnostic procedures to assess whether there is any nerve or muscle dysfunction. The results showed that I had Carpal Tunnel

Syndrome in both hands. I was told that it was likely attributed to deconditioning—something the medical community was seeing in COVID patients—as well as a result of the various medications I was administered. Remember, this thing called COVID-19 was so new that doctors weren't sure what would work and what wouldn't. They tried everything they could. When I was at my worst, they told my husband they weren't sure I would survive and if I did they didn't know how I might be affected.

Surgery was recommended to address my Carpal Tunnel. So, that November I had one hand done, then the other in December. My goal in going through this was to be ready and able to golf in the spring. In PT, I worked on strengthening my lower body. I remember being on the treadmill. If I was charged with doing six minutes, I went for 10. When my therapist asked me what goal I hoped to first achieve, I said it was to be able to get up and down from the floor so I could sit and play with my grandchildren when we visited. I worked hard to accomplish my goal and I reached it! I felt that I wouldn't let anything stop me from regaining my strength and life as it used to be. My friends called me a warrior.

Once I returned home, my youngest son, Mark, showed me a news headline he had saved as a sign of hope: "Italy's COVID-19 patient 'number one' leaves hospital after entering in critical condition and being on a respirator for eighteen days." He felt that if this man could make it out alive, so could I. My considerate husband showed me all the emails sent to and from relatives and friends—golf league members, book club ladies, fellow Mah Jongg players, former co-workers, and neighbors. I learned that many of these people had sent emails about my condition to prayer groups, church groups, etc. What an

LINDA

outpouring of love and prayers I had received. It was a scary time for everyone.

MO

To this day, the video we took of Mom in the ICU at Loyola University Hospital (gathered with the chaplain) sometimes pops up in my Google library when I'm scrolling. To date, I have not been able to rewatch it. I quickly skip over it, but I do not want to erase it. I'm not sure why I don't want to watch it. Maybe it's still too soon, and perhaps I never will. I do know, however, that what I witnessed that day was probably the most powerful thing I've ever experienced.

LINDA

In addition to the therapies that I was medically prescribed to do once I returned home, I got out every day with Mike. He would push me around our neighborhood in my wheelchair. Eventually we added stops for me to practice getting up and out of the chair and then sitting back down. Then, I progressed to standing up and taking a few steps by myself. What a great feeling! After a couple of weeks of this, I was walking. Then, Mike coached me to stop and take a few steps backward. I did it! Then he asked "Can you squat and bend your knees?" I again did it. I remember a man on his porch was watching us and clapped for me!

As we walked around our block, neighbors would stop us and ask how I was doing. It was a miracle that I lived, and they rejoiced with me. Mikey and his family came to visit. We went to the Zoo nearby. We took the wheelchair so that I wouldn't get too fatigued.

People ask me whether I experienced burnout from all the rehabilitation I've had to undergo in my recovery, or whether I feel any additional stress given what I underwent. I guess I think that what I went through was pretty much the worst of the worst, so what I've had to endure in order to fully get my life back kind of doesn't feel as traumatic. It really couldn't get any worse than where I was in that hospital, hooked up to a ventilator, no one really knowing whether I'd live or die.

I will say, as a woman, our hair is our crown. I did lose most of my hair about three months after coming home—it came out in handfuls— and I admit that was the first time I cried. It was the only time I felt defeated or overwhelmed with everything and everyone. Being of Czechoslovakian and Irish descent, my parents raised us to be strong and positive. *Bear with it, never blame*, was our family motto. Perhaps losing my hair was just that tipping point we all face at some time or another, and the tears finally caught up with me. My doctors said to wait and see before getting any treatments. They explained that hair growth is cyclical and that it was likely that it would come back. I just wore lots of cute hats. At the point I considered getting a wig, it started growing back. At first, it was grey in front, white on the sides, and dark in the back. My stylist cut it into a short pixie cut, and I persevered. Now my hair is back to its full glory!

Some still ask Mike or me how I'm doing. There are so many compassionate people in our town. It's truly amazing how impactful kindness, love, and compassion can be. I am a living testament to their healing powers. I will never fully know if I was consciously hearing the voices of my family that fateful day in the hospital, but I do know I physically responded and my condition quickly improved. It's as if my family had pulled me back to life again. My family's love and devotion never waned during those long weeks. They, along with the excellent medical care I received, brought me home again.

I am back golfing—on the course again, two years later. It's hard to believe, but I am forever grateful for this second round at life.

I *survived* COVID-19. I am alive!

CHAPTER THREE

Yuliya

I have been thinking a lot about survival; what it takes to get through or overcome something truly challenging. I have been thinking a lot about a woman from my doctoral program, Yuliya, who fled the war in Ukraine with her young son.

There are many challenges in life; never equal from one person to the next, one country to the other. History has undoubtedly chronicled numerous life-altering events throughout the centuries—revolutions, assassinations, the holocaust, nuclear disasters, climate disasters…and wars. In speaking with others about what's occurred in Ukraine, I think we are stricken not only by the shock of this war but by the unfathomable nature of witnessing an unprovoked attack on a sovereign nation; an attack so brutal, senseless, and destructive that it defies any sense of logic or sanity. My mind goes to the valor that Ukraine has demonstrated in fighting for their country; to the men, women,

YULIYA

and children that have been forced to face what has befallen them—to fight, to hide, to flee; to fear what this all means and how it will all end. In these circumstances, swiftness of action may be the only thread at one's disposal, the only thread that offers a chance for survival.

For Yuliya and the 44 million people living in Ukraine, life abruptly changed on February 24^{th,} 2022, when Russian forces invaded their country. One day they are all going about their daily routines—attending school, driving to work, sipping coffee in cafes—and the next, they are speaking in hushed tones with strangers in a cold basement, dousing all lights in their homes for fear of drawing the attention of artillery, lying awake at night while the dark skies above them fill with the sounds of explosives. As Ukrainian men between 18 and 60 were called on to remain in the country to fight and protect their sovereignty, women, children, and the elderly were left to choose—stay or flee. Decisions needed to be made in a matter of hours, days, or weeks. This is what my classmate, Yuliya, was faced with.

Yuliya is one of the most eloquent and compelling females I have ever met. Our paths crossed during our studies in the same doctoral program. I was immediately taken with her aptitude to observe and induce information abstractly and analytically. And she is funny to boot. She brought a much-appreciated sense of humor to our discussions, especially when we named our group the Bad Ass Bitches—not our cohort call, but rather what we all agreed we'd name our roller derby girl gang. Her ability to conceptualize an approach and propose a solution was pivotal to her research process and, no doubt, critical when she ultimately had to outline her exit strategy from Ukraine—when air raid alarms became a daily norm and shelter visits mandatory. To be honest, the bravery it must have taken for Yuliya to leave her *husband and her family behind in Kyiv to find a safe sanctuary with her four-year-old son, Mischa, leaves me gobsmacked.*

Amid the fear and uncertainty that war sows, innocent people are called upon to assume heroic measures—to assume responsibilities they never imagined, to summon strengths they never knew they had within them, and to make heartbreaking decisions. Amid the chaos, Yuliya found strength in the signs around her, and in her dreams. She put a stranglehold on her fear. With her young son's well-being foremost in her mind, she took control of her story and fled to Switzerland. Alone now with her son, she is still uncertain of how the future will unfold, but grateful for the peace surrounding them. She follows her instincts and trusts the process in a demanding and impossible time. She is navigating new territory, physically and mentally, striving to find some balance in tending to her son and herself, and committed to being part of the "solution" and not a victim of circumstance.

Yuliya's story depicts the bravado of those who aren't on the front lines of war but every bit in the fight. Like so many others in Ukraine, Yuliya has been called upon to be strong, brave, and bold to weather a storm that has been cast unjustly—to keep keeping on, to carve out the best existence possible, to retain the hope that victory will be achieved, and a return to home victorious. Yuliya's story exemplifies the strength of spirit I think we all hope we'd have if faced with the same circumstances; how a mother's love can summon the courage to push fear aside and just do whatever possible to protect her child—to be a haven of safety and security in the most catastrophic of times.

YULIYA

I was crying and driving a super old vehicle with my four-year-old son in the back. I was desperate. I was obsessed with my child's safety. With a friend's help, I bought the cheapest car in the garage, mindful of managing my funds. I was grateful for the transportation, but leery of its dependability with no airbag—when I so needed something dependable. The car reeked of gas, and the interior was oil-smudged; perhaps it had belonged to a mechanic. I suddenly realized that I was now a refugee, far from my home and family support—a lonely mother in a clunky car.

To fuel an empty tank, I stopped at a gas station en route to our temporary shelter in Geneva. My son, Mischa, asked me to buy him a mango ice cream. He was so joyful and excited for this little treat; a symbol of carefree, celebratory times. Seeing his pleasure in enjoying his ice cream buoyed my mood a bit—as these pure, unadulterated moments have the ability to do. As we drove on, Mischa was cheering me on from the back seat, saying, "Mama, I did not know you could drive this car!" and then, more zealously asking, "Can I play with this car and imagine I am giving you a ride?" Eventually, we arrived at our destination, our home away from home, and Mischa said, "High five, Mama! We made it!" Children are amazing. They are so resilient, flexible, and full of life. My kid is the best partner in impossible circumstances, teaching me to find a balance amid the shock, panic, and stress of being far from home.

I never imagined ever living in Switzerland. I never imagined ever wanting to leave my home in Kyiv, Ukraine. I had lived in Kyiv my whole life. Together with my husband, young son, parents, and brother, I was happy—working, mothering, and tending to my home and family in Ukraine. And like the flip of a switch, in March of 2022, I found myself navigating unknown roads in a foreign land. I remember that pivotal day clearly, though blinded by tears and in shock that war is still possible in the 21st century. The choice to leave was not easy. My husband and brother are not allowed to leave the country, and my parents feel they need to stay there. It is exceptionally difficult to leave one's home country. There is no right choice to be made in times of war. Staying did not seem to be correct, and leaving did not seem to be right either.

 Three factors impacted the decision for me to take our son and go. First, there was no proper military equipment or support from other countries to close our sky. On the international arena, there was fear that doing so would just escalate matters. While I could understand some of the reasoning, I was frustrated nonetheless. There was a constant fear of aerial attacks; we could hear and see the aftermath of explosions, rattling and lighting up our nighttime sky. As a trained facilitator and coach, I remember thinking *if nobody else will do it, I will! I will become "NATO" for my son*. The second factor that influenced my decision to flee was my night dream. In it, I was holding my son in my arms, and we were standing under a blue sky, and I realized we had crossed the border. In thinking about this dream the following day, I realized that this tranquil sky represented my "new ground," the only avenue I had that might ensure my sanity and my son's safety from this brutal war. As we knew it, the earth had been shaken and shifted with every missile that fell. The third factor was understanding that going out of Ukraine was not leaving and forgetting Ukraine. I never intended to escape the war, I wanted to face it and hold Ukraine in my heart and do what I could to help my country and my people. In discussing all of this with my husband, we decided that we needed to remain a team in keeping our son safe—whether together or afar from one another. We decided that I should take Mischa and go; that I could keep our son safe and work in other ways to be resourceful in helping my land and my people. Since this fateful decision, there have been many times that I have looked up to the sky above us to fortify my resolve; to help me breathe and cope with the scary thoughts that linger—*What if I've seen my husband and parents for the last time in my life? What if we won't be able to return to Ukraine? What if there is no home left to return to?* While we are safe and my son is out of harm's way, I bear witness to Russia's atrocities and trauma on my country, people, and extended family. The peaceful sky of Geneva—one of the most serene cities in the world—allows me to feel grounded and safe; it encourages me to remain strong and present to the war situation.

It is amazing to witness my son being resilient, like many young children are. He perceives our moving out of Ukraine as a journey and enjoys planes, new places, and people. As long as he has me by his side, I believe he has a sense of home and security. He misses his father and grandparents and knows they are in Ukraine. He knows there is a "war" going on. I am not sure he understands what war is, but children absorb so much around them. At times, I believe my son senses my mood and I cannot hide it, so I try to work on myself, and sometimes I share with my son some of my feelings to be as real with him as his age will allow. Other times, I have to quell my impatience as he insists on watching "missiles and explosions" on the news. There are so many "new normals" to navigate. There is no way to completely protect my son or isolate him from what simply is. While I do not want to create undue fear in Mischa, I do try to speak of the human side of war; how the people of Ukraine remain humane and support each other.

So much devastation has befallen my country of Ukraine. The level of destruction and harm is hard to shield from innocent eyes. The reality of war seeps through even the best-laid intentions to protect; the children see and feel it in one way or another. I've witnessed this in how my son has shifted his play, his desire to engage in a game he calls "Siren, Basement, Missile." While it saddens me to think of this activity as a game, I must settle my mind and not create more trauma. Mischa has frequent questions about missiles and past shootings on the streets of Kyiv. I can't pretend that he does not recall or know this fact. He says, "Mama, if there are missiles in Geneva, I will shoot back and defend you!" This is just our reality, and I can't fight that. I can only try to restructure the moment, and use the existing context of war for our common learning and growth.

Together we are learning to cope with strong emotions and feelings of anger. I know that it is difficult for my son, but it is equally difficult for me. At times I do not know where to channel my anger about the war, the killing of my people, the fact that I don't have my husband nearby to help raise our child and share responsibilities. I have sometimes felt completely overwhelmed and found myself impulsively directing my frustrations towards my son, which I later regret. Understanding how to channel my anger, frustration, and loneliness is something I work on every day. I am very aware of how all of this can have an impact not only on my son, but on me. I know that even in the best of circumstances, parenting can be challenging and tiring. I understand that if I want to teach my son anything, I need to start with myself. I am working on coping with the complex emotions I feel; working on being kind, loving, and patient with myself and, in turn, with my son. The last thing I want is to have an "inner war" arise within me because of the physical war we've been faced with. It is not possible (and I do not want) to separate my life from the war in Ukraine. Even though we are safe, it's a constant effort to manage complex emotions and find grounding again and again—to sustain life for myself and my son.

YULIYA

It is such a huge privilege to live under a peaceful sky. I wake up daily with gratitude, as I know many Ukrainians do not have this privilege. I will never forget the moment of crossing the border and feeling silence as there were no sirens and missiles in the air. It is hard to describe how nurturing this silence felt and continues to feel. To those devoid of the experience of war, it is difficult to convey the fear you feel; it is all-consuming—the explosive sounds; the destruction; the horrific sights; the loss of loved ones, friends, or neighbors; the need to seek safe harbor. To suddenly feel peace is a such profound relief. It took several months to recover from the intense fear that gripped us in Ukraine, to come to terms as best we could with the shock of being attacked, and to really feel we were finally safe. And, yet, fear still remains. There are just so many unknowns we continue to face. I know that I will have to learn to cope with this emotion for the foreseeable future. I can't fight our circumstances. I can't fight the fact that fear is still a part of our lives. Quite honestly, facing my fears is the most demanding work I do now.

Fear is my biggest enemy—there is the fear of war, yet I know I have no control over this war; there is the fear of being a single mother (even temporarily) and this fear is, at times, all-consuming; there is the fear of what the future holds for Ukraine, for its people, and for my family. It is something I work diligently to face and process as best I can. I come from several generations of women who raised kids and sustained life independently, despite all odds, while their husbands were at war. I recall one story about my great-grandmother risking her life to be shot by Germans in WWII as she carried a big bag of salt home on her bicycle—to add nutrients to potatoes, the only food they had for their kids. When I worry about being alone to care for my son, about the uncertainties of war, I think of these women and take their strength as my own.

While I know it will take constant work to address my fears, I do not want to allow myself to be a victim of my circumstances. I see this same resolve in a lot of Ukrainians. It is a collective victory we share! In working through my fear, I usurp the power of our aggressor into my own ability—to face my fears, not relinquish my dreams, and continue to work on myself and pursue my goals. You know, to some extent, when you are kicked out of your home and homeland, when your day to day life is upended, nothing is left except *yourself*. Take my father, for example. He is a math teacher. He loves teaching kids and training them for the Olympiads. Lately, due to the Kyiv blackout, he is not able to give classes. Yet, when I call my parents and talk to my father, paradoxically, he sounds happy. Happiness and general well-being are something that nobody can truly take away from you—even in impossible circumstances. While my father is angry about what has occurred in Ukraine, to say the least, he uses his time—with no light—to go outside and breathe the air, do some physical exercises, and acknowledge what remains of nature's beauty. He carves whatever goodness he can find to both sustain and strengthen him. I find his resilience amazing and personally empowering. This is the thinking of so many Ukrainians. It is compelling. It is a warrior's mindset—a mindset that I remind myself of when I feel fear creeping in.

Before leaving Ukraine, I worked as an individual coach and a group facilitator, consulting teams and groups on relationships, communication, conflicts, and strategy. While in Geneva, I am trying to maintain my private practice as an individual coach, working as a group facilitator for the Ukrainian community, and managing my Ph.D. My work now is mostly for free, given the circumstances. Due to my responsibilities with Mischa, and the fact that I don't have anyone to help shoulder my duties, there are only a limited number of hours that I can carve out for myself or my work. We are fortunate to have partial support from the Swiss government and lucky my husband can still earn a living. As I am part of the global leadership think tank, Deep Democracy Institute (DDI), I continue my training and teaching there—going for regular coaching sessions to allow me to face my deadliest fears, and to help me cope with my current reality. Being part of DDI guided me through many impossible situations and decisions over the years—including my PhD journey and settling in Geneva. I became a student of the DDI in order to learn facilitation and conflict resolution skills. And now, I am serving as the Director of DDI Ukraine. I co-facilitate bi-weekly community meetings—initially working with my teachers, Max and Ellen Schupbach, and later with two other colleagues of DDI Ukraine. It is work I began doing when the full-scale war broke out at the beginning of 2022, and have been able to continue in Geneva. Such meetings allow participants to raise and process traumatic topics and events together; finding unexpected solutions or new perspectives that will support our collective and individual journeys. It allows me to be useful and to apply my skills in helping others going through difficult times. It is work that has proven to be a gift for me as well, giving me quite a few "aha" moments.

    While Russia may believe their war on Ukraine is a fight against NATO and the West, what they are actually doing is attempting to extinguish Ukraine and Ukrainians from existence. They would never openly admit this, but it is what they are doing. Russians are killing innocent, civil people in Ukraine, daily and ruthlessly. "Being on the border," as the name of Ukraine literally implies, is a statement that has served more as an intent for Russians to depict Ukrainians as inferior. It is a complex so many Ukrainians have grappled with their whole lives (myself included), being a colonized state in Eastern

Europe for ages. And it's a complex that I am now working to dispel. Every day I make it my mission to support Ukraine in whatever way I can and to keep the goodness of Ukraine and its people in my heart. Sometimes this is simply sharing Ukraine's heritage and history with my son—learning about the richness of who we are and what we believe. I also co-facilitate a project that supports Ukrainian women entrepreneurs—to help them navigate the new life that war has inflicted upon them, and to offer guidance on how to keep growing their businesses, despite all odds.

Though I miss my family in Ukraine, I feel tremendously grateful to have a chance to safeguard my son. I was fortunate to have a friend in Switzerland that has helped me immensely, encouraging me to come to Geneva and helping me to get settled with Mischa. She truly aided my escape from the war and, in so doing, facilitated my son's safety. For this, I will be eternally grateful. Given the circumstances of why we had to flee, it is ironic that my friend is actually of Russian descent. Her name is Xenia. We met one another ten years ago through our work. Our friendship has spanned times of great conflict between our countries—first, the war in the East of Ukraine in 2014, and now the full-scale invasion of Ukraine in 2022. Geopolitics has challenged our friendship, but we have always chosen to work on it. It was not always easy, but we chose to remain open, to listen to one another, and to work at processing all the emotions we feel—including those of love and hate. We celebrate our special connection. It gives me hope that the war can end, that people can learn to relate to each other a little bit better.

Though the months of war have dragged on far longer than I ever imagined they would, I have to maintain my hope that victory will be ours. I find contentment in my son's safety and our ability to connect often with my husband, parents, and brother. I find joy in playing guitar with my brother over the distance, and Mischa playing hide-and-seek with his grandfather over Zoom. While these precious bonding moments do not replace my strong desire to be together once again, or quell my loneliness, they make me happy to see that my family is safe and that I'm not simply dreaming of this good fortune. This gives me the strength to keep on, proving that nobody can take happiness and freedom from me, from us. It is simply impossible.

Ninety percent of the Ukrainians that have fled the war are women and children, scattered to neighboring countries and borders beyond, with little more than what their hands could carry. Many of them are mothers like me, desperate to protect our children and find support to not regress to basic duties, but to keep following our dreams. In what seems like the blink of an eye, we are suddenly, and unwittingly, refugees. The shock of how this happened, let alone to a sovereign nation, should be paramount to all who believe in and value democracy. My story is not one of pity. It is one about becoming the self. I look at my fellow Ukrainians and feel honored and privileged to be counted among them. We are united and stand together in our resolve to protect our country, our people, and our children. I am deeply grateful to all warriors of Ukraine who so valiantly and selflessly fight on the front line, standing our ground and defending Ukraine. I respect those that have stayed on in support. And, I honor and commend the many mothers, like me, that did whatever they could to safeguard their children. No decision in war is easy. I hope Mischa and I will one day return to our beloved city of Kyiv—full of life, joie de vivre, and resilience to reunite with our loved ones. Until then, I remain committed to continuing my work as a coach and facilitator, counseling and aiding Ukrainian people at home and abroad—steadfast in fighting for a blue, peaceful sky over my son and all children of Ukraine.

CHAPTER FOUR

Brittany

I entered Brittany's home and was immediately greeted by her two well-mannered children, Tate and Quinn. Both these little beings exuded pure joy, a feeling I believe emanates naturally from this family's home. Brittany had shared that she took pride in shopping for her home and in trying to make her kids' environment more memorable. This was evident by the fun playroom that was created for her two-year old daughter and four-year-old son, in what had formerly been the dining room. And, despite having two little ones, Brittany's home was beautifully well-ordered, showcasing her knack for detail and color.

The little ones led us to the kitchen, where their dad and uncle were visiting. Soon, their grandmother joined us. In all the excitement and chatter that ensued, there was a calm presence that Brittany radiated and I quickly took note. Tate had decided

BRITTANY

it was time for karaoke, and Quinn had wiggled her way into her grandmother's arms. The children were animated and energized and, yet, Brittany managed to soothe them in a manner that reflected both her innate gift as a mother, and her innate gift for conflict resolution. It is a kid-centric home, and happily so. It is a perfect reflection of how seamlessly Brittany had melded both her personal and professional abilities.

As Brittany and I sat at the kitchen table to begin our interview, Tate kindly reminded me of the candy dispenser, filled with M&M's and Skittles, should I want a snack. As the house settled, I quickly learned that Brittany is not afraid to address complex and challenging topics. For her, this is fundamental. She makes a conscious effort to cultivate inclusion and understands being caught in the middle. "Seeking language large enough to make a difference" is where we started our conversation. We both agreed how hard it can be not to react, defend, or explain—but to listen instead—a quality that has served her well with her children and her students.

Brittany is the Community Outreach Liaison for Homewood Center, an alternative public high school—located about 20 miles outside of Baltimore—that helps the historically underserved. She and her team work tirelessly advocating on behalf of their students, focusing on efforts that will better prepare them to navigate life choices after high school—a task that is especially difficult for struggling and underserved youth.

When I reflect on my conversation with Brittany, I think of how she stepped fully into the person she desired to be and became her own North Star—not only for herself, but for her children. We both agree it's crucial to learn to heal from our respective childhoods by understanding how they have affected us, both positively and negatively. Brittany's story is about evolving from the experiences you think you can't survive and, somehow, coming through stronger than ever.

The murder of George Floyd sparked something in me. I saw a woman holding a sign at one of the protests that read, *"All mothers were summoned when George Floyd called out for his momma."* Those words broke my heart in two. George Floyd called out for his mom. I am a mom. That could have been my child crying out for help. I understood, and everything seemed to hit home at once. I, too, wanted to burn the city down.

While I had grown up witnessing outright displays of hatred and racism, the magnitude of things just seemed entirely too obvious now. I felt like part of a system that was dangerously out of balance, and it couldn't be "someone else's fault" anymore. I was shattered and empowered in one single moment. It became my charge. I was inspired to create the schools and communities I desire for my children. The feeling of knowing I had uncovered my purpose is hard to describe. Yet, I hated that it took someone being tragically murdered to make things crystal clear. I grieved for George Floyd's family— for his daughter, who would grow up without her dad. I realized my children depended on me to pave the way for them. I quit being quiet at home and work. And, I started talking about race openly in front of our family, which hadn't been done before.

I grew up in a biracial family. When I was younger, I never thought about my mixed skin tone. Mom is White, and Dad is Black. I am light-skinned compared to others, which has its advantages and disadvantages. I did not understand how to own *biracial* as my race. Still, my skin and hair tell the story of where my parents and my parents' parents come from. It all marks me a bit differently.

The murder of George Floyd prompted difficult conversations for myself and others. I think my brother, Anthony, experienced something similar. Despite our loving family, neither of us had ever felt able to fully express our feelings about how we grew up, until later in life. Watching the riots, my brother and I nearly jumped off the couch. We felt their anger. We understood their breaking point. It was everything we couldn't put our finger on for so many years. Those feelings were rising in us, seeking to be released. At the same time, it affected my husband, Kevin, differently. As a Black man, Kevin said that George Floyd's murder did not hit him as hard as it hit me and others. Perhaps he had become numb to it, having already figured out how to survive in this world with a dangerous, persistent, racial divide. This speaks volumes about how long this has been going on and how bad it is.

Kevin shared with me something his boss (who is White) said to him. Essentially, his boss was disturbed by how people were thinking about the situation and told Kevin "If your train of thought is, 'Aw man, I know police murdered a Black man, but why do they have to loot the stores like that,' as opposed to, 'I wish it didn't come down to looting stores and businesses, but I understand the outrage and feeling like there's no other way to get your point across' then you have the wrong perspective." He went on to share how powerful perspective can be when we're trying to understand another point of view.

Mom admitted to my brother and me that she didn't understand why people were burning buildings, and ruining businesses and communities. Let me be clear, my Mom is my role model and the foundation of everything good in my life. I admire her caring heart and ability to effortlessly put others first. She's the one who taught me the importance of "taking cuts to the back of the line." But she didn't get it. Maybe that's unfair. She is White. How could I expect her to really get it? But I'm still upset that she doesn't. I realize, however, that I can't make her, or anyone else, understand my lived experience.

Navigating the complexities of being biracial has been lonely. Colorism, which is discrimination based on skin complexion, plays a massive role in modern society. Growing up biracial can be complicated and confusing. I lived with two identities—bouncing back and forth from being Black to White and White to Black, depending on where I was, who I was with, and what was being talked about. I unconsciously adjusted my language. I often felt like an outsider. It is still a struggle at age thirty-two, but I identify as a Black woman and acknowledge my presence as White-passing. When I was younger, I wanted to claim one or both of my races but found that was impossible. I was also never White enough, which makes my lens unique. There were also scenarios where Black women treated me like less than them due to me not being Black enough. I have grown to have deep empathy for both sides.

I sympathize with my younger self and desire to feel "whole." Divisions can be detrimental, and I straddled many situations. I was in the Gifted and Talented English class, yet I was listening to rap music. I remember straightening my curly textured hair as a teen and feeling pretty for the first time. Then, it became an obsession. I would chill with curly hair in the house, but never out and about with friends. I had friends who didn't even know my hair was curly! This didn't seem like a big deal at the time, but now that I have Quinn, my perspective has changed. I don't want her growing up thinking she needs to change what is naturally beautiful about her just to "fit in."

My family of four lived with my grandmother and grandfather from the time I was five to around twelve years old. Having all my aunts and uncles coming around all the time was incredible! My parents created a very intentional inner circle to help raise us, and each member brought something different to my worldview. Growing up predominantly White, my identity developed around my family. I had to adjust to the many ways my Blackness was presenting itself. I felt "othered" by my friends and circumstances. As I matured and moved away from the safety of my home environment, life became increasingly complicated. My desire to belong really ramped up in middle school, and I started to feel like I didn't exist where I was existing. It felt like there was no place I could be safe anymore. I never shared these feelings with anyone. I just focused on basketball and school—which was easy to do, as both took up a ton of time. I am a first-generation college student, and that was another big adjustment. I found myself dealing with explicit racism for the first time in my life. Once, a boy who was interested in me asked one of my teammates if I would be willing to go out on a date with him. I said yes. After learning that I was Black, he canceled our date, telling me he could not subject his future babies to that.

Previous to George Floyd's death, navigating the complexities of being biracial was complicated, lonely, and depressing. Today, it feels awakening, motivating, and comforting! I am building upon the inspiring influences I had growing up and the hard-earned insights I have gained. Every day, I strive to create a space for Tate and Quinn to embrace their heritage. I have repeatedly told Kevin how grateful I am that my kids look like me. Maybe that sounds selfish, but I am so comforted by the fact that we look alike. We can relate in ways that others can't. After years of defining for myself what it means to be biracial, I now understand what it takes to own it. Embodying this unique characteristic will allow me to support my children through their upbringings as biracial people—giving me the opportunity to vicariously share the experiences I have and the pride I feel. That was never an option for my parents.

My dad is the hardest-working human I know. He taught my brother Anthony and me about his Black culture, and his community growing up. I was significantly impacted by my memories of our car rides to the barbershop, blasting Biggie. It wasn't until we had the hard conversations, following George Floyd's murder, that I realized race was a motivating factor in the work ethic shared by my dad and my brother. I guess I just thought that "hard work" was ingrained in us, something we all shared because we had hard-working parents. My mom and dad did everything in their power to provide for us. I can honestly say that most of what my brother and I have accomplished in our lives is to honor them.

My "baby brother," Anthony, started working for the Ohio State Football Team as a Student Manager—collecting balls, doing laundry, and other tasks. Eventually, he worked his way up to cornerbacks and special team's Student Assistant, then to Recruiting Assistant. He goes above and beyond daily, and people notice that. He now works in the National Football League (NFL), where he has earned multiple promotions and will ultimately become a General Manager. We all know it.

The way my dad and Anthony describe it, they had no choice but to work the hardest, to be the best, to be the first one to arrive and the last one to leave—while making no mistakes. It upset me to my core knowing that their work ethic was partly a response to the ignorant assumptions people made based on the color of their skin. I wondered how this would one day impact my son. I felt as if Dad and Anthony, though visibly hurt in those moments, felt there was nothing that could be done about this reality. So, they endured it.

On June 7, 2020, I drove to Washington, DC, with Kevin, Tate, Mom, Dad, Anthony, and my Uncle Mike. We wanted to see Black Lives Matter Plaza in person. Watching from the TV screen wasn't enough. Being there both broke my soul and filled me with hope at the same time. We were there—thousands of us! Our lives mattered. To see so much love and support during a time when it felt like all that existed was hate and murder… it felt safe somehow. Having my two-year-old, Black son there with me was surreal. I wondered if two was too young to bring him to a protest. *When does he become a criminal in the eyes of other people? Surely not at two. When do I make him aware that life will be different for him? How old will he be when people start treating him differently? Or did that start at birth?*

I took a picture of him in front of a sign posted a few hundred yards from the White House that read simply, "Stop Killing Black People." I'm not sure who told him to put his hands up, but his hands were raised as if he were surrendering. My innocent, beautiful, perfect baby boy. He is a Black boy who will become a Black kid, and a Black man. He is mine. He will always be mine. How will I protect him?

When I look at that picture, I see all of the students I work with in the face of my son. In 2013, I started substitute teaching at Homewood Center, an alternative secondary high school for grades six through twelve, located just over four miles from our home in Columbia, Maryland. After three months of working with the kids, I realized two things: the first was just how much help they needed, and the second was that Homewood Center was the best place to tackle the systemic needs of these historically underserved kids. I felt capable and qualified to fight this battle with them. I've recently become the Community Outreach Liaison at Homewood, a position that entails the constant struggle to get basic needs met. Families come to us at their most desperate. The work is endless and ever-changing. Trying to capture progress is not easy. Homewood is constantly fighting the inequities that lead disadvantaged groups to be funneled out of public schools and into juvenile and criminal justice systems. It is fundamental to acknowledge that Homewood is often the last stop in the all-too-common school-to-prison pipeline. Many of our kids end up dead, homeless, jailed, working part-time as young parents, and lacking services to meet their basic needs. Many get lost in the shuffle of the system, even if they survive and don't end up shot or in prison. It's literally do or die after they leave Homewood. This is what fuels our work. I take pride in rallying community support around my students.

It is a hard job, but there are so many small victories and moments of joy. One example that comes to mind was a trip we planned to the local library. The trip was meant to be a general overview of what a library has to offer. Our aim was to (hopefully) impress upon this group of students that libraries are safe places, full of helpful resources and caring people. When we reached the end of our agenda, we still had about ten minutes until the bus arrived to take us back to Homewood. We told the students they could browse books. One student, Jinia, picked out her very first library book and asked whether she would be able to check it out. That moment filled me up. We had planned this as an opportunity for these students to recognize the future potential of the library; that the library would allow them to access resources that would support them in job seeking, basic financial literacy, and obtaining community services—such as housing and food assistance. But this girl just wanted to check out a book. Sometimes, what our kids need can feel so complex and overwhelming. But sometimes, it is so simple.

What I want most for my Homewood kids is a future that looks different for each of them. However that lens may unfold, my hope is that they all find employment in fields they enjoy—jobs that pay a livable wage with upward mobility; health insurance to support them and their families; mental health support for their stresses and traumas; and meaningful connections in their communities, to support them when they face hardship or setbacks. I want to hand them to a community that accepts them, understands them, and loves them. It's the sort of future that I also want for Tate and Quinn.

I think a lot about how I can give my children the tools to navigate their future. But, in short, what I want them each to do is simply live their truth. That means being willing to engage in uncomfortable conversations and challenging the system. Being verbal with your intentions takes courage, but knowing where you came from and who you are is your strength. As their mother, I hope they see me as interested and engaged, working for the betterment of everyone. I want them to be comfortable approaching me with their questions and feelings. Kevin and I have had many conversations on how to parent. I love the fact that I get to raise children with him— there is no one better for the job. Even though a third kid seems completely overwhelming right now, it seems almost selfish not to consider. We have unlimited love and dedication, so why not? Fundamentally,

Kevin and I want our kids to have absolutely everything they desire. Simultaneously, we want them to be grounded, humble, independent, and willing to work their asses off to achieve their goals. Sure, we both want our kids to be standout students and athletes, but I think what will stand the test of time is helping them become good people—respectful, genuine, and loving. We both take a lot of pride in doing right by our kids, even at our own expense—and I don't see that ever changing. My hope is that that selflessness will live on through them. We both like to say we're "built for it." That's us. It encompasses so much in a few words.

     Before we even started our family, Kevin and I knew we wanted our kids to grow up where we did and attend Howard County Schools. Howard County Public School System (HCPSS) has been, and continues to be, one of the top ten school districts nationwide. However, what I treasure most about my experience growing up in the HCPSS was the economic and racial diversity. It seemed like our dream was coming true! We were in a position to leave Baltimore before our kids were school-age and possibly provide them with that Howard County living we dreamed of. But things were *expensive,* and the housing market was insane! As we were looking for a home in Howard County, we found ourselves shunning specific neighborhoods of Columbia—though these were the neighborhoods where the homes we could afford were located. I was being a hypocrite. I was "talking the talk" at work with and for my students, but I wasn't "walking the walk" when it came to my own family. I was playing both sides. I just wanted the best for my kids—the best schools, opportunities, and teachers. But what was the cost?

     I love Columbia and what it stands for. A big part of our move was to provide our kids with the same foundation we had growing up, centered around diversity and inclusion. And I knew that my children would be okay because they had Kevin and me advocating for them, no matter where they were in the world—let alone at school in one of the top districts in the nation. We found our dream house—behind a community of apartments and across the street from subsidized housing. There is a public bus stop at the top of our street, and a members-only golf course just a mile away. There is a neighborhood community center that can be reached within minutes, as well as a lake, a school, a playground, and my parents. It is the perfect place for us, a perfect blend of all that is life.

Building our dream takes work. In my own life, I am juggling many balls. I am a mother to two young children— in addition to being a wife, daughter, friend, coworker, and mentor. I work hard toward my goal of creating a better world for my children and my community. I see myself as a bridge between the past, present, and future generations. But, truthfully, I am in a constant state of go, go, go and do, do, do. The hustle is constant! I don't often take time to get my nails done or have coffee with a friend. The reason I share this is that I know how important it is. Women, especially, have the tendency to take care of others before they take care of themselves.

If I could go back and talk to my younger self—to that girl who felt like she didn't fit in or have anyone to connect with—I would tell her that she is both brave and vulnerable. I would hug her tightly and acknowledge all the pain that she has felt. Then I'd assure her that every ounce of it was worth it because all those experiences shaped her into the woman, wife, mom, and advocate she has become. And I'd tell her to keep fighting because the future belongs to the people who aren't afraid to stand up for what is right.

CHAPTER FIVE

Alix

*H*orses and happenstance brought Alix and me together. I randomly met her through a friend of a friend in Chantilly, France, in April of 2022. I was visiting this enchanting town, about an hour's drive north of Paris, with my equine-crazed husband, Tim, and our oldest son, Cole.

Chantilly is coined the "horse capital" of France, as it is the location of the country's principal horse-training center—one of the oldest and biggest in France, training more than 3,000 thoroughbred horses daily! It is also home to one of the country's most renowned racecourses, built in 1840, and the site of two of the country's four most important and classic horse races. It is here at The Grand Stables, where the country's historic passion for horses merges with the equestrian arts.

ALIX

Our visit was very horse-driven, indeed, mixing and mingling with other like-minded enthusiasts. It was at one of these gatherings, a dinner, that I met Alix.

On this particular evening, we dined at what would be considered a typical French country inn-type restaurant. I was situated directly across the table from Alix and recall taking note of her stylish, pixie-cut gray hair and sparkling green eyes. She was the girlfriend and guest of one of the horse-trainers we knew. They had been together for more than a decade, but this was our first introduction. Though Alix was initially coy about her personal life and career, it wasn't long before I realized that her resumé said otherwise.

I quickly learned that she had adeptly combined her two passions; management and horseracing. She had held the position of Head of Marketing and Development at Arqana—France's leading auction house. And she also had impressive affiliations with other organizations, such as Thoroughbred Daily News and Destination Europe Racing. We chatted briefly throughout dinner and I noted how respectfully attentive she was to our twenty-three-year-old son, Cole, the youngest member of our dinner group. The two of them had several convivial conversations which I enjoyed witnessing from afar, impressed with Alix's generosity in including Cole so effortlessly. I sat in silence, listening to the chatter around me, appreciating the evocative walls, covered in old and original advertisements, and the numerous memorabilia that dotted nearly every surface. Later that evening, Cole mentioned that he found Alix to be a remarkable listener; something I would later realize is one of her superpowers.

As our visit in Chantilly progressed, and my communications with Alix broadened, I came to learn about her lifelong struggle with mental illness and its stigma.

What propelled me to capture Alix's story is simple: it is relatable to me on a very personal level. Similar to Alix's experience, I am also a high-functioning depressed person, having dabbled with medication during distinct junctures in my life. In my family, mental illness runs rampant. My great-grandmother, Alvina, suffered several mental breakdowns and was hospitalized more than once back in the '50s, when the public defined mental illness in much narrower and more extreme terms. Surprisingly, my great-grandmother was contemporary enough to start support groups in her home to help advocate for and support others in managing their mental illness. She called these groups "recovery meetings" and held them in the hope of improving communication about the struggles of mental illness; and in the hope of discovering a broader impetus for change.

Believing in the importance of bringing the subject of mental illness out of the shadows, I was delighted when Alix agreed to be interviewed by me several months later. Though we had initially planned to reconnect back in Chantilly, I instead traveled to Paris' 20th arrondissement, located in the northeastern part of the city, as Alix's life had since turned completely upside down. She and her partner, who was the conduit to our connection, had separated. As a result, Alix had relocated to the city of Deauville, a charming seaside town in the Normandy region of France—situated along the English Channel—and renowned not only for its waterside location, but for its horseracing and related activities. Though Alix resided in Deauville, she commuted daily to her work in Paris—a roundtrip train ride of more than four hours!

ALIX

I met with Alix at Mama Shelter East, a quirky and quaint hotel located near the Belleville underground station—a hotel that very much matched the eclectic aesthetic of the neighborhood it was nestled in. We settled into a table at the hotel's rooftop bar, and Alix proceeded to distill the years of destruction she had experienced as a result of her battle with eating disorders and depression. She spoke of the challenges she faced and her quest to define the direction of the next chapter of life—as she "searches for life's purpose." She acknowledged that her connecting lines—that which propelled her personal challenges and that which offered some healing—start from her eating disorders at an early age, followed by the curative power that horses had in her life.

Alix was forthcoming. We were quick to agree that the educational dynamic of mental health can often titillate the public forum—both good and bad—but that so much was still left to do in order to truly meet the tremendous needs of the mentally ill. Millions of people suffer in silence and are left to face the reality of living with mental illness in solitude. Families barely communicate. Technology does not help. Therapy has its stigma. Stereotyping, prejudice, and ongoing discrimination against people with mental illness are dangerous. Medication, and other tools designed to provide relief, can be far-reaching and/or take time to institute. Only a few are brave enough to step forward and share their struggles. Alix is one.

Melancholy takes many shapes and forms. As a result, there is no one-size-fits-all solution to mental illness. Alix is a living example of recovery as a work in progress. She has made it her life mission to share her story, not only for herself—in an effort to find purpose and meaning in life—but to help others. She has managed to meld the pros and cons of her life, so to speak. She has an affinity for horses and their healing nature, and she struggles with mental illness. Combining these two very present parts of her life, she works as a "professional with lived experience," hired by a psychiatric hospital in Paris. She uses her expertise (her lived experience) to help others with mental illnesses. Pair Aidance, which is beginning to be implemented in Europe, and has been used successfully in Canada, is a form of peer-to-peer assistance.

I applaud my great-grandmother for her efforts to address her own struggles with mental illness and her desire to help others, and I deeply respect Alix for her work in the field of peer-to-peer assistance, as it relates to mental illness. I especially applaud Alix for having the mettle and moxie to get on stage in Chantilly for a TED talk in January of 2022, courageously exposing her soul. No matter how intense the story becomes, the discomfort of uncomfortable conversations is necessary for progress to occur. We need more people like Alvina and Alix to come forth and stand in their truth, despite their desire to crawl inward. This is the story of one woman, one brave and vulnerable soul that never gave up, that stood up and spoke her truth. And, in so doing, is bringing much needed light, understanding, and attention to the issue of mental illness.

M y name is Alix. I am 40 years old. And, I don't love life. For as far back as I can remember, I have been longing for it to finish.

In my view, humankind splits into two irreconcilable groups: those who think '*life is a gift*' and those who are certainly "*not grateful for life.*" And virtually every single thing associated with these two groups differs—every belief, want, or action. How could they ever understand each other?

The first group, those that believe life is a gift, holds the majority—the majority in terms of population, perhaps, but more so the majority in terms of respect. I mean, I think most people find it offensive not to think of life as being a gift. You MUST love life. It is assumed that this will be the case, so much so that people do not even ask your opinion before exclaiming, *"there is no greater gift than the gift of giving life"* or *"where there is life, there is hope!"*

These statements reflect personal opinions I respect, yet I have difficulty understanding them. I reside in the second group, the group that isn't grateful for life.

When I was a child, I didn't dream of becoming a princess or an astronaut when I grew up. I wanted to be a saint, so I could die young without any of the guilt associated with suicide.

As a teenager, I had depressive episodes, except I didn't know what they were yet. I also thought I was fat, as did most all the girls my age. The problem was that I developed an obsession with deprivation; an obsession that filled my life. I vividly remember the morning when I said to myself, "There is ONE thing I can control. I *can't* control the course of my life. I *can't* make other people like me. But, I CAN control my weight." This became my grand project.

Depression runs rampant on both sides of my family. Sadly, denial of its existence—in any family—causes a lot of undue harm. It is important to recognize that genetic vulnerability is valid. I did not have a traumatic childhood and, yet, at the age of sixteen, symptoms started to show. There was no stabilization. I was simply described as a sad child. I felt like I lived in a continual maze, trapped within what I was experiencing, and burdened by the very palpable stigma of my mental illness, anorexia, and suicidal thoughts. I isolated myself and my condition from everyone around me. Not wanting to eat or be alive (something I felt from the age of sixteen to forty) was a conscious choice. I wore a mask to disguise the pain I felt, both inside and outside, for years. Even at thirty years old, I would return home from work crying, eat, and throw up. This was grueling on my body. Physically, I looked and felt awful. The body dysmorphia was ongoing. I felt dizzy and I had teeth issues.

Anorexia is a hard drug. Under the influence of the lack of food, your body goes into survival mode, and you have a kind of adrenaline rush—it's totally addictive. Once you get into this vicious cycle, *"nothing tastes as good as skinny feels."* It was Kate Moss, the famous British model, that made this statement, but I certainly bought into it. For a long time, I thought I just had a problem with food. In fact, the first doctor I went to thought the same thing. He asked me, *"Do you smoke? You don't? That's a shame. You could have had a cigarette instead of making yourself vomit."* I also consulted nutritionists, who made me write down everything I ate or didn't, to no avail.

So, it took me a while to realize that my problem was not eating too much or too little. It was life itself that I was throwing up. After seven years, I went to a psychiatrist who prescribed me antidepressants. Little by little, I found that I could distance myself from my addiction and regain some sense of self-confidence. At first, whenever I felt better, I tried to stop the treatment. I wanted to stand on my own two feet, without a crutch. No sooner would I do this than I would relapse. Once, when I returned with my tail between my legs—after another attempt at quitting my medication—my doctor said, "You know, you won't get a medal for stopping." Somehow it registered with me that taking my medication was not an act of weakness, so I decided to go along with it.

I used to ride horses, and while I was a student, I discovered racehorses. And, in so doing, I also discovered that my body could be useful. Suddenly, my body was no longer this cumbersome thing that I needed to pare down to a bare minimum. Instead, my body served a very important role—it was the means by which I could access the most magical sensations. To be able to feel the exhilaration of speed on a thoroughbred at full gallop, I had to be strong. I had to be fit. I had to have a clear head. I had to feed my body because I NEEDED it for an activity that gave me so much pleasure.

So, for 11 years, I remained on the same antidepressant and did relatively well. I worked and I had a boyfriend. I had the kind of life that was judged respectable by the majority. In the summer, with sunshine and good weather, I'd sometimes experience periods of mild euphoria. I would sleep and eat very little, work tirelessly, and party every night. Everyone thought I was great company. I noticed how pleased everyone was to see me in such a good mood.

Every winter, however, was an ordeal. The low I felt when winter rolled around became more and more pronounced, to the point that I thought I wouldn't be able to see it through. As a result, every two years or so, my doctor had to increase my antidepressant dosage in order to keep the medication working. Then one day, I felt that all the fences I had built up over so many years—between me and suicide—were giving way. I asked to be hospitalized and was told that I was suffering from "melancholy." There is nothing romantic about melancholy in psychiatry. It is the *melan-cholia* of the ancient Greeks, etymologically the "black bile," the ultimate darkness.

    I remember going to the breakfast room on my first day in the hospital. There I sat looking at the other patients who, after having had their coffee and toasts, would spend time out in the garden. Once outside, they either paced in small groups, sat on a bench to have a cigarette, or chatted with others. I couldn't comprehend where these people—who also suffered from mental breakdowns or they wouldn't be there—found the will to engage in such futile activities. My will had vanished. There was absolutely nothing that would drive or push me in any direction. I sat there for a long time…and then I collapsed.

    I was given some potent drugs to "ease the moral pain." I turned into a shadow of myself.

    Every morning, the psychiatrist visited my room. He never needed to ask me how I felt. I guess my whole attitude—my look, my demeanour—spoke volumes. In those early days, the doctor seemed almost as depressed as I was when he retreated from my bedside. In an effort to find some way forward, I was prescribed a whole battery of antidepressants, anxiolytics, and mood regulators—in various combinations and dosages. After one month and several failures, my doctor took a chance with a drug designed for Parkinson's disease; one which has been observed to have an antidepressant effect. A few days later, on waking, something felt different. I no longer felt as if my head was being held underwater. It was a radically new outlook on life. After a few days, I told the doctor I was feeling exceptionally well and couldn't wait to leave. I was amazed at how quick and profound the improvement had been. To my surprise, the doctor didn't seem to share my joy. Instead, he said "I was going to tell you that you have started a manic swing. We're going to stop this drug immediately and keep you on lithium." So that was it. I didn't merely have melancholy, but bipolarity as well. Still, I felt a glimmer of life was running in my veins again. And, it hasn't stopped since.

During my time in the hospital, I had been with many patients who had been waiting for months to find a treatment to ease their anxiety or dark thoughts, to no avail. When I left, I knew I had been fortunate. A clever combination of molecules had succeeded in repairing my malfunctioning brain. That isn't the case for everyone, as many suffer in silence. I learned that melancholy is often fatal and that 30% of depression cases go untreated.

I also realized that mental illness *still* frightens people; many recoil from any conversation on mental illness. Sadly, my partner never showed any interest in visiting me while I was hospitalized, and I noticed that he seemed to shut down whenever my condition was mentioned. When I finally returned home after seven weeks, I also discovered that he hadn't said a word about my condition or hospital stay to anyone—so our mutual friends greeted me as if I'd just come back from a long holiday, even though I honestly didn't look like a holidaymaker.

Despite my partner's disinterest (or embarrassment), I felt like talking about what had happened to me. I had a vague feeling that I wasn't the only one to have had the experience I had and I felt that sharing it could be helpful to others. So, I started to talk about my experience quite freely, notwithstanding my partner's appalling looks or disrespectful queries— "So you told him you were crazy?"

As I became more and more interested in my mental health and how my experience might help others, I came across a job offer that was a bit unusual. There were two prerequisites for applying: a graduate degree and having spent time in a psychiatric hospital. "For once," I said, "I tick all the boxes!"

My job involves accompanying people with mental health issues, based on my experience as a "recovering" patient. We say 'recovering' and not 'cured' because recovery is an ongoing process, like a tightrope walker whose equilibrium is always uncertain. In real terms, it means that I am still undergoing treatment—that I will be in treatment for the rest of my life. And that therapists are still monitoring me to ensure that caring for others does not cause me any harm. But that doesn't stop me from recognizing the significance of what I AM and what I DO. I can be both carer and cared for. Even the expression of my vulnerability gives a specific value to my words. On my badge, it says *Peer Support Worker*. And "peer" is understood to be in relation to the patients.

So, now it's official! Everyone knows I'm "crazy," as my former partner found such satisfaction in coining my condition. My challenge is now my superpower. And that's exactly why I'm called in.

I work with patients between the ages of 16 and 25. I try to assist them with living with a mental condition. Sometimes an appointment is spent scheduling a weekly routine for a teenager who no longer gets out of bed. Sometimes we discuss how it feels to have been diagnosed as mentally ill, how it shapes our identity, and how to distance ourselves from our symptoms. Sometimes it is parents that I try to advise. Sometimes the session consists of going to the market with a young girl with an eating disorder. Every day is different. And every day, I am amazed by the willpower these young adults display. Despite their depression, bipolarity, or schizophrenia, life is still a gift for most of them.

While I have made great strides, there is still an ongoing stigma that surrounds mental illness; one I continue to struggle with, one that impacts how I process the social norms of what it means to survive and thrive. The idea of being whole was something I longed for but did not feel attainable. Exposing myself, and my words—through a TED talk platform in Chantilly, France, in January of 2022, and now to you on the S.H.E. stage—is a way to structure my story and express how I have expelled the black bile (the melancholia) from my body.

The lack of emotional validation from others, including my partner of ten years, taught me the importance of having a relationship that values closeness and connection; a relationship that recognizes that vulnerability is an asset. It didn't take long for me to realize that these key elements of a healthy relationship were missing from the relationship I had with my long-time partner. First, he never made any effort to visit me during my seven-week hospital stay, which says a lot about his character. And, after my TED talk, he would not speak to me. While it made me sad to be denied or dismissed solely because of my condition, it certainly wasn't surprising. I am much relieved that this relationship is now behind me—though I do find it sad that the stigma attached to mental illness played such a heavy role.

The slight change in my personal organization was another obstacle to overcome. Starting over in a new city, on my own, and a bit of a commute to my work and doctors, definitely added some complexity to my ongoing recovery. Yet, it is but one more lesson in adaptation that I have met head on, and been able to find my path out of the darkness and into the light. There are, however, still challenges. The stereotypes are accurate. The fallouts can be draining. My purpose moving forward is not specific. But, I am grateful to have a medical solution to the problem around which my existence used to revolve—the problem of *how to stay alive*. It took time to find a resolution to the nuances in my emotional state. Having found such a solution compels me to share my story with others on depression/melancholy. It is important to impart that there IS light at the other end of the tunnel!

I feel fortunate to convey my experience with others, hoping that what I share might serve as an aid in their own paths to recovery. During my TED talk, I mentioned being "crazy," which may not be a suitable word when advocating for mental health awareness. My intention was to offer language that would accurately convey my condition: my brain is not functioning correctly, and medication and therapy can help me alleviate the pain. Let me just say that me using this word in reference to myself, versus someone else using the word to describe me, is vastly different. The fact is that the word "crazy" implies a characterological issue or flaw in personality, rather than a brain illness, which is misleading when dealing with mental illness.

Each hardship or problem (or terminology quagmire!) I have had has helped me to improve and understand aspects of myself that I was previously unaware of. I certainly did not have the proper guidance early on, and the road to finding the right medication has been highly frustrating. If you have a broken arm or if someone is ailing from either cancer or diabetes, the goal is to fight to find the right remedy. Locating the proper medication is never a one-stop shop. The struggles and ups and downs of finding the right doctor, medicine, or therapist can be infuriating—and significantly impede progression. Remember that doctor that told me I should start smoking to resolve my bulimia! I'm so thankful my journey did not end with him. Don't give up, no matter how many roadblocks appear.

Sharing my experience and allowing others to connect with my innermost feelings is the best way for me to add value to this world. Mental illness knows no pedigree. It afflicts young and old, rich and poor, and the good and the evil among us with equal ferocity. As an educated woman—from a privileged background and a supporting family—I feel it is incumbent upon me to share my story. There is no shame in mental illness. There is no need to conceal its existence. It is an illness of the brain and should be addressed with the same dignity and respect we reserve for the remedy of the many illnesses that exist—cancer, diabetes, heart disease, arthritis, etc. I hope that in speaking my truth, in sharing my story, that others will be encouraged to speak up, to seek the help they need, and, ultimately, to dispel the myths surrounding mental illness and, with them, the silent suffering so many have needlessly endured.

CHAPTER SIX

Bailey

*L*ife *is not fair. You hear this statement flippantly delivered time and again to account for virtually any challenge life might present. While it may fall flat, it is in the most egregious of life's challenges that the concept of "fairness" loses complete relevance. There is simply no meaningful way to rectify fairness when it comes to events in life that cause immense pain, sorrow, anguish, or trauma.*

Abuse is one of these events—an act so inhumane that its existence in our society defies belief, or fairness. And yet, abusive behavior is quite prevalent worldwide—emotional, psychological, physical, verbal, sexual, etc.—with a host of ramifications. Victims of abuse can feel isolated, fearful, and distrustful—all of which can manifest into lifelong psychological consequences such as low self-esteem, depression, self-harm, and trouble forming and maintaining relationships. When that abuse is suffered as a child, the path to recovery is evermore laden with challenge as there is no sense of self or maturity to begin to comprehend the transgression.

This is the story of Bailey, an amazingly captivating, vividly mature, intelligent 21-year-old woman who just two years ago felt her life might not be worth living. She had reached the pinnacle of her pain, feeling that her hurt had become too great a burden to bear. Until the age of 10, she had suffered sexual abuse at the hands of her grandmother's husband.

My first conversation with Bailey began as an interview to discuss the possibility of her being an artist for S.H.E., Volume Two. However, early into our chat, she asked if and when I might be writing Volume Three. Perhaps sensing my surprise at the question, she immediately said that she had a story that she might now be "ready to share." Needless to say, this revelation changed the trajectory of our conversation. After several more discussions, Bailey agreed she was willing to be the artist and the storyteller for her own chapter in S.H.E. This is the first time I've encountered this swift change of track, but I'm so honored for Bailey to share her story. Not only is she brave in doing so, she is generous. I believe that sharing frees our souls, but also reaches out to others in ways that can make us all feel a little less alone, a little less trapped. If we see some of our own pain in the expression of another, there is a connection that can form and allow healing. And with healing comes empowerment.

Bailey is in the process of transforming trauma; working through it rather than existing in it. We all work through "stuff" at various points in our lives, some more burdensome than others. For many, even believing an outlet of hope exists is hard to fathom. It is somewhat redeeming for another to hold space and understanding for our stories—our pain—allowing a purging of sorts to safely occur; allowing a new perspective to surface; providing a life line out of anguish. Bailey's ultimate experience with therapy offered her this life line. For myself, therapy has been pivotal in healing my own trauma. Interconnection, support, and social cohesion are paramount to my being able to process and repair the broken pieces of myself. To varying degrees, we are all a bit of broken porcelain in places. Understanding that there is help out there to restore us to our best selves is the first hurdle to getting to the other side of pain.

In discussing the process of healing with Bailey, I was reminded of the Japanese artisanry known as kintsugi, meaning "gold seams." It is a process that was introduced centuries ago in Japan, whereby artisans use lacquer and gold pigment to put shattered pottery back together. It is a repair method that is still going strong today. As an artist herself, I'm sure Bailey would relate to this correlation. Japanese artisans revere this technique, viewing the highlighted cracks and repairs as events in the life of the object—something beautiful to acknowledge and celebrate. They believe that allowing the mended objects to continue in service, as opposed to disposing of them, is honorable. To view the mending of our souls in this same manner is a comforting thought—an endeavor where our broken parts are literally seen as worthy of repair and beautiful in their imperfection.

Bailey and I both confessed that our initial experiences with therapy were daunting. This is not uncommon. It can take time to acknowledge that you are ready and want help, and time to find someone you really connect with. The key, and difficult part when you are in the midst of struggle, is to keep after it, to commit to finding and making that connection. Thankfully, Bailey did in June of 2021, and it is proving to be *a life-changing experience. I think one of the most profound revelations that Bailey made early on in her process of recovery was the realization that dissecting trauma from the soul of who you are allows it to be viewed as its own apparition, apart from the essence of you. With the help of her therapist, also named Shannon, Bailey is learning to reclaim herself, and take her power back. She is incredibly thankful to have found a therapist that she truly feels safe, confident, and comfortable with. She credits Shannon with helping her to restore her sense of well-being.*

It takes courage to demand a new way forward—to work through the many pitfalls that trauma presents and determinedly forge forth. The fortitude it takes to seek, commit, and stay on a path to recovery develops skillsets that improve over time. As her therapist, Shannon, expressed to Bailey, her goal as a therapist is to train Bailey to be her "own therapist." I feel this approach is so empowering. Bailey is already making inroads on a better and brighter path. She is not only a talented, self-trained artist, she will also graduate in December of 2023 with her Masters in Architecture. She obtained her Bachelor of Arts in Architecture in only three years, at the University of Kentucky, which is truly extraordinary. What the next year of her life will unveil is yet to be written—but I trust it will be just as extraordinary as she is.

Bailey believes in her ability to evolve and sees that freedom is on the other side of fear. In connecting with her over Zoom, I found comfort being in her presence. There is a captivating vibe that people who are willing to grow radiate, and Bailey definitely exudes this. Though our one-to-one chats were via video, I still felt like I was a welcome guest in her home; a space that warmly mimics her personality. Her bookcase is lined with meaningful knick-knacks that bring her joy, and volumes of psychology and architecture paperbacks bookended by Corinthian column-looking sculptures. She is a prolific reader and seeker of knowledge. Her feline, named Kitty, offers her immeasurable support and companionship. If not slinking about, she is nestled in a hammock that hangs in the front window; a secure perch to witness the day's happenings, including Bailey's every move. In a comfy leather chair that sits nearby rests a pillow that I think says it all: "Enjoy Today."

While Bailey is learning to step into herself, she is already an expressive (and impressive) young woman. Clearly indicative of her creative nature are the beautiful tattoos she has thoughtfully chosen to represent herself. Each one of her tattoos symbolizes a significant story. On both of her forearms are columns. On her right arm, the column is coiled with a serpent. On her left arm it is coiled with ivy. The near-mirror imagery represents the duality in her life—architecture and life, broken and together. The octopus on her shoulder represents a time in high school when she was printmaking. She sketched the art for the one on her chest, of a Gemini—a nod to her astrological sign. And on her back is the Pantheon—a fitting symbol of protection. The dome structure of the Pantheon was intended to represent the continuity of the heavens, with those under its canopy watched over by the gods. It is also beautifully representative of Bailey's own artistic skills.

At the heart of Bailey is an urgency and curiosity not to rush past her hurt, but rather to move fluidly through her pain in order to fully understand it. I respect Bailey's openness in sharing her involvement with therapy and how it has allowed her to face her fears in a safe space, learning the skills that will help her process her feelings and emotions in a healthy way.

She is teaching herself how to deconstruct trauma and lean into her discomfort, knowing that vulnerability can be excruciating, but also empowering. I am so grateful that she is sharing her story here in these pages. Her story is about overcoming childhood trauma, but is also about so much more. It's about bravery, fortitude, perseverance, honesty, empowerment, self-love, and generosity. So, thank you, Bailey, for entrusting us with your words and, through your words, helping others that might also be struggling. When we shine a light on darkness, others can also see.

Trauma is something that happens to us, not who we are.

It takes a long time to fully comprehend the significance of this statement and just how impactful it is in the process of healing from trauma. There are so many habits and things that we do that are engrained from traumatic experiences; things that become entangled in our psyche and difficult to extract.

For me, the road of healing and undoing trauma has had many bumps, turns, pits of despair, and, sadly, no bypasses. It wasn't until the last year and a half that I have felt hopeful. With the help of therapy, I have grown tremendously and learned things about myself I never knew were buried under years of trauma responses. While it took some time, I do believe this is something that anyone can achieve. It is so common for humans to get caught up in the past and relive trauma, allowing it to consume our lives. Getting out of your head and thinking about *why* you do *what* you do is imperative to the healing process. My trauma and experiences have led me to where I am today. Two years ago, I would have never believed that was possible.

The specific history of my trauma is not worth getting into. What I can say is that my step-grandfather sexually assaulted me as a child, up until the age of ten. I did not tell anyone until a couple of years ago, silently harboring this secret for more than ten years. This monster is now in jail and will remain there for ten more years.

Needless to say, my childhood did not follow the innocent trajectory that should be the norm for all children. Beyond the abuse inflicted upon me, there was instability in other parts of my life. My father is an addict and also spent time in prison during the early part of my childhood. Apart from a brief three-year period where I split my time between his home and my mom's, he wasn't a huge part of my life. And this arrangement only lasted a few years because he relapsed when I was seventeen, sending my life into a spiral just six months before I was supposed to leave for college. He lost his house, my car got repossessed, his wife spent my college funds on drugs, and I saw her overdose (too many times to count). A year after all this occurred, in March of 2020, I was in a serious accident while in Florida with some girlfriends. We were all in a golf cart getting a lift back to our place when we were hit by a drunk driver with a blood alcohol level of .256. (I'll interject at this point to just say that the driver of our golf cart was sober.) The accident was incredibly scary and left me with lasting health issues. Because of the harrowing nature of the accident, tensions escalated—trauma can do that—and friendships ruptured.

I had internalized my childhood trauma for so many years by this point in time. It was like a cancer, eating me from the inside out. And the challenging life experiences that continued to plague me certainly didn't help. All of this just manifested into a host of problems. I struggled with an eating disorder, depression, anxiety, and extreme anger. The anger that burned within me started around the age of fifteen, and progressively worsened between the ages of nineteen and twenty. I lost friends, drank heavily, took drugs, and used sex to escape. I was also suicidal. My anger would get the best of me at bars. My friends would use me as a party trick—decking forty-year-old men who would hit on my girlfriends was like a walk in the park. I tried multiple therapists, went through a few boyfriends, pushed away all of my friends, and relied heavily on self-medication (drugs and alcohol…a lot of it!) to feel afloat in daily life. Somehow, I always managed to be on top of schoolwork.

I was eventually diagnosed with post-traumatic syndrome. I had huge insomnia and struggled with safety and trust issues. I was merely existing. My whole life was spinning out of control, though I gave the outward impression that I had it all together—inside I was a wreck. I was oddly self-aware of the façade I had created, though it was a vicious mind loop and definitely taxing to maintain. While therapy would likely have proved beneficial at various points, I wasn't ready. I know this is probably hard for someone who has never experienced trauma to understand, but there is an internal instinct to just try to be normal, functional, okay—to just keep trying to push away the negative thoughts that drag you to the abyss. I know that I would have manipulated any therapist, saying what I believed they wanted me to say in order to bypass questions and conversations I did not want to have. I did know how to influence what I wanted.

Then approximately one year ago, I woke up heavily hungover and looked into a mirror, finally witnessing someone

I felt shameful and disgusted with. I decided I had only two options left to consider: take my life or go to therapy. I looked at myself and asked, "What do you want to do?" In those first moments, my thoughts went to suicide and what might be least painful. I then wrote out some of the things I would want to say to my loved ones. But then, as if a bolt of lightning hit me, I gained perspective and decided that I could not let the bad shit win. I knew deep down that I was too smart for that. I knew that life was more than that moment. I knew I was worthy of much more, even entrenched deep in that dark hole in my life. I threw up, googled a therapist near me, and decided to come clean. I began going to the gym regularly; I ghosted some toxic people and created boundaries for others; I quit my job at the Tilted Kilt (which didn't help with my body issues…it's the Irish version of Hooters); I stopped drugs and alcohol; I started meditating; I found new friends; I started eating healthy; I focused on school; and I read a ton on psychology and self-improvement. I was doing some serious self-work!

I knew there had to be light somewhere in this tunnel I had been in for years, and I was determined to find it. The first step was therapy. After trying treatment multiple times throughout my life, I was always told that I was capable of solving my own problems—the result of having lied throughout the process in order to make everything seem picturesque, precisely as I had done as a child. I would always push my trauma back down, painting this perfect life picture, hoping it would one day go away and finally leave me alone. Through years of doing so, it began coming out in other ways—the suicidal thoughts and plans, the fits of extreme anger, and the self-isolation. I knew my biggest struggle was my own mind, and therapy had never worked because I never let anyone see my problems. I had a tremendous fear of being rejected or shut down. Being at my lowest point in July 2021, I decided maybe it was time to seek professional help and try to be transparent, for my own sake. I found a therapist I liked, and it turns out that asking for help is better than protecting your ego. I was finally on the road to self-help and healing.

A few months ago, in May of 2022, I sat looking at this adorable scrapbook my young mother wrote for me to look back on once I grew up. I began to cry as I turned the pages and looked at this sweet, innocent child. *How could someone look at this little girl and do such awful things to her?* In addition to the incidents I vividly remember, I couldn't help but think, *were there occurrences earlier than my first memory?* A beautiful photo album of baby pictures—something so sentimental that follows you through your entire life—instead triggers an automatic state of anxiety in my brain, all due to someone else's actions. Repeatedly returning to situations where I was subjected to physical, sexual, and emotional turmoil as a child caused my brain to develop a constant state of overwhelming hypervigilance. These memories don't just go away, I know they are with me for the rest of my life. It now comes down to reevaluating how I process them, recognize that they represent what happened to me, but do not define me.

I will permanently grieve that lost childhood. I remember vividly sitting next to my attorney two years ago during a sentencing hearing for my step-grandfather. I had prepared a statement for the court that my counsel read to the packed courtroom on my behalf. While listening to my attorney, I kept replaying these words in my mind: *Breathe. The end is near. I was not ready to stand up.* I was still stopping the cycle of torture in my mind. Potentially facing the future and working on releasing that part of my past was still painful.

When I heard the lawyer read my words to the court, I felt like I was reclaiming my power and standing up for myself. I share my statement here with you:

My step-grandfather forever affected my life with his wrongdoing. The acts of this man have left me with still current mental effects of isolation, pain, and toxicity. I still, to this day, never feel safe in any environment, and I seek safety in all of the wrong places.

My traumatized brain has to learn how to maintain healthy relationships. Most cases like this go unresolved, and victims like myself deal with the repercussions of others' selfish actions forever on their own. Not this time.

Thank you for the opportunity to express my feelings— the child in me, my current self, and the future adult needed this to heal and move forward on my self-defined path. This does not define me, but it does describe and portray who he truly is, and I hope that is all he sees when he looks in the mirror over the next decade.

I chose to grow from these words and this courtroom appearance, to use the difficult emotions I harbored as fuel to better myself and live a happy life. I learned to break free from my thoughts, live my life for myself, and realize that people do not care as much as I think they do. I don't let my trauma control me anymore or wish it would go away; that is a freeing statement.

Trust is still a hard one for me. I have not mastered it yet, but recognizing healthy boundaries helps, and realizing I do not have to do everything alone is encouraging. Because I never had the opportunity as a young child to develop trust, building it will take time. My anger is still present. And letting go of unhealthy patterns remains an ongoing battle. As part of my healing process, I journal, work out, and meditate every morning with self-affirmations. Some of my favorites are: *I am safe. I am in control of my thoughts and emotions. I release my past self peacefully.*

I like walking into this new self—the era of Bailey, the architect and artist. On my fridge are four magnets I made, each with a different quote from the book, *Four Agreements*, by Don Miguel Ruiz: *Be impeccable with your word*; *Don't take anything personally*; *Don't make assumptions*; and, *Always do your best*. I made a set for my best friend, too!

My mom has always been an active and avid advocate in my recovery. She once said, "I wish I could stop giving a shit about things, and not let them bother me like you have been able to do." What she doesn't know is that people and situations do affect me. It's a continuous process this work of healing. I don't want to disassociate from people, sabotage, or damage relationships, and I know I can do this. I want to be in touch with my true feelings, needs, and thoughts and not get triggered by my past. Detachment is a protective mechanism. It can definitely serve that role, but it can also create a lack of connection with oneself and others. This is not the goal I want to achieve. My therapist, Shannon, and I have been working towards understanding this, and my being in touch with the "why" that underlies all this behavior. This has been helpful.

Lately, I have told people, "The universe is in love with me." I do feel this. Shannon has been instrumental in my journey. She is my angel, sensitive and gentle, but restorative to my sense of who I am and what I am made of. She has presented me with books to read, such as *It Didn't Start with You; How Inherited*

Family Trauma Shapes Who We Are & How to End the Cycle, by Mark Wolynn, and *Waking the Tiger: Healing Trauma*, by Peter Levine. When I read them, I realized two things: how far I have come and how far I have left to go.

When I went to Europe in the summer of 2022, my therapist gave me a brown leather journal to chronicle all my experiences. When she presented it to me, she pointed out that the words etched on its front cover were the same as those depicted in the tapestry that hung on the wall of her office. It was such a fitting gift to take with me on my travels—symbolic and useful. I carried these words, written by A.A. Milne, with me through Europe: *"If ever there is a tomorrow when we are not together, there is something you must always remember. You are braver than you believe, stronger than you seem, and smarter than you think. But the most important thing is, even if we're apart, I'll always be with you."*

I am thankful to continue to experience all that is ahead. It was magical when I visited the Eiffel Tower in Paris in July of 2022. We had just left my birthday dinner, and I was standing right in front of one of the world's most magnificent structures. I never would have thought, just a few years ago, that I would have made it to witness this at twenty-one years old. I have so much self-appreciation and respect for the path I have traveled these past couple of years, and for how far I have come.

Trauma is something that happened to me, it is not who I am.

CHAPTER SEVEN

Sharon

*H*aving grown up in Michigan, I know firsthand that May in the Midwest can be moody. On this particular day, however, the sun was shining and it was a balmy 71°F. I recall feeling thankful for the atypical forecast—as if a nice day makes a difficult conversation any easier.

Vibrant annuals and multicolored river rocks lined Sharon's front walkway, offering a cheerful path up to her ranch-style brick home. Sitting on her front porch were two antique stone dogs, each holding a basket of flowers from its mouth, like perfectly-trained, obedient pooches. I rang the doorbell, admiring Sharon's lovely garden as I waited, noticing how incredibly smooth and green her lawn appeared. Looking back, I think I was far more aware of my surroundings than usual. The cheery entrance to Sharon's home was in such stark contrast to *the story of grief she had agreed to share with me—a reminder that beauty and sorrow co-exist.*

When Sharon agreed to our meeting, she was very frank in saying, "I'm willing to give it a try. I don't talk about their deaths that much, but I think it might do me good." She is a firebrand at five-foot-four—a stature that belies the mental and emotional strength she has had to call upon so often in her life. It is unimaginable, yet Sharon understands the fragility of life; death no longer scares her.

We were scheduled to sip our Diet Cokes in her backyard garden; however, her three-year-old rescue dog, Luke, made it quite clear that he was not in the mood to calmly socialize. Sharon quipped, "He's a little on the wild side." She explained that Luke didn't mix and mingle much, and that she was his sole buddy. She had hoped that he would be a good boy, but he had other plans—in contrast to his stoic brethren standing guard at the front door. In an effort to give us a more peaceful setting, Sharon quickly called her friend and neighbor, Joni, and we ended up sitting in comfy-cushioned wicker chairs gazing out on the tranquility of Joni's pool. We both appreciated the calm, and the gooey marshmallow treats Joni brought out.

I could not help but think how hard it must have been for Sharon to meet me on this particular Monday—the day after Mother's Day. And then I thought about all the Mother's Days she has endured, and the magnitude of that void—the loss of all three of her beautiful sons.

Sharon has been silently grieving for more than three decades. We touched on the complexity of grief, ranging from the delight she feels talking about her boys to how rage and resentment still linger. She hesitated to describe her emotions, and I understood all too well. After losing my thirty-year-old father at the age of eleven, I am still learning how to name my own emotions. I can say from experience that grief never entirely goes away.

I noticed on her wrist a tattoo affirming, "to live is an act of courage." Sharon and I agreed that you never "get over" the loss of loved ones. Grief—the pain, the anguish, the loneliness—has a way of finding a home deep within. Sharon is still calibrating her sense of love and loss. She described the sharp-edged suffering that still stabs her; a reminder that grief comes in many forms. She admits it is not easy for her to dredge up the past and that she has cultivated an inner life that seeks to distance herself from dark feelings. I treaded lightly, listened intently, and asked her hard questions, which she bravely spoke to.

Sharon's story reminds us that grief is an inevitable part of the human experience, an ongoing conversation between celebration and sorrow. I recently read that if you rearrange the letters in depression, you get "I pressed on." I like this reminder that our present circumstances are not our final destination, however difficult that journey may be. Sharon's story is proof of the inner strength that can pull you along—even in the moments you'd rather it didn't.

I don't cry.

And, I have never fully shared my pain with those close to me, because how would they ever really understand.

By not talking about the deaths of my boys, I've managed to never address my feelings. I've mastered how to avoid them! I know I will never make peace with losing my precious children. Perhaps this is why I chose to suppress my sadness instead. I only went to therapy for two or three months after my youngest son, Mike, died. I probably should have gone after the death of each of my boys. Perhaps if I had gone when my husband Jim died, fifteen years after Mike's death, I might have learned some tools that would have helped guide me through the heartache I had yet to discover lay ahead. Not sure what I can do about it now, at age sixty-nine.

It was hard returning to work after each death, but going on helped keep my mind occupied. I tried to think about what good things I had left in my life, but seeking comfort in this got harder and harder.

My family lives nearby. I have two sisters and two brothers. I take care of my dog Luke, and enjoying gardening and cutting my lawn. My place is quiet except for Luke barking at the birds in the backyard. A typical day for me now is a walk with my identical twin, Cheryl. After running errands or getting my hair done, coming home to an empty house can be lonesome. Having dogs in my life has given me something to live for. Luke is my life now; he is all I have left. I rescued him when he was two years old, even though his pit-bull and bulldog mix can sometimes be naughty.

I was close to my parents. The boys and I spent a lot of time with them. My mother, Kathlyn, was seventy-seven when she died suddenly in 1994. I miss talking to her every day. I can still hear her say, "Smile, darn you, smile!" That was her favorite catch phrase. I still feel guilty about not seeing her the night she died. And, I miss watching the Detroit Red Wings with my dad. His name was Howard, but people called him Pete. He was older when he died in 2005, and I felt it was a blessing for him.

My husband, Jim, died in 2006. He was fifty-three years old. It was a mutual attraction when we first met; we noticed each other at a gas station! It was owned by a family friend and we used to hang out there. Jim had big blue eyes and straight, dark hair. His personality was the opposite of mine. Jim would push and push until I got mad or he got his way—which usually happened simultaneously. I remember one-time canoeing down the Rifle River, with Jim all the while telling me I was paddling wrong. He kept pushing my buttons until I snapped, and shouted, "Jesus Christ, enough!" He smiled and said, "That's not my name!"—in typical Jim fashion.

Jim and I were married for thirty-one years. In his forties, he was pre-diabetic and diagnosed with multiple sclerosis. He traveled extensively for his consulting job and would frequently be home only on weekends. One project took him to Tennessee for a year; another to New Jersey for several months at a time. As the boys grew older, I often spent weekdays home alone with them, and was thankful my family lived close by. Jim died unexpectedly—in his hotel room—while working in Cincinnati. My life changed drastically that day. I not only lost my best friend, but I lost the person I most turned to. The loss of a husband, though immensely painful, is a different type of heartache than the loss of a child. I found comfort in knowing that Jim was with our youngest son. I tried not to question God, but it was tough.

But my boys— I will never stop missing my babies. Jamie, Ben, and Mike were everything. I wish all three of them were here and I was teaching them in Sunday School again. Part of me doesn't want to grieve for them. They are my world, and I don't know that I will ever find meaning in them not being here with me. I sometimes ask myself why would I want to get over the loss of my three boys. I've closed myself to those emotions. Life without them has been lonesome. I have Luke and my memories to fill the holes in my heart. I never imagined life would be like this. I never pictured needing to grieve for the loss of a child, much less the loss of all three of my children, and my husband.

If I could transport in a time machine, I would return to the summer when Mike was four years old, Ben was six, and Jamie was ten. I can still see the boys, at these ages, in the place we so loved. For two weeks every July, we would make the six-hour trek north to St. Joseph Island in Ontario, Canada. I remember the happy feeling of crossing the bridge, knowing the boys would run out of the car to start playing with their cousins while the adults unloaded all the provisions. We couldn't get to our lawn chairs quick enough— sipping our rum and cokes and watching the sunset over the water, while the kids all played baseball. The cabin was too rustic for my husband; he preferred the hotels he was used to. But the boys and I did not mind.

If I close my eyes, I can hear the boy's laughter and smell the sweet maple syrup on a stack of steaming hot pancakes. The best maple syrup comes from Ontario; each of my boys would agree. We would catch walleye and northern pike, deep-fry them, and serve them for dinner with homemade coleslaw dotted with pineapple bits. The boys and I would hike to Camp D' Ours. I can still see Jamie and Ben giggling together in that blue rowboat. The memories made with all the cousins and family will always make me smile. Those times spent together on Gawas Bay will live with me forever.

Mike is my youngest son.

He was born on November 2, 1984. I will never forget thinking how large his head looked! I know that sounds strange for a mother to say, but he did have a big head. His beautiful brown hair and big blue eyes were equally prominent. My son was also born with a heart murmur. At the age of four, he was diagnosed with aortic valve stenosis.

Mike never let his heart condition hold him back. I loved watching him ride after his brothers on his red Huffy two-wheeler. He was always trying to get his older brothers in trouble. And, when he somehow got caught being the instigator, his punishment was not being able to watch Alf on TV. He was also a Ghostbusters fan! Mike loved teaching his cousin, Doug, how to be cool, and the two of them had matching Teenage Mutant Ninja Turtle outfits. I will never forget when he said, "Mom, that was the best burger I have ever had!" Of course, I did not make it. I'm pretty sure it was a Banquet frozen TV dinner.

Mike never complained. Only once did he ask, "Why do I have to get bloodwork, and Jamie and Ben don't?" In December of 1990, Mike's doctor advised us to take him to the hospital at the University of Michigan, in Ann Arbor, to undergo a heart catherization. Though Mike was just six years old at the time, the doctors needed to perform this diagnostic procedure to better assess our son's heart condition, and this is when we learned that he was going to need surgery to repair a valve. He made it through the surgery and we thought we were on the road to recovery. Sadly, the relief we felt was short lived. My spunky six-year-old died on Martin Luther King Day, January 21, 1991, due to his irregular heartbeat. Before his open-heart surgery, I remember Mike saying to his dad, "You have stinky feet." It was such a silly, sweet moment. I will forever miss my son's voice and the way he used to belt out the Beach Boys' song, "Kokomo," while in the car waiting to pick his brother up from school. I like to think about seeing him again in that tropical paradise and giving him a big hug.

Ben is my middle son.

He was born on October 13, 1982. Mike and Ben shared a room, and they were very close. After Mike died, I never considered how looking at his toys and empty bed might affect Ben. At the time, we all thought it was best to keep Mike's memory alive. With an eight-year-old and a twelve-year-old, we had to figure out how life went on. We did talk about Mike's death, but maybe not enough. I think Ben may have shouldered more than I realized at the time. He definitely struggled with his brother's death, and also had a hard time with his emotions. Eventually, we began to see this struggle come out in his actions.

With Jim traveling so much, I was unsure how to handle Ben during his teenage years. I missed my big-hearted boy who was open about everything. In time, Ben found an outlet in skateboarding. He was a fantastic skateboarder, but as he got older he started hanging out with the wrong crowd. His behaviors and personality started to change. He struggled with substance abuse. We sent him to a facility in Montana for one year to help with his behavior, and to help him understand his relationship with drugs. He came home and graduated high school, but the ups and downs were still there.

SHARON

After graduation, Ben moved to Florida. We would talk on the phone every night when he lived there. Jamie eventually followed him down there for a short time. They lived together and continued their love/bicker brother relationship. Ben dated a girl for two years, and they broke up but were able to remain friends. As a mother, it's hard to see your child hurting; sometimes, there's just nothing you can do to ease their pain.

Shortly after Jim's death, Ben and Jamie decided to move back to Michigan. It was nice for us to be back together again. Ben always wanted me to make spinach and ricotta stuffed shells with Prego tomato sauce. We would sit at the table together and talk about random things. It was nice not to be alone and have them both home again. Ultimately, however, they decided to head off to Chicago, like they had always talked about doing one day. It helped to know they were together, but Ben was still struggling with using drugs.

I remember one night when the boys were home for their dad's funeral. I had just gone to bed, and Ben came in and laid beside me. He shared how worried he was about his past behavior and did not want his dad to be mad at him, let alone not love him. I convinced my middle son that his dad loved him and forgave him. That was tough.

My charismatic twenty-six-year-old son died on February 21, 2009. I will never forget that call and Jamie's shaky voice. He found Ben, his younger brother, in their Chicago apartment deceased from an accidental drug overdose. I felt numb and remember thinking, "*Losing one son was enough*! *Why do you have to take two, God?*

Reflecting back now, I realize it must have been hard for Jamie to call me when he found his brother. I know he blamed himself. He said that when he went to bed, everything seemed fine. He didn't find Ben until the following day. During that heart-wrenching phone call, he talked about the song "*How to Save a Life*" by The Fray. The lyrics get me every time: "*And where did I go wrong? I lost a friend somewhere along in the bitterness. And I would have stayed up with you all night had I known how to save a life.*" This became our song for Ben.

I know I am biased, but my two grown sons were both such caring and good-looking men, especially when they dressed up. Ben in his name-brand clothes, and Jamie in his second-hand store finds. That was another thing they would tease each other about. Ben was so different from his brother. He was comical. I wish I had saved the messages he would leave on my machine. He would call and say, "Boni and Zoey, do you want to go for a walk?" After hearing his message, my Great Danes would go nuts! He loved dogs, just like I do.

I wish we could have helped Ben with his inner demons, but we couldn't. His recovery was never consistent. As a family, we tried to understand his addiction. We were told that genetic and environmental influences could play a role, as well as mental health and self-esteem. Both Ben's grandfather and father had addictive personalities. There might be some genetics involved there, I guess. It was difficult to really get a handle on as Ben could be so convincing. He was adept at masking his inner pain. I blame myself, at times. Rationally, I know we did what we felt was best at the time to help Ben, but that offers no real solace. I always told Jamie that I knew he tried to help his brother.

SHARON

Jamie is my oldest son.

He was born on March 21, 1978. Jamie was always a careful kid. I miss seeing his bearded face and sun-kissed tan. He had the most beautiful hair, just like his dad's, very striking. And like Jim, he knew how to "push buttons" to get what he wanted! After Ben died, Jamie and I would drive together to the Upper Peninsula of Michigan, or into Canada. We had some fun, goofy times together during those five-hour drives with the windows rolled down and Jamie's dark hair blowing in the wind. Our trips became more sporadic when he moved to Grand Rapids, the year after Ben died.

That was when he started seeing Liz. She and I were never close, but they dated for five years and even got engaged. I suspected she wanted to keep him away from his family. My gut told me she was not good for him. I tried to be nice, although I once asked why he was with her—maybe not my best mom moment. They broke up shortly after they set the wedding date. The best thing Jamie got out of the relationship was Moose, their gentle, but powerful mastiff mix.

On July 11, 2016, Jamie called to tell me he was coming home for a long weekend. He was going to the annual Greek Festival with a friend and told me he would stop by later. I was at my sister's house when George, Jamie's childhood friend, called. I was told that Jamie immediately started gasping for air and choking at the festival. Almost an hour prior, George had given Jamie some laced "medication," unbeknownst to me. I later learned he didn't tell the police what type of drugs he had given Jamie, how much he had taken, or where they came from.

I rushed to the hospital, but Jamie was unconscious when I arrived. He remained in a coma for two weeks with minimal brain activity, but no movement —alive but unresponsive. I visited my oldest son daily from 8 o'clock in the morning until 10 o'clock at night. One of the nurses, Justin was his name, was so kind. He guided me through what was happening and even prayed with me. Eventually, we had to decide whether to end Jamie's life or put him in a convalescence center. There was no guarantee he would ever regain consciousness. I held his hand, stroked his beautiful dark hair, and permitted him to leave me. My easy-going, thirty-eight-year-old son died the next day, on July 12, 2016. All I could think was, *"Really? Another one, God?"* I believe in God, but I was— and still am —furious at him.

I have a hard time remembering some details, to be honest. All I can say of the pain of losing a child is that nothing compares to it. If there was a state beyond numb, that's where I went with each loss. After Mike died, I went to Compassionate Friends, a support group for losing a child. They wanted to relieve my suffering and pain, but talking about the pain hurt too much, and I stopped going. I went back to work, ignored my sadness, and focused on Ben and Jamie. I remember Jim being much more emotional than me. He cried and was angry. I think he drank too much too.

It was different with Ben and Jamie; they were both older and had their own places. Having to empty each of their belongings was tough. After Ben died, I did go to a psychic in Fenton several times and started feeling hopeful again. She told me that Mike, Jim, and Ben were OK, wherever they were. I remember her stating, "Jamie is going to be fine." I lost all hope when this did not prove true. This seems random, but I also watched several seasons of the show *Charmed*. Maybe I was drawn to the three sisters fighting evil and wishing I had the powers to undo the darkness in my own life.

Internalizing my grief just felt right. Why would anyone want to hear about my pain? Of course, I want my three boys back! But I was raised not to show my feelings, to handle things on my own, and to never appear weak. I got that trait from my independent mother. I think back and remember my mom when she lost both her parents and a husband. She was pretty young when she lost the father of my brothers, who at the time were three and six years of age. I remember that she had a hard time with Mike's death, but she sure kept up a strong appearance. I guess I got it from her.

Now, I am left with a mother's guilt and wondering what I could have done differently. The only thing that keeps me going is the hope that I will get to see all three of them in heaven. I do believe in God. I was raised in the Presbyterian Church, as were my boys. My parents also believed in God, though they didn't make us go to church every week. I've never contemplated suicide because it's nothing I would ever consider, and the Bible considers it a sin. I want to see my sons and husband again, and I don't want anything to get in the way of that.

I wonder if I will ever be able to forgive God for taking my boys. After Mike died, I wondered why God did not take me instead. When Jim, Ben, and Jamie died, I wondered if this was really God's plan for me. The only thing I could come up with was I must not have been a good enough mom that my boys are better off in heaven, where they are safe. After all these years, I still have anger and sometimes self-pity—moments of wondering, "Why me?" Hopefully, if I get to heaven, I'll understand what God's plan was and whether or not this hell was worth it.

My rescue dog, Luke, gives me purpose. Nobody I know would be able to take Luke in because he is not good with other dogs. So, I guess I need to be here as long as he is. I don't fear death—I am afraid of living too long! When securing a space for me, the Oakwood Cemetery said they could "squeeze me in next to my husband and children." This tiny plot, I learned, is located right next to the road. I quickly quipped, "I might get run over."

Honestly, life sucks. But complaining doesn't get me anywhere and definitely won't bring my boys back. I like hearing people mention the boys, which is not too often now. I don't like people asking me, "How many kids do you have?" I am unsure how to answer because people get uncomfortable with my response. Sometimes it's hard listening to people whine about stupid stuff. I just want to scream back at them, "That's nothing! Let me tell you about losing my whole family!" I guess it's true, we can survive a lot of things. What other choice is there?

Do you see this tattoo on my wrist? At sixty-five years old, I decided to get inked instead of constantly questioning God. My niece and I went to the Drunken Monkey together. Her tattoo reads, "there is a reason for everything." People say mine is upside down, and I always tell them it's for me to read, not them. It's a friendly reminder.

My daily dose of reality: "to live is an act of courage."

CHAPTER EIGHT

Dr. Debby

*D*uring *my brief doctoral journey at Union Institute & University, I came to know and truly value a particular professor of mine. Her name is Dr. Debby, and the course I took with her was "Engaging Differences." At the start of each class, Dr. Debby would close her beautiful brown eyes as she recited the day's affirmation, meditation music playing softly in the background. It was such a positive and welcoming ritual that took only a few minutes, but was always incredibly uplifting. Following this welcome, she would transition the class into discussions of the various ways that our understanding and construction of self, and others, result from both philosophical and concrete dimensions of difference, each with social implications.*

Cheery and always front and center on Zoom, Dr. Debby would wear the most vibrant turban-like head wraps each class. I always looked forward to seeing which wrap *she would have on—each as colorful and exuberant as she is. Being a bibliophile, I also admired the background in Dr. Debby's Zoom calls. It was not the virtual, customized images that are often used, but rather a real-life background of white wooden bookcases. Each shelf was loaded with inky treasures—extensive and eclectic. Among the many titles, there were two that always caught my eye: <u>Becoming</u>, by Michelle Obama, and <u>Miracles and Mysteries</u>, edited by Jean Watson. I recall one day asking Dr. Debby if she had a favorite book, and she said, "Believe it or not, it's <u>Valley of the Dolls</u>, by Jacqueline Susann." She said she read it in one sitting and could not put it down. I still smile thinking of this book choice—a pop-culture classic with the time-honored message that fame and fortune do not buy you happiness.*

Dr. Debby had a way with words and introduced us to various texts, giving voice to how each of us has multiple perspectives on how we view the world. She encouraged the class to pause and reflect on the varied topics we covered to better assess and understand our viewpoints; to prepare for our weekly conversation concepts, which ensured deep, thought-provoking discussions; and to view our work with an eye toward the culture culmination projects we'd present. She often reminded us to let experiences in life be imperfect, like the world which unfolds around us. Her lessons were not only life orientations, they were instrumental in prepping us for the research studies we would conduct toward our dissertations.

I never had trouble connecting with Dr. Debby. She was always an available, resourceful, and supportive professor, a valued anchor for me as I navigated the PhD program. Her energetic spirit is simply inspiring. Though I missed her virtual Juneteenth presentation in 2022 ("Time Vault for SOUL = <u>S</u>elf <u>O</u>thers <u>U</u>nity <u>L</u>ove"), this event truly represents what this woman of wonder is all about. Dr. Debby strives to invoke in all her students, myself included, a historical "awakening." She compels her students to ponder their pasts and be mindful of what continues to emerge in the present. And in so doing, she allows her students to expand their learning while navigating and adjusting to an ever-shapeshifting world.

Her course challenged me to participate in a deep exploration of my own cultural identity, values, and biases in varied areas—my childhood, family, social class, gender, and the privilege of being a White female. Self-exploration was a strong aspect of her course. It proved to be a valuable tool for understanding my personal perspectives. She even had us keep a journal along the way, with specific sections to note our personal awakening/growth, consideration of difference and sameness, thoughts about inclusion and exclusion, and overall reflections regarding the material we were given to read and dissect.

During my time as a discussion leader, I delved deep into Critical Race Theory (CRT). I became knowledgeable on how this theory showcases how prejudice is deeply entrenched in our culture. Dr. Debby's lectures were a discourse on difference and the dynamics of diversity as they play out in various areas—race and racism, gender relations, and intersectionality. She understands how to help her students question fundamental assumptions. She is an agent of change. She has taken the extraordinary moments that took place early in her life and managed to transform them from pain to gain. She models a way for all those she encounters to chisel away at their state of feeling sad and struggling, to be a better version of themselves.

I invite you to listen to Dr. Debby's words below. Her story is one that showcases the importance of embracing our cultural *identity; of recognizing the numerous signposts that appear in our lives and what they are trying to tell us. This awareness, as Dr. Debby attests, can have a profoundly advantageous impact in shaping our lives and perspectives.*

Can you believe a pimp saved my life? Well, he did.

The fact that a pimp saved my life created the swirling alchemy that allowed me to accomplish amazing things. In that alchemical cauldron, I found motherhood, love, empathy, higher education, and opportunities to give back to the community. One specific moment, at such a pivotal period in my maturity as a young woman, opened the door to a life I had only dreamed of.

The purpose of this story is to share my lived experience of loss, motherhood, and love through a narrative that I hope will be one that will be both healing and empowering. I invite you to join me as I re-travel parts of the path that brought me to this point in time and space; how the profound loss I experienced as a young teenager first altered my life's path and how one moment in time radically shifted that trajectory to bring me to where I am today.

I was born and raised in Boston, Massachusetts, where people of different races and cultures lived in their own communities. We only mingled at Haymarket Square, an indoor farmer's market open to the public year-round. I remember how fresh everything always looked at the market, that you could smell all the citrus fruits in season and the salty seafood pulled from the ocean. I enjoyed what Haymarket Square offered— a larger lens on humanity and a visceral sense of a greater connection. This appealed to me. It broadened my sense of community. It also stood in stark contrast to what I could never have anticipated would lie ahead for me in terms of my own little community—my little nuclear family, living with my mother and my step-sister.

At the age of fifteen, I lost my mother. She passed away after a lengthy battle with breast cancer. Unfortunately, this was at a time when there were not the advanced methods for treatment that we have today. Suddenly, with no parents to look after us, my sister and I moved in with my grandmother. And then, as life would have it, our grandmother passed away one year later. To make matters worse, my sister and I have different fathers, and her father's family did not want me. *Where was my father? Who knows?* I honestly do not know who my father is, or was. This was not an ideal situation for me. My sister and I were awarded a state-appointed guardian to handle our mother's estate, so when my sister went to live with her father, I moved in with my mother's best friend. My new family consisted of the mom, five girls, and me. I shared a room with two of them, who were also teenagers. Those girls were always arguing, and it was hard to concentrate on my homework and prepare for tests. Living in that chaos was more than I could handle. After much foot stomping and hissy fits, my guardian reluctantly permitted me to leave. I found myself on my own at fifteen, still in school and with a job.

I had sought help from the Urban League, headed by the late Vernon Jordan. This non-profit organization helps African American teenagers get jobs in the community. I landed my first part-time job (New England Telephone Company) and many more through that agency.

Every day after school, I took the train to my job as a researcher at the New England Telephone Company in Cambridge, Massachusetts. One day after work, I noticed a large brick building, the Franklin Square House, a rooming house for young women. I was delighted to find that it had a vacancy. And, just like that, I moved in. The rent was $35.00 a week. I could afford that much because I had a job, and my mother's estate covered the rest of my expenses.

At this very young age, having gone through such a significant loss and separated from my only living family member, my sister, I quickly learned the challenges I'd face. I had no one to advocate on my behalf, but me. And the system was not tilted in my favor. I was thrown into a world filled with racial disparity. (Racial disparity refers to the imbalances and biases thrust upon underrepresented groups.) I was, essentially, a young, orphaned, Black girl. I was left on my own, facing unknown challenges in a complex world, with a feeling of despair and abandonment. I experienced a deep, melancholic sense of loss. (Melancholia is a state of lingering depression that is not easily shed.) I will say that, over time, I have found that the artistic process—whether it be visual, spoken, or performance—is a cathartic way to work through this state of despair, and one I have tapped into often in my life.

I felt fortunate to have found the Franklin Square House. There were nurses, secretaries, and "professional" women living there—all so impeccably dressed. I was in awe of these women, all seemingly in charge of their lives. I befriended a few women and spent the next several months cooking meals together and enjoying their company. Soon, however, I noticed that the few times we went out, there was always a man with them.

Moreover, I noticed that he was very protective of them. The man was, like the women, impeccably dressed. He always wore a navy blue, three-piece, pinstripe suit with a grey topcoat trimmed with a silver fox collar. In addition, he had patent leather boots, a wide-brimmed silver hat, and sunglasses. And, no matter the outing or terrain, he carried an intricately carved cane with a silver wolf handle. He was a pimp, though this honestly didn't yet register with me. This was during an era when pimps were considered powerful in their hoods. Most of the pimps in the '70s were men of color. They were consistent in their attire, meaning they dressed from classy to flashy and characteristically donned a hat and a cane.

One day, without any warning, I felt a presence behind me when I was putting my key in the door to my apartment. I turned around and that same man that was always with the women I had befriended was standing there. He said, "Debby, I do not want you to hang out with those women anymore. You cannot see them again." His voice was stern but not threatening. I looked at him and said, "Who are you?" He responded, "Slickback." And, as suddenly as he had appeared, he turned around and walked away. I went into my room and closed and locked the door behind me. I never saw the women or him again.

At this point in my life, I had lost my mom, my grandma, my sister, my home, and nearly everything. Although I did not know it at the time, it was a wake-up call and a precursor to everything else that would happen in my life. I never dreamed that so much trauma could result in a positive change. It felt like my world was still coming down on me, but I did what I had to—I picked myself up, dusted myself off, and went forward.

Given how abruptly my initial friendship connection had ended and how it was severed, I began to define the meanings of the people who surrounded me. It wasn't long before the lightbulb went off and I realized precisely what Slickback was and what the women who were with him did. I was immediately educated on the definitions of a pimp and a prostitute. I understood that Slickback was a man who took women for granted by having them engage in sexual acts, taking a substantial percentage of their money. And, in contrast, I knew that a prostitute complies with her circumstances for fear of ending up on the street or worse. Looking back, this experience was truly a blessing in disguise. I had likely been pulled from the edge of a precipice (and would ultimately be very grateful), yet, at that moment, I again found myself alone. Despite my new circumstance, I was determined to continue to thrive and make good choices.

I soon became enamored with watching the Rev. Dr. Martin Luther King, Jr. on television, listening to him speak about the concept of a beloved community. That idea really resonated with me. I remembered how much I enjoyed the communal feeling of Haymarket Square—the idea of people coming together from varied cultures and traditions. I don't know what the specific catalyst was, perhaps having lost so much, but I immediately knew that as I grew older I would try to create a beloved community wherever I went and in whatever I did. I began to volunteer and, as I did, I felt appreciated. I was experiencing the joy of what it meant to both give back to my community and, in turn, to give and receive gratitude. That, to me, was the meaning of beloved community.

It is through volunteering that I first discovered how important it is to love. How giving love begets love and my helping others made such a positive difference in my life. This, for me, was such a pivotal awakening to the beauty of individual and communal healing. Today, I continue to volunteer with various groups and I believe I make a difference in many people's lives.

When I had my first daughter, I understood the meaning of love and motherhood. It proved to be a far more profound experience than anything I had previously experienced. That intense mother-daughter bond is what has kept me going all these years. Yes, we have spiraled in and out, and each time we grow closer to one another. It is as though the web of life can tear and be rewoven in a way that can redirect our course and deepen our understanding of how the universe works and the roles we, as individuals, play in creating our reality. We have the power to lift ourselves from melancholia and to reweave the fabric of our lives.

Had I not had the experience I had as a young girl, living alone at the Franklin Square House, I might not have become the woman I am today. Had my encounter with Slickback gone any differently, had he not warned me to stay away, perhaps my life would have taken a far different course.

I had always dreamed of being a teacher but lost sight of the dream amidst the responsibilities of supporting myself and my family. One day, out of work and hopeless, I sat down to watch *The View* on TV. Something clicked when I heard Barbara Walters ask the panel, "If you only had 20 years, what would you do with them?" I suddenly thought, "Wow, I surely have 20 more years, at the very least." At that moment, I realized that being laid off was not an ending but a new beginning. I knew instantly that I had it in me to dust myself off again and start a new journey. Prior to having this epiphany, I would have thought that twenty years seemed like an endless time to suffer until retirement rolled around. Instead, I felt that those two decades could be the beginning of a new life and, possibly, the career of my dreams. I found that I was ready to go back to school to follow my path to teaching. And more importantly, I felt my dream seemed attainable. It was that simple. In one fateful moment, I saw a future—one that I had begun to dread—in an entirely new light.

I took my first leap of faith by attending Diablo Valley College, finding it a joy to be back in school. From there, I applied and was accepted at John F. Kennedy University to finish my bachelor's degree in Philosophy and Religion. At that point, I was on a roll and applied to the master's program in Consciousness and Transformation. I loved every moment of my studies! I was introduced to new ways of thinking and even found that I was unusually familiar with many of the concepts being taught at a deep level of consciousness.

As I was approaching the end of my studies, I realized that I did not want to stop. I found the California Institute of Integral Studies in San Francisco and applied to the Transformative Studies program with a concentration in Consciousness Studies. As a doctoral student, I was stretched in all directions. My mind, body, and spirit joined an alchemical spiral that transformed me to the core. This journey proved to be the most exciting and fulfilling of my life.

Who do I credit besides myself and my family for the successes and shifts? I credit the pimp that saved my life. Had it not been for Slickback's warning to stay away from the women I had initially connected with at Franklin Square House, I might not be who I am today. Who am I? I am a woman, a mother, a grandmother, a feminist, a scholar, and an activist. The spiritual journey of every being is to explore the divine relationship of the self to the higher self. In this context, the higher self is our total soul consciousness. When individuals enter a harmonious alliance with the universe, they can view the world with an enriching sense of hope and inspiration.

One of the significant shifts in my life as an academic came when I was asked to teach a course on diversity and inclusion. Although I had thought about it and been faced with it every day of my life, I now had to delve into the depths of what it means to be a Black woman in today's world. In Michael Eric Dyson's book, *What Truth Sounds Like: Robert F. Kennedy, James Baldwin, and Our Unfinished Conversation About Race*, published in 2018, he recounts a conversation he had with Kamala Harris, in which she states that "to talk about race in America requires one to face the truth in terms of disparities that exist based on race. And the truth makes people extremely uncomfortable" (p.75-76). This is to say that you can't talk about one without the other; to know that the conversation may stir up things within that could have a chance to emerge, be recognized, and become something more significant.

This book definitely made us think deeper about race in America. Having a greater understanding of racial disparity created a sense of deep melancholy and sadness within me. It propelled me to reevaluate my experiences with Slickback and the women I had initially befriended. I could see the racial disparity within their community. They were all Black, but I was not welcomed in their group for whatever reason. Though I am thankful I was spared a fate I may have been too young or naïve to have dodged on my own, I questioned why. *Was it because my skin color was lighter than theirs? Was the discrimination due to my age?* I will never know. It demonstrates that racial disparity is not just a Black and White thing, but can happen within various racial groups. I have, over time, realized that we must stick together as women—regardless of race or profession.

I also had the opportunity to speak on a panel about melancholia's impact on women of color. Years ago, the word melancholia was a diagnosis of depression in women. Later it was used in songs like *Melancholy Baby* to express a sense of loneliness. I wonder if, in retrospect, Slickback's women suffered from melancholia, which in turn caused them to form emotional attachments to him as their pimp. If they (or Slickback) severed that attachment, the women could have ended up living on the street, selling and taking drugs and eventually meeting their demise.

This was a time of great introspection for me, and again, I was fortunate enough to have the courage and wherewithal to dust myself off and face my melancholia. Though I was alone in this effort, I felt a sense of strength, self-sufficiency, and fearlessness. I felt like I was taking control of my destiny; I had to. Melancholia could not win. I found a strong sense of faith that allowed miracles to come into my life and flow with the river that would lead me to the here and now.

The intersectionality of motherhood, loss, love, racial disparity and melancholia are woven into my life, as they are for many women like me. This intersectionality of congruent elements often lies just below the surface of our consciousness, understated and quiet. Yet, it is crucial that they be heard and seen. They should not be dismissed or glossed over. As Ms. Harris shared in her conversation with Michael Eric Dyson, the *truth can be uncomfortable*. But you know what they also say, the truth can set you free. Looking at this intersectionality through a creative lens has always aided my perspective. I imagine motherhood, love, loss, racial disparity, and melancholia swirling in a cauldron, melding together into gold that fills my mind, body, and spirit. This new alchemy creates the new gold, not money, but heart.

I ache to know, even these many years later, if the pimp who saved me would be willing (or even interested) to listen to the intricacies of the story of my life. *Would knowing how his words changed my life for the better impact him in any way? Would he know me if I had the opportunity to meet him again? Would he care?*

And then I think about a more plausible scenario and pose the question: Did Slickback have any sense of care for me that afternoon when he followed me to my room, or was he merely trying to look out for himself and his girls—in some perverse sense of ownership?

I believe there is a degree of goodness in everyone and that for that one shining moment, Slickback knew he was saving my life and thinking of me and my future.

Hey, Mr. Slickback!
You were the pimp I knew at an early age.
We crossed paths to thine be known the reason.
I met a family I longed for in that Franklin Square House.
Oh, those fabulous fun women and the fun we had,
In the kitchen, pots are clicking, and music is playing,
Sashaying about as the aromatic flavors permeated the
air each day until one day
The sun set on those happy moments in my life.

Wherever you are, I give gratitude as you truly saved my life.

I wish to leave you with an affirmation: "We are all phenomenal beings, and we will survive."

CHAPTER NINE

Izza

*T*he world was enriched when this "femme fantastique" was born in Casablanca in 1942. Known as the "Godmother of Moroccan Film," Izza is not only a filmmaker and producer, she is a profound storyteller. Her films explore diasporic identity and Moroccan-Jewish history and heritage, with a focus on narrative documentaries—topics quelled through the rediscovery of her childhood roots and the music of her North African nation.

Morocco is a Muslim country with a strong foundation in the family. "An unforgettable journey with complete sensory overload" would be the easiest way to describe how I felt visiting this country, located in the northwest corner of Africa and approximately the size of California. While in Marrakech, I visited Musee de la Femme, a museum that pays tribute to all women of influence. During my stay, the museum was showcasing a beautiful exhibit of Izza's work; a wonderful multi-media display featuring photography, music, and an amazing video loop of vibrant dancers and sweet singing.

Izza's story represents unity between her family roots in old-world Morocco and the guile and flair of France, a country where she and her family migrated to further financial opportunities and personal expansion.

Connection to home, profound in most all cultures, can be a complicated journey for those whose lives are uprooted due to environmental, political, or socio-economic reasons. Migrating to another country in search of a better life—whether fleeing religious persecution, seeking personal safety, or desiring greater opportunity for prosperity and stability—is a tremendous uprooting, nonetheless. Migrants can experience a very palpable sense of loss, a void within that can often go unanswered.

In Izza's story, she came of age in Morocco during the French Protectorate and, like many educated Moroccans, willingly turned her gaze to France. Her story is one of a family's migration in search of a better, more prosperous life; a story of disconnecting from one's heritage—familial roots established over centuries; and a story of just how profound the ties that bind can illuminate and fill the void in one's psyche. The reclaiming of her homeland led this remarkable woman on an amazing, 40-year journey, establishing herself as a formidable documentary filmmaker—witnessing and keeping record of her homeland through great changes in its political and social dynamic. Her work has garnered her numerous accolades and recognitions, including that of being the first Moroccan woman *truly devoted to the documentary form—although she was not really concerned by her gender in the political background.*

I first met Izza and began our conversation several years ago, at her office in Paris, in October of 2019. Sitting in her workplace, I was enamored with the Moroccan influence her office exuded in this Parisian environment. I distinctly remember asking her if there were any challenges she faced being a woman filmmaker in the '70s. Her curt response that rainy afternoon was textbook. In between two sips of espresso and one bite of her buttery croissant she said, "I never thought about it."

Given the travel hiatus that COVID-19 imposed on all our lives, Izza and I didn't reconvene again until three years later, in July of 2022, for a casual interview in her apartment in Paris. There are many beautiful places to live in France, but none are as magical as the City of Light. Of course, it's a major metropolis; however, Izza's Haussmann-style apartment, with its tall and drafty windows, was awash in the most dramatic natural light. Getting there did prove to be a bit of a logistical exercise—locating her residence within the city and then navigating through the several gates and doors to reach her unit. But it was worth every step. She and her husband, Gerard, were lucky to find their creative space in the early '70s. Despite its limited size, it is a charming gem.

At eighty years young, Izza continued to impress, preparing the ultimate brunch spread of something sweet, something fresh, and something savory. Brigitte, her niece—a conduit to our introduction—happened to be in Paris from the States on the same day I was interviewing Izza. What are the chances? I mentioned kismet. Izza corrected me, while artistically arranging her table, and said, "magic."

IZZA

It was a delight to witness Izza's culinary finesse. A variety of beautiful French cheeses were arranged on a wooden board. Salmon was set perfectly alongside mini blinis and crème fraiche—little bitesize wonders. The olives in the orange salad she prepared were taken from a tree in her friends' riad (the interior courtyard garden of a traditional Moroccan house or palace) where she had stayed just a few days prior. She even made Moroccan eggs with special spices called Piment D'Espelette—a smoky cumin being one ingredient. All of Izza's creations were artfully arranged atop a delightful white linen tablecloth dotted with blue and yellow flowers.

Alexis, Izza's great-nephew, arrived shortly after we began brunch. He lives in Mexico City, but was traveling and had been to Croatia and Montenegro. And then, shortly before I was about to leave, the door flung open, and in walked her doting daughter, Joanne (she also has a son Guillaume, who was not present). Joanne was classicly attired in a black shirtdress sprinkled with white florals, or as the French say, "chic decontracte"—the right balance between effortless and elegant. She kissed her mother on the top of the head and went into the kitchen to clean up.

Izza taught me so much that day. The best part of the gathering was when we sat together and shared stories, time, and experiences. Stories were told about life, living in dual cultures, and what it means to "just smash life." The exchanges we shared that day are embedded in my psyche forever. Izza's life and career are a testament to the enduring nature and significance of "home," and the remarkable way in which one's heart can recapture and sustain the richness of their land and culture through art. During our time together, Izza introduced me to the song "Gracias a la Vida," sung by Argentinian folk singer Mercedes Sosa, which encapsulates the essence of this lively filmmaker and producer. She softly insists this be played at her funeral. As Izza sincerely states, "these song lyrics have given me smiles and have given me tears." I leave you with a portion of the refrain, and the lyrics are straightforward, just like her: thank you to the life that has given me so much.

In 1960, I migrated with my parents from Morocco to Paris, leaving behind a country my family had known and lived in since the early 1920's. I was seventeen years old and the youngest of nine children, many of whom had already made their way to France during the time of the French Protectorate.

For more than sixty years, I have traversed the sophisticated streets of Paris—with its charming boutiques, brassieres, and overall je nais se quoi—in complete contrast to the roads I traveled in Morocco as a young girl visiting the many and diverse souks of my homeland with my father, a grain wholesaler in Casablanca. The essence of Paris is noteworthy in my story as it accurately encapsulates the dichotomy of who and what I correspondingly represent, evident in the push and pull of the lens on the two countries that ultimately won my heart.

I studied Literature at the prestigious Sorbonne University and shortly thereafter became involved in festivals and the exhibition of films. Ironically, one of my first jobs was working in a private movie theater, the Club 70 (where 70mm films where screened). In 1973, together with Louis Malle and Claude Nedjar, I created the company SOGEAV, utilizing the professional-based, private screening room at Club 70 to predominantly screen films in pre- or post-production that would not normally be seen in mainstream cinemas. And, in that same year—one which marked a pivotal transition for me—I expanded the company to specialize in the distribution of French films in French-speaking African nations, and made my first sojourn back to Morocco. This visit was truly the beginning of rediscovering myself.

Among the sights, sounds, and people I interacted with—many of whom remembered my family—I realized just how disconnected I felt and how energized I was to reintegrate and re-identify with my homeland—catapulting the beginning of an unparalleled career that eloquently interwove all that I had accomplished living, working, and thriving in France, with the foundational fabric of my childhood and country of origin.

In my twenty-plus narrative documentaries, the messaging in my films transcends time. I grapple with my diasporic identity, Moroccan heritage, and the music of a country I and my family left for a more prosperous life. As a Moroccan diasporan, I believe my films provide a means to connect our bodies and souls to our home.

In 1981, I served as the producer of a film, entitled *Transes*, showcasing the concert of one of the most influential music groups in post-colonial Morocco, Nass El Ghiwane; a production that I later expanded to a full-feature film. It was this experience, immersed and electrified by the music of this band, that I credit as having had one of the greatest influences on my career, as it was the music of my land that brought me back to myself, essentially pulling me back and reminding me of home.

My reconnection with Morocco, after a 13-year absence, fueled a fire within me to reacquaint myself with the country of my origin—through its culture, its language, its music, and its very nature. I had already attached myself to the cinema of Morocco through my work in producing and distributing Moroccan films. Yet, my discovery of the musical treasures of Morocco became my North Star, setting me on a course of dedicating myself to documentary work—rebranding SOGEAV to OHRA, under which I continue to the present day to produce and distribute my work.

In 1987, I embarked on a formidable project entitled *Maroc Corps et Âme* (Morocco Body and Soul), a work of ten short documentary films, each focusing on a different region and musical tradition of the North African kingdom—a compilation of work that truly established me as a film documentarian. In 1994, I produced *Return to Oulad Moumen*, a film capturing the nostalgic reunion of my family in Morocco, and the story of our migration from our small village of Oulad Moumen to Paris over a number of years—retracing the circumstances of my family's departure from our North African home amid the social and political climate of the country.

In all of my work, throughout the '80s to the present, I credit the music of my native land as the light that guided me back to myself. While I specialize in narrative documentary, the music of my native country has served as the common thread in my storytelling, exploring all sides of Moroccan heritage: the Berbers, the Gnaouas, the Sufis, the Andalus, the Aïta of the Cheikhate, and the songs of the Sephardic Jews. I believe my work authentically captures and visualizes the music and essence of Moroccan culture—filming musicians and dancers in the space they exist, in a manner that allows their souls, voices, and words to truly resonate. I take pride in my ability to balance my outsider status and still utilize my transnational identity within Morocco to effectively document its varied musical landscape—people, songs, dance, culture—believing that music represents the hope that there is a common human experience that can comprehend the other across borders and cultures.

Undoubtedly, it is my most recent documentary, *My Thursday Souk*, that brings my story full circle. It is a piece of work that I am currently ready to release, and one that is near and dear to my heart. The memories I recall of those reminiscent open-air markets in my vivid country were with rigor and roust, matching the personality and core of who I am. *My Thursday Souk* is a film that recalls my sensory experiences and the imprint of the time spent with my father at this enormous market in El Gara, and what our time together there meant to me. While watching the rushes of film we shot in El Gara in 1994, the Moroccan village where I spent so much of my childhood trailing alongside my father as he worked selling grain, I realized that it was precisely this place that I was founded in mutual recognition. It was here, in El Gara, that a seed was sown in me so many years ago, germinating decades later in the host of films I produced and made on Moroccan culture. Images of this grain village named Boucheron—under the French Protectorate when we lived there—recalled in me the weekly Thursday market (souk) I visited with my father; and, illuminated the vibrant heart of commercial activity and animation, meetings, carnival, pleasures of music, and horse fantasias I remember from that time. This film has served to enchant my child's soul, to recall and record a time left behind, yet ever so important to the woman I am today.

The shooting of this film was providential in more than one way, beginning with the fortuitous encounter with the icon of the popular song Hajja El Hamddaouia—who died at the age of ninety-one in 2021, precisely three days after my rushed screening. Accompanied by the El Bouazzaoui brothers, these emblematic musicians of El Gara, we were offered the invaluable gift of a spontaneous concert from which Jean-Claude Lubchansky's camera did not let anything escape. In this intimate relationship to place, people, and events, the film, *My Thursday Souk*, aims to explore, through never before published rushes, real treasures that had been lying in boxes since 1994. Magic!

While dreams of emancipation directed me toward the West as a young girl of seventeen, my interest in cinema and my fateful return to my homeland 13 years later, fortuitously reconnected me to my roots, my past, myself…and my sense of home.

CHAPTER TEN

Mia

*T*he tween years are a monumental time of transition—no longer little kids, but not quite teenagers. At twelve, Mia is in the eldest tier of Gen Alphas—the first group tagged as experiencing a fully digital world—and the youngest SHERO in this book. I felt it important to share Mia's story in an effort to bring greater insight into the world of today's tweens—and the ever-accelerating digital landscape that is quickly outpacing that of previous generations. And, in so doing, hope Mia's story will forge greater understanding and embracement of this generation of digital wonderkids; helping to bridge the gap between all our generations.

Mia is a young storyteller on social media. I was thrilled when a friend of mine recommended I speak to Mia based on how impressed she was with her interactive social skills. And, impressive she is, exuding confidence and maturity well beyond her barely double-digit year. How often does an adult compliment the behaviors of a young person these days?

As a member of the Gen X generation, I had to rethink and readjust my viewpoint as the mother of two technologically-savvy Gen Z sons early on. I adopted a contemporary approach, having them educate me, collaborate, and equip me (and them) with information on navigating cyberspace and connecting with technology—smartly and safely, instead of preventing them from using it altogether.

Mia is cheerful and spunky. Like most teenagers, she struggles with fitting in, managing insecurities, and getting braces. When I see someone like Mia charting a course that allows her to express herself authentically, I smile. For any tween girl, finding a place that feels good—that makes you feel confident, that empowers you—is not always easy. Self-doubt, jealousies, and bullying permeate the tween and teenage stratospheres. Finding something that grounds you at these ages can make all the difference in your journey. Mia found her steady foundation in using her voice. She likes creating original content to share knowledge and educate her family and friends. She is not interested in being an influencer to build a brand and popularity. Mia does what she does not for the notability, but for the love of being helpful and creative. She insists the number of followers she has does not matter.

Mia's mother, Lisa, approved of my interviewing Mia. However, Mia was the one who took the reins in scheduling our time together. She picked her favorite restaurant, En Fuego Cantina, a historic spot in Del Mar, California, meeting me punctually at four o'clock one afternoon, following her gymnastics class. We chatted about how she determines the material she wants to share—ultimately creating lively videos that expressively showcase make-up tutorials, meal choices, and recipes she favors. Each clip is captivating and imaginative and showcases this extrovert's charm. Her language use is mature, witty, and fun. She keenly understands that stress and self-care are essential at any age.

  Following our conversation at the Cantina, we decided it was best to meet for a second time at Mia's home to delve deeper into who she is and where she creates content for her TikTok and YouTube videos—all of which begin with her standard greeting: "Hello, lovely ladies and gents, it's Mia, and I am here....!" Before my arrival Mia again called me one hour prior to confirm our meeting, offering explicit directions on finding her home and where to park. Mia gave me a tour of her bedroom, where all the magic happens—the domain where she spreads her sunshine. Her room was inspiring, with a positively cheerful aesthetic that matched her personality to a T. Her space was immaculate, peppered with bold displays that honor what is important to her. There's a hand-me-down grey desk displaying her essentials, from makeup and lotion bottles to a unique bottle of tajine (she loves the chili lime seasoning and sprinkles it on everything). She uses a desktop selfie ring light to create her video content. She even had framed vintage pictures of three generations prominently displayed—showcasing her grandmother, great-grandmother, and great-great-grandmother. As we conversed, I kept reminding myself of her age! Her sense of maturity, responsibility, communication, family, and joy contradicted her tween stature.

  Lisa has been instrumental in allowing Mia the freedom to explore who she is and how life can give you lessons at any age if allowed to learn them. She has outlined parameters *within which Mia can express her creativity—ensuring that she understands that utilizing an online platform requires acting responsibly and within internet guidelines. Mia has a strong command of language and communication skills. While some young influencers are using their voices and videos to fight against social injustice, bullying, and environmental issues, Mia enjoys entertaining and sharing her insights—keeping her audience engaged with her talent through tips and tutorials under the username @miashay_show on Instagram and TikTok. She started these platforms during Covid. They helped her keep busy and made her feel like she was engaging with others during a time of great uncertainty, especially for many kids who suddenly lost all direct social connections.*

Mia is not your typical tween. She is contagiously enthusiastic and quite mature. She bravely opened up during our conversation, sharing her struggles with anxiety and providing insightful information on how her parents' divorce has affected her. Mia effortlessly creates awareness and educates on everything from how to make French toast to random life hacks. Her drive and determination landed her a place in Volume Two, perhaps because I see a little of myself in her. I want to champion that young, inspiring girl to continue to believe in herself, to express her creativity, and to stand firm in her conviction that what she is doing feels right and joyful.

She is a poster child of the Gen Alpha generation, which is moving swiftly into an advanced world where automation and innovation dominate. The speed of this progress means that as their mothers and mentors, we must stay engaged, ride shotgun and guide their course, learning and growing with them along the way. To be fearful and attempt to tamp down this acceleration into the digital world will do nothing more than topple the bridges connecting us to our youth.

I have always liked talking. My mom told me I started babbling before I turned one. I have always had that "jazz hand spunk" of a personality. I watch home videos now of when I was a baby and laugh at myself. Technology helps me find new dance moves, recipes, or how to make a movie using various applications. I like to share what I learn. My friends and I talk about how long it would take to get things done or access information if we did not have the technology we have today. TikTok and Instagram (social media platforms) allowed me to express my emotions when I couldn't talk to my friends during Covid. I was in the middle of fourth grade at the time, and I was lonely at home. My brother was occupied in seventh grade, and my mom was trying to make both of us happy. Covid took away my life's social aspect for a bit, so I looked for other opportunities that interested me.

You have to be thirteen to have an account on TikTok. At ten years old, I had a public account. They realized I was too young and were like, "bye," and kicked me off! So, I opened a private account and turned it into just family and friends instead of the whole world. I started my "Mia Shay Show" because my friends and family liked my material. I have always talked to myself and have always been a "viewer of myself." In putting together ideas for content, I showcase a lot of things my mom initially taught me and I now do myself, adding my own creativity—like how to make eggs, organize, and put on makeup—because this is what I have fun with.

At my age, other people might see me as too young to give advice. They want someone older with more experience, but I don't do it for their opinions. I like to help people learn what I know.

Hello lovely Ladies & Gents, I am Mia, and I am here!
Here to show you that a young creator like me...
can offer you food, fashion, and fun varieties of life—
in ways, you'll want to learn about it!

I will be showing you...
how to do things, and where to get things.
If you want to stay, hear, and see all my "how to's and life hacks,"
watch my videos!

Let's get started....

As I've said, I talk a lot. I am lucky to be able to make many of my own decisions. My mom gives me the freedom to be me as long as I understand the rules she sets to keep me safe. If I do something wrong, she teaches me another way and the lesson. My basic boundaries include my location being permanently switched on with my iPhone, no sleepovers on school nights, and no going out after dark. There are more—I just can't remember or want to list them. I was raised under the "see something, say something" philosophy. A couple of months ago, a friend of mine was rude to another friend and I took her aside, privately, and told her that she shouldn't treat our friend the way she did; that maybe talking it out together is better. I try to treat people the way I want to be treated. I like to provide happiness to others by being nice.

When I was young, I would sing, dance, and teach myself different things. My mom, Lisa, brother, Miles, and I moved to

California when I was nine. I was born in Tulsa, Oklahoma, and my brother is three years older than me. My parents' divorced when I was one and it has not been a struggle, but more of a learning experience. I get to live full-time with my mom and see the difficulties of my other friends with divorced parents, having to move back and forth between their moms and dads. The only thing that makes me sad is that I don't see my dad that much. I visit him once a month but never spend the night at his home. He doesn't live near me. Divorce seems common, and I don't think it's bad. I want both my mom and my dad to be happy.

I have also been struggling with eczema since I was an infant. Creams and medications will work for a small period of time and then I am off to find something new. It's been an endless cycle. The struggle has affected me harder as I've gotten older, especially when participating in activities that make me sweat—LOL! My discolored skin prompts some people to make comments. It's not always easy to cover-up. I'm not able to use all the make-up that my friends do because it's not all eczema and sensitive-skin friendly. I would break out if I did. As I have gotten older, I've realized that the anxiety I can sometimes feel in having to manage my eczema will actually cause flareups. It's not easy if something unkind is said to me at school, or with friends. Like any other struggle in my life, however, I have learned how to better process what I can and cannot control. This mindset has helped me overall—making me more resilient. I find that when I focus on being with my family and friends —spending time in my room making videos, and learning new things—I am at my happiest.

Hey, my lovely Ladies & Gents; I am Mia, and here today to show you...skincare from Sephora.
I want to point out I have had eczema since I was little,

using oatmeal and other lotions for a long time—they didn't work... but this cream called "Skinfix Barrier" face cream has a silky texture, and at the same time, it is very moisturizing—my skin and I just love it!

Until I was seven, I enjoyed ballet and hip-hop. Then I tried acting at eight years old. I learned early on that being an aspiring actress was not in the stars for me. I was a big Jennifer Aniston fan and connected with her character on Friends. I felt she and I were similar—funny, caring, and extraordinary. She was my inspiration, and I thought I wanted to be a movie star. I remember auditioning for a commercial and getting the part. It felt natural, but I was told I would only be commercial material. So, I stopped acting.

I kept talking to myself and seeing myself as a viewer. I decided if I could teach myself things, I could teach others. This was when I started creating social media content and not getting down when people told me no; I just found new things to explore.

I know this about myself: I am both interested and interesting. At times, I feel older than I am. Saving money is important to me. I am proud of what I have put in my bank account. I walk three dogs, three times a week. They are Lola, Coda, and Scout. Scout is a King Charles breed and the friendliest dog I have ever met. She is so chill and gorgeous. I sometimes just hang out with her because she calms my anxiety. Scout's mom lets me go over and play with her for free.

Being responsible feels good, and I know how to ration my earnings. I save more money than I spend. After school, I like to go to Starbucks with my friends and do homework—

if I am not at gymnastics practice. I use my money to order a Mocha Cookie Crumble Grande Frappuccino—no whip, double blended, with extra crumble and a straw. I am getting braces in three months and eating all the sweets and sushi I can until then!

My best friend is like me. We met on the first day of school in seventh grade. I do talk about divorce with my friends. I have a close friend who goes through the same situation as me with her father down to the bone, but I have also talked to other people on other occasions.

Calm sometimes can be dull. I like to be busy and have fun. To me, it's more interesting. There is pressure to perform in school with my friends. It may sound weird, but I like when things are hectic. I have four hours of homework due tomorrow. Thinking about it does not make me feel calm, but being in my room with candles and crystals around me will help get it all done.

I am not allowed to have my phone at dinner. My mom insists my brother and I interact while eating her crockpot chicken chili with cornbread. My homework must be done before I can be on my phone, and I have to turn it off by 10:30 p.m.

I love Algebra. I really hate reading. My favorite thing about school is helping make campus decisions, as I am on the Student Site Council. I am good at problem-solving. I like being helpful. I also like being back at school instead of on Zoom. English is a subject I am not very good at. I am a good talker but not as good when it comes to writing and reading.

For a short time, I had panic attacks. I was scared I would lose my mom because she lost her mom at a young age.

My separation anxiety has lessened as I've matured—knowing that everything happens for a reason. I don't need to be scared of anything because I'll never have to do it alone. I usually use a comfort method (doing something I enjoy that will distract me), such as making a video about makeup or what I'm doing the next day. Still, most of the time, I lie in my mom's room and watch *Grey's Anatomy* or *Friends* because those are two of my comfort shows.

I am close to my brother, Miles. He just got a job at Jersey Mike's. When Miles comes home, my mom makes him dinner, but on special occasions I will make him dinner because cooking is fun. My mac and cheese is a favorite of Miles, along with my mashed potatoes. I won't tell him my secret ingredients. I will never forget going to the park near our house when we lived in Oklahoma. The tire swing was something fun that my brother and I did all the time. I have a picture framed of the two of us.

Hey, my lovely Ladies & Gents, It's Mia,
and I am here to show you another one of my easy, favorite,
and simple snacks!

This one is not necessarily a snack but can go into
a really great meal. Like I said in my last video with
Maybelline's Sky-High mascara, we know her we love her,
but this time it's my love of Chipotle white lime and
cilantro rice, and I have the perfect four-step recipe that
will make your heart melt like every time you go and
have it at Chipotle.

Everything in my recipe today is from Trader Joe's.
Step one starts with buying white Jasmine rice, fresh limes,
and cilantro. Keep listening for further instructions...

MIA

Mom and Mia days are the best. We hang out all the time —from going shopping and just watching a movie. We both like to shop and then go to dinner. Our favorite meal to share is sushi, especially tuna, cucumber, cream cheese, and avocado sushi rolls. Once I have my braces on, I may switch to soy paper sushi to make it easier to eat. I also love ice cream—rocky road is my favorite. My mom likes salted caramel. I am happy we don't have to share when it comes to ice cream!

I like how I can tell my mom everything. I am very blunt and honest with her. She trusts me and lets me try new things. If I ever have a question, I tend to not always look it up. I try to always go to my mom first because I trust her opinion more than anything—especially when dealing with interesting comments on social media. They are annoying but don't stop me. I just ignore them. I don't want rude people or remarks to ruin my day. When they sometimes do, my mom helps me get through it. My mom reminds me to love myself first and better myself every day.

Hey, my lovely Ladies & Gents, I am Mia, and I am here!

Today, I will show you my outfit and where everything I have on is from.

OK, here we go; these super cute little yin-yang earrings are from CVS... and these bulky boho earrings are from Amazon.

*Oh, this loose, long sleeve, oval-cut shirt is from Forever 21;
I just love it so much—
my high waisted checkered pink pattern shorts are from Zara
and, finally, my brown, super comfy Doc Martins with these fun
yellow laces are from Dillard's.*

Oops, I forgot, one more thing, this stretchy, turquoise bracelet is from my favorite local store in Del Mar—so amazing!

Thanks for watching.

Like writer's block, I get talker's block. Sometimes it seems like everyone has already done everything, so how can anyone, myself included, show the world something new? Someone said something like, "Creative burnout is real," and I agree.

My goal is to be a fashion director or a business manager type. Directing runway shows and making all the magic happen would be a blast—not being the designer or the model, but the person who coordinates the whole fashion show. I could see myself running a business in New York City, maybe even having my own boutique. My town has a fantastic boutique, and the owner, Julie, is lovely...and smart too. I like her so much. Her store is bright and full of cool clothes, books, and candles. I go in there all the time. Maybe when I am old enough, she will hire me. There is something for everyone at her store.

I am proud of everything I know how to do at my age, like being responsible for household chores, cooking for myself and my older brother, managing money, overseeing my dog walking job, doing my homework on time, and caring for my dog, Sassy. (I really don't like to do laundry, though!) Doing these tasks makes me feel good, and if I can teach my friends and social media followers these life skills, they might feel good about themselves too. I found this quote a couple of weeks ago, and it's one of my new favorites. "A successful woman can build a firm foundation from the bricks others throw at her." I take this to mean that whatever you're dealt with, you can make a good life and good decisions—maybe even help others by sharing what you know, or creating new products or services from what you've learned. I will keep being who I am—learning, sharing, and being kind.

CHAPTER ELEVEN

Tomoko

Do you ever feel that there must be more to life—that you have a greater calling? Or, you yearn to build a more meaningful and fulfilling existence; one that aligns with your values and leaves the world a better place? I think, deep down, most people do at some point in their life's journey.

I wonder how often we ponder these feelings of belonging to something bigger; of feeling that there is a seed within us that we must nurture, despite all odds. And whether we listen. As Mary Oliver brilliantly stated, you have "one wild and precious life." It is up to each of us to grab ahold of our life, to be stewards of our own fate as best we can—to own it and live it!

I am grateful and humbled to introduce you to Tomoko. She is a woman who knew, from a very early age, that she was drawn to music and song. And yet, apart from her grandfather who encouraged her to learn and broaden her horizons, Tomoko's family did not value her interests.

While it took years to finally reap the rewards of self-awareness, self-confidence, and determination, Tomoko is a woman that did not crumble under the pressures of culture and family in her efforts to forge her one wild and precious life. She never gave up on that feeling that there was more out in the world for her; a life that would value what she herself valued.

I spoke with Tomoko for over three hours on a beautiful, clear-skied day in Marina Del Rey, California. It felt like a brain-huddle strategy session, putting our heads together and diving deep into questions that were bigger than us; questions on how best to be oneself in the face of adversity. I instantly connected with her understanding of who she was at a very young age (vis a vis who she is to date)—that lost-in-the-sea feeling of overwhelm, perfectionism, and self-doubt that can drown youthful ambition and self-worth. From the time Tomoko was a little girl, she knew she was going to have to rely heavily on herself. She knew that she would need to shed the voices that wanted to restrict or diminish her. Releasing the past that often holds us down is freeing. Both Tomoko and I connected on this profound realization. And we agreed that sharing our lived experiences—how we persevere despite the roadblocks we encounter—can bring about pure human transformation and empowerment. It can be life-altering, as Tomoko's story proves. I walked away from our conversation thinking this most subtle and sophisticated woman was a rebel at her core.

While Tomoko's journey may have been a leap into the unknown, it was time and tolerance that allowed her to create a new paradigm. Faced with obstacles that could easily have deterred her from her love of music, she continued to seek new paths to follow. Music had always been her sanctuary—it gave her hope, eased her pain, and maybe, most importantly, helped her to heal the wounds of her childhood. Music is what gave Tomoko the courage to stand in her truth; to quiet the voices of disdain.

What I respect about Tomoko is she is still connecting the dots of her life as she charts her unique path. At her core, she is a non-conformist. She refused to accept life at face value; refused to allow disrespect to govern her journey, to be labeled "problematic" simply because she sought out something different than what her family deemed meaningful. She was not afraid to admit her natural desires and what she wanted to accomplish. Now, as an adult, she wants people to find the courage within themselves to be honest about what matters to them.

I asked Tomoko what she would tell her younger self, knowing what she knows now. Her response was quick, "Don't give up; trust the process; life is hard, but I am here for you, my perfect precious self." Her quest for self-discovery is inspiring. Not many want to do the "inner work" and heal our generational gook, as I call it. Being honest with ourselves—about what we want in life—is not for the faint of heart. Tomoko's story is a testament to the beauty of forging on, despite all that may stand in your way; to believing in that deep-down voice within you that tells you that you are capable, worthy, and able to achieve your dreams.

Building a life that one loves takes a ton of courage, but you don't have to do it alone—even though Tomoko did for the first half of her existence. She is proof that everything changes when you believe you matter. Believing you are worthy doesn't

TOMOKO

make your journey easy, it simply gives you license to move forward; to make decisions with your own self-interest in mind. It can feel like a leap into the unknown—trusting oneself to craft the narrative. And leap she did! At the age of twenty-seven, in desperate need of a pivot and respite, Tomoko boarded a plane from Tokyo, Japan, to Los Angeles, California, carrying one suitcase, half-empty; knowing no one, and having only a limited grasp of the language. She planned to live with a host family for one year. However, a chance encounter just days after her arrival, changed the trajectory of her life completely.

My most significant source of joy is singing!

From the time I was a very little girl, I wanted to be a singer—something that was not seen as being of much value on a farm. Deep in my soul, I always felt there was more for me to experience than my small village might offer. This made me different. This, and, perhaps, the fact that I was not born a boy. Though it took me nearly thirty years to reach my destiny in life, everything I went through led me to where I was meant to be.

My life began in a small farming village in rural Japan, 100 miles from Tokyo. I grew up in the same house with my father, mother, grandparents, and two older sisters—Aiko, who is five years older than me, and Emiko, who is three years older. The village we lived in was very isolated, but near Tokushima. We lived in a modest, two-story white house. We grew mushrooms on our farm, as well as oranges and other vegetables. And, we had chickens, rabbits, and cats.

After having two girls, I think my parents (especially my father) may have hoped that their third child might be a boy. Instead, they got me. My mother even tried for another child after having me, but miscarried. Given that a son is seen as the one likely to carry on the family farm, I always felt as though my arrival was a disappointment for my parents. Perhaps this is why I felt dismissed by them and other members of my family all my life. As early as three years old, I was able to sense the emotions of other people through their eyes and voice. I vividly remember extended family members coming to our house and sensing their negative energy. They were mean, especially to me. (People's eyes always tell their story.) This is my earliest memory of feeling unwelcome in my family, and with my father.

In most stories, you hear of people getting bullied by their friends; in my story, all the adults in my life (with the exception of my grandfather) bullied me. I was an inquisitive child, which was not appreciated. I would question *why should I do this?* Only my grandfather appreciated my desire to know the "why" of things; he understood my desire to learn. He was my friend and my teacher. I was curious about life. To me, sameness felt dull; there was no growth or adventure to repeating what I already knew. I just had different ideas from those around me of what I wanted out of life. Because of this, I was called a troublemaker. I felt like my parents and my teachers hated me.

My grandfather was the only family member that truly took note of me; the only one that valued my individuality. I remember listening to the radio together. This was when I had my first introduction to the English language. My second exposure was watching television. I will never forget how inspired I felt watching people sing on stage. I was mesmerized by artists like Aretha Franklin, Chaka Khan, and Mariah Carey.

TOMOKO

Mariah Carey's Diva's Live performance was so riveting that I remember watching it over and over and over again. I felt like I couldn't get enough. I was so moved and amazed by her talent. This particular time in my life was so impactful. It was when I truly embraced the realization that I wanted to be a singer. I wanted to belt out songs and feel like the singers I watched on television. Watching celebrity life and listening to vocalists gave me something to strive for. Hundreds of miles away, the people I saw on this small box were more relatable to me than the people in my village.

Music was a sanctuary to me, from a very early age. I remember listening to my sisters' piano lessons when I was just three. I would try to mimic what I saw. At the age of five, I would lay in my bed and stare at the stars, feeling that life was more significant than where I was. It was around this time that I witnessed a shooting star, which is rare to see. I felt this was a sign supporting my feeling that the universe was big, beautiful, and shiny; that someday *I would be special*, and this specific time was meant for me to see that.

At the age of six, I started playing the flute and piano. While much of this gave me some joy, I still felt very much alone. At seven, I stopped talking to my family, but would talk and be energetic at school. To my family, I would only answer with yes or no. I did not show emotion or smile. I would erase myself rather than be dismissed. At eight years old and not feeling welcomed, I found a piece of broken glass behind the science room at school and tried to cut my wrists. I saw suicide as my opportunity to leave the place I was in. However, the glass was too dull—which made my unsuccessful attempt even more painful. To date, I still have a small scar as a reminder of how sad I felt inside during that time in my life.

At the age of ten, I went to America with my family. We visited a farm in Yuma, Arizona, where my father had studied agriculture as a young teen. We traveled to Portland, Oregon, and then to California, visiting San Francisco and Los Angeles. I was so impressed with the freedom of expression I witnessed in our travels. Looking back, I know I was meant to take this trip; to see the potential that existed beyond our family farm. I was especially taken by Los Angeles and immediately felt I wanted to live there. I, too, wanted to get my ears pierced, my nails polished, and have the ability to express myself. Culturally, none of this was allowed in either my home or school in Japan. Regardless of these strict rules, I did pierce a pin through my right ear upon my return to Japan. Though it was painful, I felt proud of my act of independence. However, my sister and teacher found out and I was locked in a storage shed as punishment. I remember crying out for help, alone in that creepy, unlit shed, but no one heard me through the thick wood door. I chalked the experience up to just another thing to get through.

When bad things happened, or I felt sad, I turned to nature. Growing up surrounded by mountains and the vast countryside instilled in me a deep love of nature and animals. As a child, this was my playground and my haven. When I needed to get away, I would go to a special place down the narrow road from our home. It was a small hillside near a river. I would wander to a shrine that was nearby that was just the size of a birdhouse. In my culture, a shrine offers protection. There were large, old oak trees there that covered much of the area. It is there, under the branches of those trees, at the age of twelve, that I found peace—both internally and externally. I would feel comfortable and contemplate why I felt different and how I struggled with fitting in, not just with my friends, but also with my family. I truly believed no one understood me, and almost everyone considered me difficult and sensitive.

    As a child, I was sometimes shy, but I wanted and could be outgoing when people were not mean. Sometimes, I would wonder how I could change my situation or if I was delusional about dreaming big; whether I could make it out of my village to the big city and learn English, which was my goal. Contemplating and agonizing about who I was and how I could fit in consumed my thoughts throughout my entire childhood. Even through boarding school and high school, I was bullied and made to feel small. Singing, like nature, was a haven. It made me feel free; it gave me that avenue to express myself, as I so longed to do. I like the free and structured elements that create exciting music. I feel this dichotomy represents how life should be—a balance; notes are balanced in music, as roles are meant to be balanced in a relationship. And, of course, there are the lyrics of a song, which can elicit a range of emotions—hope, sorrow, love, anger, joy, etc. It was around this time that I became acquainted with Cyndi Lauper's song, *True Colors*. The music and lyrics of this song became an anthem that played on repeat in my mind.

> *You, with the sad eyes*
> *Don't be discouraged*
> *Oh I realize*
> *It's hard to take courage*
> *In a world full of people*
> *You can lose sight of it all*
> *And the darkness inside you*
> *Can make you feel so small*
>
> *But I see your true colors*
> *Shining through*
> *I see your true colors*

S.H.E. SHARE HEAL EMPOWER

And that's why I love you
So don't be afraid to let them show
Your true colors
True colors are beautiful
Like a rainbow

My first experience truly expressing myself in song was in high school. I had joined a band and we played at a high school festival. We performed "First Love" by Japanese singer Hikaru Utada. The music hall was packed. I remember feeling so free and awesome. I also recall how strange it was to see the girls who were so mean to me now crying in response to our moving performance. Having moments like this helped to soften the hard shell I had formed as protection against all who had belittled and dismissed me all my life. The birth of my niece also contributed to this softening. I remember thinking: *What is this creature? She is so innocent and exudes such pure energy. She makes everyone happy.* I wanted to do the same, to express my true self and experience happiness.

While everyone in my family expected me to attend University, I was tired of the school system and wanted to taste more of my newfound freedom. I moved to Tokyo, which is a showbiz place in Japan, and enrolled in music school in an effort to appease my parents and also honor my passion. I knew the first day it was not for me. My parents paid for a whole year, but I started working with a producer, and we began creating music together. For five years, I sang professionally in Tokyo. Then at twenty-five, I started having panic attacks. The pressure became bigger and bigger. I was writing music, singing, and performing in front of more and more people. Then, slowly, my producer and all those around me started changing my genre. My lyrics and my music moved further and further away from who I was. My singing was praised, but my producer took credit. Eventually it all became too much and I lost my passion, and myself in the process.

During this turbulent time, I was diagnosed with nodules on my vocal cords. For one month, I was very sad; I had to refrain from everything that might tax my voice. I stopped singing, talking, drinking alcohol, and smoking. I was a heavy smoker in Tokyo, but the thought of losing my voice was enough to make me quit cold turkey. Thankfully, my voice returned to normal. I saw this experience as a sign that I needed a change, something different. I knew this was my chance to attend language school in America; my opportunity to finally live in Los Angeles.

When I started planning everything, I almost forgot that I ever had nodules on my vocal cords, I was just so excited. At twenty-seven, I was finally doing something I always dreamed of doing. I had every intention of spending one year with my host family, learning the language, then returning to Tokyo to marry my Japanese boyfriend. I had only been in LA for one week when my friend from language school and I went to Hollywood to attend a going away party for another classmate. At the end of the party we got separated, as my bus schedule and her time management did not match. She made her bus, but I missed mine. There was no UBER, and I tried to call a taxi to no avail. There I was, on the corner of Santa Monica and Westwood boulevards, waiting for the last bus of the night, floundering with my phone and slightly peeved that I couldn't remember the number of my host family, when a nicely dressed man in a suit drove up. While this was certainly a scenario where alarm bells should have sounded, whatever initial concern I had with this stranger seemed to quickly dispel. The man offered to help me, showing me his driver's license and business card to legitimize his identity. For whatever reason, I just felt confident that this man, John, was a good guy, trying to do a good thing. I am happy I allowed myself to trust my gut. It was late and I knew I needed help in getting home. As it turned out, my intuition proved fortuitous, as John eventually became my husband, and Los Angeles my home!

  One day, I asked John why he wanted to marry me and he said, "In your life, no one was in your corner. Someone has to be there for you. I want to be that person." And he has been in so many meaningful ways. One especially poignant moment was when John asked me, "What do you wish to do?" I answered quickly and honestly that I wanted to take vocal lessons from the legend Seth Riggs, who has been the master behind the magic of several superstars, including Michael Jackson. For one lesson, it is costly, like $500 per hour. John's response was short and simple, "I will pay for you. You must keep going if you have a dream. Take the lesson." I was so overwhelmed by his support, something I had lacked my entire life. And, here he was, totally and completely supportive of my passion for singing.

  My career path, however, was not a straight line. Acclimating to a new culture was challenging. Learning English was challenging. I dabbled in Reiki healing for a bit and continued my vocal training work—something I had started while in Tokyo and was working to establish in Los Angeles. Then, at the age of thirty, I finally received a recording contract in Hollywood. However, it was short lived. I gained hope only to lose it again when the recording project did not work out. Then, at the age of thirty-two, I had an enlightened experience while watching Christina Aguilera on the show, *The Voice*, and learned of the term "belting." This moment was a turning point for me and for my vocal training work. I knew instantly that I had found my mission.

"Belting" is essentially a contemporary singing technique that allows a singer to produce a high-intensity (powerful) vocal sound by carrying their chest voice beyond its natural break; singing notes in their head voice range, with the power of their chest. If done incorrectly, it can damage your voice. If done correctly, it's magical! Once I discovered "belting," I knew I had found my purpose and saw a very clear vision. Since then, I have worked hard, challenged myself, and developed what has taken eight years to create: a vocal training method for Japanese people to sing like American singers—singers like Mariah Carey, Christina Aguilera, and Lady Gaga.

I believe many talented artists take rigorous vocal training that doesn't teach enough technique, and then they blame themselves for not progressing. This was something that I experienced in my own vocal training in Japan. I met many of those kinds of teachers, paying a lot of money only to be demoralized. With my training method, I take both the person and their gift into consideration—caring for the artists' voices and their minds, as I see many of them experiencing the same struggles I went through. In many ways, the turmoil I experienced as a child and young adult—trying to make my way in life, without the support or care of my family—now serves as an asset in my work. I am now channeling the youthful "rebel" Tomoko in building my business; recognizing that "being nice" is not an attribute that should be bestowed upon people who are unkind. In finding my purpose in life—what I am truly meant to do—I also found my confidence. I am a recovering people pleaser!

Today I work with many clients from Japan. I find this to be especially gratifying; to know that I am able to change some of what I suffered from is so healing. Too many talented artists are shrinking and doubting their abilities, while teachers threaten them and steal their money. This is still common in Japan. I try to inspire the vocal trainers to work in a fulfilled way and explain to them how they need to change how they educate singers in the system. I don't want to see people suffering from their voice, limiting their ability, and not shining in this world. I am doing what many say is impossible, "the Japanese cannot sing like the Americans." It's not only the singing. It's about seeing the person and listening to the heart's voice.

Now, at the age of forty, I am proud of what I have accomplished in designing my vocal training methodology—what I have coined the Rebelting Method. The irony that "rebel" is in the name is not lost on me. I now consider myself a rebel in the best of ways—proudly and confidently believing in the skills I can offer vocalists; believing in myself. Everyone who completes one of my voice master courses says, "This is life-changing. Thank you very much."

As I look back on those first 27 years of my life and see where I am today, I realize that the struggles we endure in life can oftentimes provide us with our greatest motivation. My grandfather taught me to have faith. This allowed me to persevere. My parents were strict and challenged me in ways that felt harsh, yet I now know gave me strength and a dedicated work ethic. For all of this, I am grateful.

My name, Tomoko, means *the wisdom of a child seeing God's truth*. It truly is so fitting. While the scars of childhood do not leave you, I do believe that the difficulties in my life have made me a humble person. I am still learning from them. The anxiety, worthlessness, and loneliness I felt growing up are now what I channel to motivate me. I know I am worthy and I am loved. All the thoughts I had that there was something bigger out in the world for me were true. It just took some time for it all to come to fruition.

Life is an ebb and flow; a give and take; a rhythmical dance. Like musical chairs, you don't know when the music will stop, or where you will end up. As a little girl who just wanted to be a singer, I am grateful I persevered; grateful that I never let the thoughts of that young girl— believing there was something bigger in life—ever get lost in the noise of others that tried to dampen her dreams.

CHAPTER TWELVE

Monay

The surf and turf restaurant that was the site of my meeting with Monay in the fall of 2022 was particularly welcoming—a cozy little spot with a uniquely chic hunting lodge vibe, and a picturesque bayside patio that offered views that stretched far out over the inland waters of West Traverse Bay. I immediately felt it was the perfect setting for our conversation— casual, yet warmly inviting.

I spotted Monay sitting in a circular booth at the back of the restaurant. She was fiddling with her curly blonde hair; wisps twirled between her fingers as she gently furled and unfurled the ends. I immediately hoped that she was comfortable with our meeting. As I approached the table, she looked up and smiled, and I was straightaway taken by what I can only refer to as a "movie star" smile—that of a Hollywood starlet's dream. The warmth of Monay's smile conveyed a sense of self assurance and comfort.

After our quick hellos and introductions, I learned that Monay had a specific reason to be beaming so brightly: a day on the links! She enthusiastically shared that she is an avid golfer and any day spent golfing, even that particular day which was quite rainy but eventually cleared, was a good day. Shortly after we settled in at our table, Matt, our attentive waiter, approached to take our order and quickly embraced Monay as if they were long-lost friends. They are, in fact, great friends and coworkers, as Monay is also an employee of the restaurant, working as a server there since 2020. I was touched by their evident friendship and ease of connection, further confirming my impressions of how warm and kind Monay came across. We placed our orders—a margarita for her and a glass of French white wine for me. And then we settled in to chat.

Revising our life scripts often creates uncomfortable conversations, yet breaking ideas and versions of what people think and want of us, or what we perceive they want of us versus what we wish for, can be soul-quenching. All of us want to live happy lives—no matter how that journey is defined. And each of our travels through life is as personal and unique as a singular snowflake—for no two snowflakes are exactly alike.

All the narratives I share in this book showcase women— their resiliency, struggles, and empowerments—and I feel it's about time we acknowledge trans women[1] in this tribe. This may be a touchy subject that many feel uncomfortable having (or, perhaps, disagree with); however, I believe it is crucial to have the conversation.

With all of that, I introduce Monay.

Monay is a 54-year-old statuesque blonde at six feet in height. She is a dedicated and loving parent and a hard worker. She has, as I mentioned, a truly captivating smile, a heck of a golf game, a devotion to the Denver Broncos, and an easy demeanor. She is also *a transgender woman. I am purposeful in using the term "also" in this last statement because—like each of us here on Earth—we are all so much more complex than one term or adjective can convey. We are all composed of "alsos."*

Monay has been existing and exploring a change cycle for decades. Just sit with that for one moment. The resilience and strength required for one to seek out and follow a path they know in their heart and soul to be their only true course in life, and one in which others may have difficulty accepting, is astounding— more so when you consider the time Monay has been on her journey. From the start of our conversation, she was extremely straightforward, explaining how she had always realized who she was: a woman. It took her over thirty years to confront the truth about herself and begin the process of transitioning.

She talked in detail about dealing with the confusion and embarrassment she felt for forty-plus years, expressing how she always felt caught in the middle of two personas—hiding who she felt she was with the façade of how she entered the world. Through various points in her life, the puzzle pieces shifted and aligned, becoming easier to decipher and understand, ultimately allowing her greater clarity and strength to begin her journey in earnest.

"Live and let live" is such a powerful and selfless statement. I only wish it was universally truthful in the actual

MONAY

comportment of humankind. I think, especially in the case of understanding the trans community, it is difficult for many to comprehend "not" being in concert with the body you were born with. The ease imparted to the cisgender[2] population to enter life and be totally in tune with their given gender assignment is not lost on me. Yet, it is not universally recognized. The cisgender population's gender assignment at birth is just a given; a "pass go card" undealt to the trans community.

    This is the story of a brave, transgender woman who always knew who she was, even when it was uncomfortable, scary, or too soon to share her truth. She lived her truth in silence for so many years. This is her unique story, as no two stories—regardless of your lot in life—are the same. And that is true as well for the trans community. Monay's is a story of "one foot in front of the other"—a constant march toward the light she knew was hers to reach, in her time, in her way. The more we can understand, empathize, accept, and embrace one another, the better we will all be in "living our best lives—in living our truths." What Monay shares may resonate with others. That is my hope.

My whole life, I have been embarrassed to say what I always knew: I am a woman trapped in a man's body.

    For so many years, I lived in continual fear of people discovering me; unveiling my truth. While at times I felt I could handle it—would welcome unburdening myself by finally speaking my truth—I feared the humiliation of my family, especially that of my father and daughter. That fear was bigger than me. Growing up I just never felt like I could be truthful with my dad, I was so concerned with embarrassing him. Teasing was such a huge and painful part of my childhood that I just couldn't stomach my dad being teased by family or friends; or in being disappointed in me. I do believe that the thought of letting down someone we love and look up to, typically our parents, has a lot to do with transgender people hiding who they are. Timing is so critical in all aspects of life, and the timing of finally making that decision to be truthful with my family was no different.

I was born William Morrison, with everyone calling me "Mo," but my dream was to be Monay someday. I remember the first time I shared my desire to be a girl. I was in first grade and I was visiting my Grandma's house on Skidway Lake with my cousin, Danny. We were nestled in our bunks, chatting away about a variety of things, when Danny shared that he wanted to be a hockey player. I recall my words freely floating from the bottom bunk to the top bunk where he was laying, "I want to be a girl when I grow up, with big boobs." Danny laughed and said, "no way, you can't!" As is the memory of most six-year-olds, nothing more was made of the exchange except that it was the first time I felt my bubble had been burst; that my desire in life wasn't going to be as easy as simply saying what I desired—and thus making it so. I recall this moment so acutely, as it marked the beginning of my being in constant conflict. As I progressed through school—second grade, sixth grade, and onward—I feel I lived a continuous "bubble bursting" experience as I never felt I could freely express who I knew I was, and who I knew I was not.

My mom and dad were married for six short years. After they divorced (I was six and my sister, Stacey, was one), my mom moved to Colorado. I loved to visit her. She was full of adventure and was even a fire department volunteer. My favorite moment with her was when she allowed me to drive her yellow Ford Mustang. It was a stick shift. I recall so many fun moments with my mom, including the times we'd belt out "We Will Rock You," by Queen, at the top of our lungs. She was vibrant and fun, but I think she also struggled with depression. She left this earth too soon, with lupus and kidney failure eventually taking her life when she was just in her mid-50s.

Other than the occasional visits with my mom, I lived with my dad. Growing up, my dad had "Bill Cosby" vibes—in a good way, as he was always calm and fun and everyone who met him instantly liked him. He remarried a couple of times, which wasn't always easy. His second wife, Connie, truly hated both me and my sister and was unfairly strict with us. She and my dad had two other children together. I remember Connie catching me in her closet on several occasions, trying on her clothes. I'm sure this didn't contribute to her liking me any better. She told me what I was doing was wrong and continually called me a sinner. She explained how God made me a man, not a woman; that I was going against God; that I was sinning. She said that I would go to hell for this behavior. This experience is what drove me away from the Catholic church. I am still spiritual, but not Catholic.

My dad and Connie eventually divorced. He now lives on Pine Island with his third wife, Jackie. They have been married for twenty years and seem happy together. They golf daily, and seldom leave the island.

I've always felt my dad was my biggest inspiration. While he was known for his good nature and calm demeanor, that briefly went by the wayside when, at eighteen, I got my then-girlfriend, Dawn, pregnant. My dad was irate. He kicked me out of the house. I remember the day his anger with me finally came to a head. He lit a cigar, which was always a sign he was furious. He forced me into the car and drove to the county building. He grabbed my ear and did not relinquish his vice grip. We entered the building and went down several hallways to the last room on the ground floor, where he said to the army recruiter on duty (while still gripping my ear), "take this little son of a bitch, right now." He later added, "the army will make a man out of you." I think that as long as I am alive, I will not be able to rid that voice inside my head—the harshness of my father's tone. I certainly feel like I tried to be a man and father for many years, but it just never stuck.

I served four years at Fort Polk in Louisiana. Dawn's parents took me in for that short time, but insisted we marry, which we did in 1987. My daughter, Marisa, was born in January 1988, shortly before I left for the army. Her mother and I divorced in 1992; Marisa was four. I had completed my service, I was newly divorced, and I was a father. None of that changed my feeling of being in constant conflict. I continued to feel caught in the middle. There was no place for me. At times, I feared the life I yearned for inside me would bust out as I hid my desire to be a transgender female from my daughter for years.

At fifteen, Marisa moved one state away to live with her mother's sister. Her friends at the time were bad influences, and my dear daughter needed a strict influence in her life. My desire to be a woman and the love I have for my daughter caused me constant turmoil during that time; I just never wanted to do anything that might harm our relationship. This concern, along with being raised to be seen and not heard, made my desire to transition more difficult. My family life never involved communicating or sharing feelings. Being on that bottom bunk back in 1973, sharing my desire to be a girl, was the first time I expressed my feelings out loud. I had to put the idea out of my mind for precisely forty-two years. While the voice within me said otherwise, I kept suppressing her, purging her from my mind—until I couldn't anymore.

Finally, I told Marisa in 2006, when she was eighteen. I felt that if the timing was ever going to be right, this was it. She was a young woman now. She needed to be the first person I told because she is the most significant person in my life. This was literally a life-changing moment for me. I had always been Mr. Mom raising her, as Dawn's impact was limited. Yet, in a way, I was taking away her dad. I assured her that I would still always be "Dad." I will never forget her comment about her biological mom not ever being there and how refreshing it was going to be to have a "mom." Given that I had only visited my own mother sporadically before she passed, I wasn't entirely sure of how to be motherly, but I was determined to do my best.

Sharing my truth with my daughter was the catalyst that allowed me to finally move forward, though it wasn't easy. I had been working at a lawn and garden equipment store for almost nineteen years. I could talk shop with the guys, listen to them, and was trained to sell and source any or all battery-powered apparatuses to lawn mowers or generators. As I began to transition from a guy to a girl, during the last couple of years of my employment, I suddenly felt caught in the middle again. I decided to be both Mo and Monay, simultaneously.

My first wig was my favorite. The natural long and curly blonde extensions cost me $500, but it was worth every penny. From 2008-2015, I was living a double life as Mo and Monay. I started attending a local dance bar, a lowkey LGBTQ[3] place to dance and be oneself. The bar's motto is "Not Just a Gay Bar! Gay, Straight or Bi – Everybody's Welcome!" It was here that I met Shawn, who was from Texas. Shawn is now Misty. Having someone to share my feelings with helped me plod my path forward and encouraged me to go out and be open with who I was, allowing my softer voice to settle in serenity.

In 2015, with my father living in Florida and my daughter living three hours away, I began being open and stopped living behind closed doors. All I have ever wanted was to be accepted and called a female. The journey has not been stress-free—there have been a range of emotions and experiences—but feeling like I no longer had to hide and could live my life in the wide open felt freeing. Though my dad accepted me, I do think it is still a process for him. He often refers to me as "him" or "he," which is a bit awkward at times. I do think that his ability to accept me was partly the inevitability of it, as he was well aware of my forays into my stepmother's closet; a closet he eventually locked me out of! Perhaps it just finally made sense to him.

As I began my journey, I decided to find a job as a woman. Being a part-time server at the Olive Garden was an experiment for me. I was shocked they hired me. I worked there solely as a female, which was a changing point for me. I recall one interaction with a customer—a reminder of my own youthful innocence—which made me appreciate how brutally honest kids can be (as I was back in 1973!). It was a little awkward in the moment but also a great gift in that it made me realize that I needed to work on my voice. A little girl, maybe nine years old, said, "What's going on with you? You look like a girl but sound like a man." I remember saying, "You're right. I am both." I left the exchange at that, though I think her parents were embarrassed that she was roasting me. I really appreciated the moment, however, as it proved two key things: 1) I was able to get a job, and 2) I needed to take voice lessons, which I began in 2014, right after I acquired new teeth— too many years of Kodiak tobacco in the army.

Some people transition socially, legally, and medically, which is what I have chosen to do. Some may transition only socially, and some may not do any of these. I guess it may be prudent to explain transitioning. The idea is simple, but the act of it is not.

Changing the way I look and how people see me, so I can become the gender I have always felt on the inside, was important to me. As stated, the process is different for everyone. For some, it involves medical treatment and hormones. Others may only change their name and preferred pronouns (she/her, he/him, they/them) to match the gender identity they wish to be. And, for still others, it can involve changing one's appearance and dress, or coming out to family and friends. Not all transgender people transition. For those who do, not all transition in the same way. For me, it has been a very long and ongoing process.

I never got to be what I wanted, which was a girl. I needed to find my identity, and therapy was my first stop. There was a local psychologist at the VA, named Jeff, that I began seeing. As I recall, I had to write down my feelings and answer questions about how I felt being a woman trapped in a man's body. This is when I learned I was not alone. There is a technical term called gender dysphoria[4]. I was diagnosed with this.

Many people before me led these doctors to agree that embracing one's inner self—listening to that voice inside you— is the first step. Then, a protocol of hormone therapy allows the body to undergo the necessary changes to conform one's physical appearance with one's gender identification. This experience reminded me of something I had forgotten from a psychology class I took in college. In discussing sex and gender, we learned that they are uniquely different. "Sex" refers to genitalia, and "gender" refers to one's individual personality, portrayed as either male or female, especially when considered with reference to social and cultural differences, rather than biological ones.

 This insight was significant to my better understanding who and what I am. I recently came across an article wherein the manager of a youth and education non-profit stated that "transgender people live in a sort of awkward misalignment reality," that "their physical exterior is at odds with how they internally see themselves."[5] This was so enlightening and profoundly well-stated. Just because I have male sex genitalia doesn't mean my soul is male.

 My hormone therapy included Estradiol, a form of estrogen, and Spironolactone, which blocks testosterone. My goal was to create feminine characteristics such as a softer voice, less body hair, muscle tone, and redistribution of body fat to develop breasts. I am unsure if I will get implants to augment what I currently have. I do know I will never have a period or get pregnant. I am now in the queue for sexual reassignment surgery. I am still debating penile inversion vaginoplasty, which is the creation of a vagina by inverting penile skin.

 I do find it funny now when I recall how my dad made me enlist in the army, against my own wishes, and that it is the military that has helped me become a woman. The veteran's health benefits that I reap as a servicemember are endless. I was fortunate to obtain dental work, psychological training, hormones, speech classes, and surgical procedures to alleviate gender dysphoria.

Assimilation is often noted as one of the hardest hurdles for the transgender community to crest; the idea of being accepted or absorbed into the population as YOU.

Matt, my coworker and friend, has shared a few experiences with me that his wife has had in overhearing rude transgender comments coming from one of our coworkers. He said it was driving his wife, Anna, crazy. While I certainly don't appreciate the disrespect and lack of compassion, I told him, "I don't give a damn." I feel fortunate to have open-minded people like Matt (and Anna) in my life. And most importantly, feel incredibly grateful for my dad and Marisa, my daughter. I remember once telling Marisa that I thought I could conquer the world— screw anyone else. Though it's a constant process of evolvement, the truth is that nobody else's opinion—apart from that of my daughter— means shit anymore. I know that if my daughter were against my transition, I would not have pursued this path to Monay. I will forever be eternally grateful that she was not. Having Marisa at an early age was a massive benefit to us both. We often joke that since we are only nineteen years apart in age, we will enjoy each other way longer!

Today, Marisa is married. She met her husband, James, in high school and they have a son named Cameron, who we call the Cam Man. I have already bought him a golf set, and I am hopeful we can connect on the course like my dad and I have. It is hard being so far away from them. My grandson calls me "Nay Nay," which melts my heart. Early on, I did worry about Marisa feeling betrayed, though she has never once complained about losing a "dad." We all know I'm still here, just better. The funny thing is, now I only receive Mother's Day gifts. My daughter knows me, and my gifts are always golf-related and usually involve some marijuana too. What can I say? As long as Marisa is good, I can live with everyone else who may not be on my side. She even bought me a mother-daughter necklace two years ago. I treasure it. I am fortunate to have friends that continue to grow and evolve with me, who speak up in batting down transphobic comments, and are committed and compassionate in knowing me as Monay.

Though my dad is in Florida, we do visit one another, and play golf together every year in a summer tournament. At the time of this writing, we are set to play a tournament with my childhood friend, Waldo, and his daughter, Ava. Waldo came from a conservative, but loving family. He couldn't comprehend how I learned separation from people, or myself. In explaining myself, I reminded him of my broken family and the many homes I have had. Reinvention, re-entry, restarts—however you want to term that continual process of healing, of finding your footing, of learning a new environment. Those experiences of my youth are all intertwined with who I am and how I navigate the world. There is no right or wrong way. Learning to lean into my life is what has giving me the greatest joy and what I believe I have done best.

I currently live with a roommate, Michelle, who transitioned eight years ago. She enlightened me to the fact that as I started to shift my identify—taking hormones—that I would discover my attraction to men. Though I doubted her, she was completely right. I had to eat a little crow when, in 2019, I had my first relationship, albeit brief, with a man. I can't explain how, when, or why I changed, but Michelle was right. I only see myself dating and marrying a man. I was blown away. I can tell you that being with a man made me feel like a woman more than ever before.

Like the rest of humankind, I am many things. I am the proudest mom (in 2020, Marisa asked to call me "Mom,"—oh, be still my heart!) and grandmother; I am a caring and supportive friend; I am so appreciative for my father, who has done so much for our family, and I'm continually patient with his own process of seeing and accepting me as Monay; I am a huge Denver Bronco fan (John Elway is just yummy); I am an animal lover (I have named birds and cats Elway, and today have a black lab-cattle dog mix named Ellie Mae…it felt fitting); I am an avid golfer (as said here many times); I am respectful and compassionate with others; I am a hard worker; *and*, I'm a transgender woman.

Who and where I am now is what I deserve—this person, myself and all her glitz, glory, and golfing ways. The woman inside me has finally taken over. There are plenty of good years ahead. I look forward to sharing my life with my daughter and grandchildren—the life I always knew I should have.

---

[1] A trans woman is a woman who was assigned male at birth and has a female gender identity.
[2] Cisgender denotes or relates to a person whose sense of personal identity and gender corresponds with their birth sex.
[3] LGBTQ stands for lesbian (L), gay (G), bi-sexual (B), transgender (T), and queer (Q). While there is no official entity responsible for determining which letters go into the LGBTQ initialism, as the communities continue to evolve, so does this acronym. The LGBTQIA+ initialism adds intersex (I), asexual (A), and more (+). These acronyms serve to describe the community of people who do not identify as heterosexual, straight, or cisgender.
[4] Gender dysphoria is a term that describes a sense of unease that a person may have because of a mismatch between their biological sex and their gender identity.
[5] https://www.bridgemi.com/michigan-health-watch/quiet-decision-michigan-continues-medicaid-coverage-gender-changes.

CHAPTER THIRTEEN

Ania

*T*hroughout my life I have been drawn to people leading lives of meaning. It fascinates me to try and understand what they've done to put their lives on the right track—to discover how they found the definition of "meaning" that aligns with their being. How did they find their purpose? Finding joy, like defining happiness, can often feel elusive.

On one of my treks to Phoenix, Arizona, to visit my two sons, who are in their mid-twenties, our conversation turned to the topic of what a happy, authentic, meaningful life looks like. We all agreed our ultimate goal is to live a more meaningful life, filled with awe-inspiring moments that embody fun, laughter, and love—and a sprinkle of self-understanding—is it that simple? How do we get from defining our vision, to living our vision?

ANIA

Ania may have the answer.

Our friendship began several years ago in a place of idle equanimity. We sat and socialized on a wooden park bench near an open grassy space with the sounds of sea birds echoing around us. At first glance, Ania is striking, carrying herself with an assuredness that aligns with her statuesque posture (which forced me to sit straighter). Her confident, down-to-earth, determined nature was quickly evident—very in line with her Taurean character. Not one for small talk, our conversation quickly moved to deeper topics of finding our true purpose while balancing the responsibilities of work, marriage, motherhood, friendships, and family; of letting go of fear; of connecting with our innermost selves; and of unleashing the constraints that restrict us from achieving our true potential in life. Interruption (a sea change in circumstance or self) and/or introspection (a desire to know more about why we think or feel the way we do) are often the catalysts that drive this search. Both were true for Ania.

It was in 2014 that Ania found herself at this crossroads where interruption and introspection collide. Her marriage had come to an end, she was the mother of two young daughters, and she was dissatisfied with her career working in the accounting field (equipped with a degree in Finance). Ania was more than ready to redefine what her new life was going to look and feel like. With drive, dedication, and a lot of self-reflection, she remade her life in the image of how she wanted her story to unfold; a life more fully aligned with her authentic self.

Born in Poland, Ania came to the United States in 2001. While her Eastern European ideology certainly influenced her approach to challenge—specifically her early visionary *mindset and work ethic—she is her own mental guide. She understands that the body is a doorway to greater things. And this understanding is foundational to how she realigned her life. Though she always felt a deep mind-body connection, it wasn't until 2014 that she was forced to truly look within and discover who she was and what she wanted—diving deep for the first time into how mental modes can galvanize us into greater connection or disconnection with ourselves and others.*

In one of our think tank sessions, we both realized our fascination with the brain and neuroplasticity. Sharing how each of us views the mind and its powers became a cross-pollination of epigenetic talk—an invigorating discussion about gene expression and the environmental factors that influence them. Ania mentioned Bruce Lipton's book, <u>The Biology of Belief</u>, as having aided her in her journey. I had read his recognized research when studying epigenetics in my doctorate program and turned to his book, <u>The Wisdom of Your Cells</u>, as my biological bible, of sorts, when trying to better understand the workings of our behavior at a cellular level. Ania and I truly channeled our inner nerdiness in these discussions, but came away with the same sentiment: our cells, those little engines of life within our body, are affected by our thoughts which can build up or tear down our physical and mental health.

At a time of great uncertainty, it was Ania's ability to understand the importance of a strong physical and mental foundation that enabled her to reimagine her life. She committed herself to healing layers of doubt and insecurities while recognizing the difference between co-dependence and interdependence. She took heed of the positive impact that yoga had on her attitude during the last years of her marriage, weaving this discipline into her healing process and mindset of growth moving forward, ultimately coming to the practice of Pilates. Pilates became a life force for Ania, a physical modality that promotes greater emotional well-being. She forged forward—ultimately becoming an owner-operator of four Pilates studios—championing women, business ownership, and chakras.

The impetus for reframing her relationships and reality was a desire for self-healing; and just as important, a desire to avoid passing any generational gook onto her girls. Another Taurus trait is the refusal to give up, which has been another vital attribute in accomplishing what Ania sets her mind to. As a single mother of two young girls, she was acutely aware of how her actions would impact her daughters. She was determined to be strong in her approach to redefining her life, and in turn, theirs.

Ania and I discussed marriage and motherhood, topics intrinsic in both our lives and elemental to the decisions we make personally and professionally. We acknowledged that forming loving and lasting relationships can be challenging, agreeing that effective, clear communication and openness is critical to establishing long-term connection. Motherhood is complex, but also incredibly important in each of our lives—notwithstanding the constant battle of balance and sense of guilt that comes with prioritizing time for our children and ourselves. As most women would likely agree, this is a difficult tightrope; one that Ania has managed to stay atop, believing that finding one's own joy and purpose is a healthy and profound example to portray to your children.

Ania and I concluded our conversation and final interview over FaceTime. She shared that a change cycle continues to flow—family is family, business is business, but *sometimes something shifts, and you reflect on how flexible you can be and how far you have come. The series of events in Ania's life—that collision of interruption and introspection—led her to look inward with compassion, and outward into the world with grace. She stepped fully into her destiny—envisioning, imaging, and crafting a path forward with intention. I feel fortunate to have Ania share her story in S.H.E. As she says, "I need to keep pushing past my fears; that's where the growth lies." Perhaps this is the answer to finding our own true meaning and purpose in life: push past fear, one step at a time. It's not easy, but certainly possible, as Ania's story illustrates.*

When I decided to take the first step over the bridge toward what my heart was longing for, I was surprised to find a community of people waiting to welcome me. Once I started formulating my thoughts and feelings, it became clear this was a sign for me to surrender what weighs my heart down. It's not for me to carry. It's not for me to overthink and worry. When the idea of me sharing my story was presented, I was not convinced. I had to release myself from that quiet little corner and open my heart to complete my growth—to again, push past fear.

  What is valuable to me is to feel lighter and to move at ease in my life and work, while growing and healing alongside others in my orbit. I have experienced firsthand that everything has a way of working out. It may be painful at times, but working through that pain will always deliver you to the other side, and allow you to reimagine a new way. It is through this process that an amazing exchange of energy occurs.

ANIA

I am fortunate to be the founder of Pilates of San Diego, and a lead instructor of a community of health-oriented individuals attracted to mind, body, and spirit synchronicity. Pilates is a form of exercise that has gained popularity over the years for its numerous health benefits. Developed in the early 20th century by Joseph Pilates, it focuses on core muscles and improving posture, balance, and flexibility. For the past seven years, I have been unlocking the power of Pilates in my life and that of others for both physical and mental healing.

Pilates, for me, has had a positive impact on both my physical and mental well-being. Because there is always a choice, I chose self-love. What that means has changed over the years. I believe reforming your body translates into improving other aspects of your life. So many of the fears we have are self-inflicted. Pushing past fear is a constant force in life; a process that I have learned to accept and value as it is what allowed me to persevere in healing myself and in building my business. Each of the Pilates studios I opened serve as a testament to overcoming my fears; symbols of greater self-understanding and maturity.

When I began understanding why the quality of my life was not precisely where I wanted it to be, it became crucial for me to break generational cycles for myself and my children—to step away from dependencies that rob the soul. I have been the best project I will ever work on. Realizing this was pivotal to my getting to where I needed to be—to my most authentic self.

In the '80s, the world seemed much more straightforward. I grew up in a small Polish town named Radom which is in central Poland, 100 km from the capital of Warsaw. My parents were traditional. I didn't consider whether we were rich or poor back then. All my friends lived parallel lives, so I assumed that's how life went. I never really felt like I fit in. Schooling and socializing were not the issues; it was more profound than that. I felt a sense of detachment that I could not really articulate at the time. I saw the matriarchal strength in my mother and grandmother—they were the lifeblood in our Polish household. I recall watching them prep meals and remember the pleasant smells that resonated from the handmade mushroom and sauerkraut pierogies they crafted. I did not have a close relationship with my dad. He and my mother divorced when I was six years old. I longed for a father figure.

Together with other Eastern Bloc countries, Poland was considered a satellite state in the Soviet sphere of interest until about 1990, tainted with all the things Soviet influence might entail. There was communism, quite a bit of Russian control and meddling, and probably some other crap I missed since I was too young. People were super-structured. Eastern Europeans are somewhat known for their stoic nature, with little display of emotion. We tend to hold feelings inside and never talk about them (a recipe for promoting negative energy in the body!). Life was tough. Given the political regime and the communistic environment—an atmosphere that does not champion freedom of mind or creativity—I knew early on that I wanted more than what my life in Poland (or the Eastern European mentality) could offer me. I knew I wanted to exist beyond the day-to-day routines of mundane life.

Obtaining good grades was easy for me in both grammar and high school. As a senior, I taught basic English after school to kindergarteners—the alphabet and numbers. During my second year at University, I enrolled in the student exchange program to visit and work in English-speaking countries. The first summer, I was sent to a city on the border of Mississippi and Tennessee to work in a casino as a cocktail waitress. It was a cultural shock. I enjoyed my time there, and especially, the money I made. Once back in Poland, I bought my first car—a small, black Fiat. But, as luck would have it, my newly-purchased vehicle had a very short life. Fortunately, I did not receive the same fate. The last day I drove my little Fiat, it was raining. I was motoring along, listening to the Irish musician Enya's song "Only Time," the irony of which is not lost on me. I knew every line to those lyrics—*Who can say where the road goes? Where the day flows? Only time. And who can say if your love grows as your heart chose? Only time.* Maybe I should not have been putting on my makeup, but the street was empty, and I was heading to take an exam. The next thing I knew I was being pulled from my car by emergency personnel. It was a miracle I survived. The roof of the car broke in half, but I somehow walked away unscathed, not a scratch.

The accident I experienced in my teens made me recall something that occurred when I was twelve years old; an experience that, to this day, provides me with solace—in moments of uncertainly or fear—that I am safe. Pope John Paul II, the head of the Catholic Church at that time, was visiting my hometown. Though the streets were lined and packed with people, I managed to sneak to the front row of those assembling for a view of the Pope. As he passed by, we made eye contact. I could feel his eyes penetrate me, a surreal sense of magic. Call it a blessing or a chance of fate, but I interpreted that encounter to set the stage for protection and grace throughout my life.

As an adult, I do believe reality begins in the dream space. There is a power and potential that exists within, intertwined with inner vision. The key to unlocking this energy is to act.

Between the ages of eight and ten, I was unsure how to analyze my dreams—reoccurring dreams that were both peculiar and powerful. In one that gobsmacked me, a random man drove up in a convertible and asked if I wanted a ride. (This, in and of itself, is peculiar as hardly anyone sees a convertible around where I grew up. It's unheard of.) The faceless man said, "Do you want a ride to America?" Hearing this, I ran away as fast as I could as I had been taught that strangers were terrible. In reflecting on this, I could understand the correlation of a stranger and fear, but wondered about the significance of the vehicle and the specific query. It seemed odd, but also in line with the peculiarity of my dreams.

My second exchange program experience took me back to the United States to work at Sea World in San Diego, California, and brought that childhood dream full circle. Though I was again working as a restaurant waitress, this second program was incrementally better than my first experience. My boyfriend, at the time, was with me, but things were not going well in the relationship. During this summer spent in sunny Southern California, my life went in a different direction and I met my future husband. Despite the thirty-year age gap, there was a strong attraction—a magnetism that could not be denied. He was not only charismatic, but a successful businessman who did not take no for an answer. Given my own dogged determination, I could relate to his refusal to give up. When he first invited me to dinner, I told him "No, I have a boyfriend." This did not seem to matter, as he was relentless in the ask. Now, here is the crazy part. A couple hours later, as I was walking down the street that same day, I saw him. As I turned around the corner—there he was. He pulled over in his convertible and asked, "You need a ride?" That reoccurring dream I had as a young girl became my reality. The whole universe was pushing me toward this man, only now he had a face. We dated for five years and then married.

For years, we had a functional marriage that produced two beautiful daughters—the joys in my life. To think we created these two tiny beings from within and watched them develop into little humans with personalities and traits like no one else, leaves me awestricken. My oldest was born in 2007, and my youngest was born in 2008. I always wanted kids, but nothing can prepare you for motherhood and marriage. Motherhood brings out the best and worst in me. It's messy and crazy and can be completely depleting and exhausting. Yet, it's also an incredible journey filled with joy and pride. It is the greatest love I have ever felt and the best part of my identity. I see in my daughters so much of myself. They are my grand mirror to truly see myself in action, learning what I am made of.

When the girls were seven and eight, my husband and I divorced. The reason I stayed as long as I did was out of fear. I could not see a way out, and the voices in my head didn't know which way to turn. Trust me when I say fear is not something that should hold a marriage together. It was tough. I was devastated and at a very low point in my life. I went back to work and moved out of the house. I mentally went back to my childhood and remembered how my mom survived; she and my grandmother were such headstrong women. I knew I had those characteristics within me. Their genes were prominent. I just had to wake them up from their dormant slumber. Two years before the divorce, I started yoga. This was when I started realizing the environment I grew up in—the Eastern European mentality of *who cares how you feel, just get it done*—was part of me, but not my entire embodiment.

During my yoga experiences, I began seeing and sensing the whole mind and body connection. I began to feel. Things started bubbling up, becoming turning points in my life to analyze. I started to analyze things such as healing and trauma, not just my physical body but that deeper desire of what I was missing and longing for. The years of heaviness—the weighty burden that generations of oppression created—began to surface in ways I had never previously thought about or experienced. During yoga, I realized I had not felt good in my marriage. My root chakra was fucked up, deep in survival mode, and I needed to shift fast. I opted to take the teacher's training program to further my education and abilities in yoga and quickly realized that the Polish mentality of "practicality" did not align with this passion. The guise of my upbringing had always been to do what is sensible to support yourself, not what you like. I was learning that this no longer served me. I started to become an internal seeker as opposed to the external seeker I had become.

Attending workshops and healing through yoga was intensely gratifying and felt effortless. Ana Forest and Shiva Ray were prominent mentors in my life. Connecting my generational dots was empowering. I started teaching yoga privately. I began noticing how I was helping my clients deal with significant issues, which I discovered helped me. They changed, and I changed. I began to realize this was my gift—channeling what wisdom I had and using the energy of the body to promote greater healing, strength, and confidence. It was natural for me to adjust their poses and help them through their pain, building together. Through mindful movement, I have come to recognize trauma lives in the body, and we need to break it open. It is literally "trapped energy" that needs to be converted into something else. This realization was such a powerful epiphany; it reenforced the fact that I needed to heal myself before I could heal others.

Then, as karma/kismet would have it, I met someone caring and compassionate shortly after my divorce; someone who became a huge help during this transitional time for me. I believe God sent him as my angel. Meeting the right people at the right time is being in the right channel of inner knowing, just like my Pope John Paul II encounter. I finally felt content, knowing my passion and purpose were filling me. My boyfriend became instrumental in supporting me with opening my first Pilates studio in downtown San Diego. Our serendipitous meeting was through a client referral. I was helping him resolve sciatica pain. Long story short, he said, "you have supernatural powers and should open your own business." We dated for seven years.

At that time, Pilates was all about structure, which was relatable to me from growing up at the cultural crossroads of Eastern and Western Europe. Pilates is a form of exercise that concentrates on strengthening the body with an emphasis on core strength. Similar to yoga, Pilates focuses on posture, balance, and flexibility. The practice is comprised of a series of repetitive exercises performed on a reformer machine, which is a piece of equipment that looks like a bed with springs, a sliding carriage, ropes, and pulleys. Some newer clients are intimidated by the system, but once they begin, under the guidance of a trained instructor, they become hooked—just like me! The founder of Pilates believed that change happens through movement, and movement heals. I agree. I am grateful to my boyfriend for being a tremendous driving force for me to become independent and share my gift with others. He always said I had an amazing touch and strongly believed in my talent. I recognized that Pilates could become a considerable business perspective for me. I wanted what I did next to be both sustainable and lucrative for my mind, body, and balance sheet.

When I saw the airy open space in San Diego's Marina District, I knew precisely where the eight reformers would be positioned. I opened my first location in 2015, in a residential building underneath commercial space in a high-rise building. The business went very well, and the response was positive. In 2016, the second studio opened in East Village, next to Petco Park. Again, eight reformers. In 2017, I noticed a need for Pilates in North County. We opened up in the charming seaside village of Del Mar with four reformers. This space is much smaller and more intimate, but matches the area's particular demographic. We do many private sessions there. Fairbanks Ranch was opened in 2018 with six reformers, and I cannot say if there will be another studio at this moment. Each studio is bright and airy to help improve mood and aid in concentration; natural light from oversized windows helps to create spaces that are both emotionally and mentally calming.

While finding my purpose through Pilates redirected my life in an incredible way, my greatest joy has been having my two daughters. They are my most marvelous masterpieces. I thought I worried a lot when they were little. Now that they are teenagers, I would give anything to simply worry about sippy cups and nap times again! Seriously, I had no idea how hard it is to manage everything; it's not easy and highly chaotic. My best driving force is figuring it out as I go—hard work pays off. Incorporating mindful movement through yoga and Pilates has given me the power to adapt to the needs of reality. Flexibility and adaptability can be our superpowers, allowing us to go with the flow of life. Life is a balance of holding on and letting go. I am still mastering it.

There is no perfect equilibrium. I am a single mom raising two teenagers and running a business with a strong work ethic engrained within me. I am a multi-tasker and know how to set boundaries. There is no doubt that guilt can bubble to the surface when wanting to be with them, and at the same time, be at work. I juggle the girls between their dad's house, school, and schedules. Work is not a chore, it's pure pleasure. This is my passion and calling. I trust the girls notice I am practicing what I am passionate about. They have grown up fast and had to be mature, making their lunches and figuring things out on their own, similar to what I am doing.

I am often asked if I miss Poland. Maybe the culture and the people. I don't think that sense of your homeland ever leaves you. It was definitely a challenge to relate to a lot people I met in the U.S. at the beginning—they seemed to lack willpower. There is a different mentality growing up in a war-stricken setting. While I am happy where I landed, I do still love Europe. There is something magical about the history, architecture, and soul of its many old countries. It feels grounded in its identity—an appealing quality!

We are all on a journey to our more profound truth, learning to grow into self-love and reclaim our true identity. Many clients come in and see me feeling disempowered by their physical ailments. As we work together, they feel supported to overcome these physical obstacles and genuinely step into their power. I think trusting my intuition has helped me interpret energy—theirs and my own. My practice of Pilates offers my clients a path to healing and total embodiment of mind, body, and soul. Through a curated movement experience, specific to their individual needs, we work to quiet the mind and focus energy to strengthen the mind-body connection. Everyone operates from their own level of consciousness. By quieting the mind, we are able to see each other as energy. Some negative energy may be trapped in trauma. Watching a client accept and witness the trapped trauma is nothing short of remarkable, as it begins to vanish just by noticing it and naming it.

For a long time, I felt like the air around me was thick, dense, and intense with emotion. It felt suffocating, but I worked my way through that to find my flow in life. I have learned not to carry any attachments, frustrations, or pain in my body—acutely aware that the energy that becomes stuck can often be the beginning of a disease. I want to help others to move through deep trauma, as I did; to relinquish the negative energies that fuel pain and suffering; to enhance their physical and mental well-being. Yoga and Pilates have been my soothing salve, an art of mindful movement teaching me to exercise my mind and body smarter and more skillfully.

A quote that I have always been drawn to is by L. Thomas:

"Every day, the world will drag you by your hand, yelling, this is important! That is important! You need to worry about this! And this! And this! And each day, it is up to you to yank your hand back, put it on your heart, and say, "No, this is important."

Each year tests my resilience to heed these words. Finding one's way is rarely a smooth path, yet I know from experience that it is a journey worth embarking on. I am grateful for the generational baggage I have carried. Sometimes it takes sorting through all you have dragged with you through your life to finally purge what no longer suits you, recognizing that the burden must be released in order to reclaim yourself. It is, at times, scary to deal with trauma and pain but I am an example of someone who emerged completely transformed from looking fear in the face. My relationship with fear still exists, but I am certainly healthier for having done so, and hopefully wiser. I appreciate everything and regret nothing.

As I look to the future, I smile. Raising my two teenage daughters and launching a luxury line of essential oil blends called De L'essence brings me joy. I am also creating a non-profit that will benefit girls rescued from sex trafficking—to help them regain their lives. The journey for me was one step at a time; that is how it all began.

CHAPTER FOURTEEN

Jamie

*T*he brick building at 1325 Cherry Street stood firm in the May morning sunshine. I arrived promptly at 10 a.m., walked up the two front steps and through the sage green entry door. Immediately upon arriving I could feel the sense of refuge this space offered. The Mustard Seed Shelter has been a home to struggling women since 1995. Their mission is to provide a safe space where these women can find their way back to life—physically, spiritually, and emotionally. By "watering the seed of inner strength" we all possess, they have helped over 1,400 women make a better life for themselves and their children.

On the morning I visited, the building was a beehive of activity! Leona, one of the Mustard Seed's three foundresses, was standing at a sink demonstrating how to stuff an oversized turkey with lemons, onions, and a bouquet of herbs. The back door flung open, and a crying little girl flew through with her mother trailing closely behind. Another volunteer walked in with a grinning young gal who had been practicing parking in the back lot in preparation for her driver's license exam. There was a lot of seed watering going on!

Amy Bartels Roe, the Executive Director of this amazing women's shelter in Saginaw, Michigan, was just finishing up one of her many meetings when I arrived. She has been providing this ministry with life-changing leadership, community outreach, and fundraising for eight years, which is nothing short of remarkable. The guests of the shelter call her Miss Amy. She was kind enough to offer me a quick tour of the premises before introducing me to Jamie, the woman I was there to interview that morning.

Jamie became part of the Mustard Seed family in December 2021. On the day we met, she was still recovering from a near-death experience with COVID-19, and her asthma symptoms had flared due to a lingering cough. Miss Amy led the two of us to the computer room in search of a little privacy and quiet. Two women were just finishing up some work online, to acquire their birth certificates and IDs, but wrapped up their project quickly, leaving us a quiet workstation to begin our chat. Jamie and I settled ourselves on a comfy green velour couch in the room, which we coined the "parlor," pretending to hold dainty cups of chamomile tea in our hands. We laughed at our lady-like impressions, breaking the ice a bit. There's always that moment of unease before you engage in a what you know will be a raw and heartfelt conversation. It's not usually long-lived, thankfully. I've learned through experience that it's best to just get into it.

My first question to Jamie was, "How do you want to tell your story?" She began by firmly stating her strong belief in God and that He made possible the divine appointment for us to be together that day. For Jamie, faith is inseparable from trust. As she shared her story, it was clear to me that she was a woman well-equipped to not only handle the writing of her narrative (she had spent years expressing herself through journaling about her life's experience), but also a woman whose strength and faith in God has offered her salvation from the years of hardship pressed upon her from the time she was a young girl.

At the age of twelve, Jamie was pushed fast forward into the adult world. For years, she feared her father's wrath and abusive behavior, and dealt with a mother that suffered from mental illness. Beginning at the age of fifteen, she would embark on a journey of survival that would last more than twenty years. And it has taken her forty years to fully celebrate her perseverance and poise—and she does so with her distinctive honesty, humor, and prose. She has come to realize that rejection can often simply mean redirection. I am honored to have Jamie share her story here in S.H.E., Volume Two, and thank her for entrusting us with her words and wisdom. She is a remarkable woman of grit, fortitude, and perseverance.

I am an ex-prostitute. Yes, that's a big statement for a Christian woman to make. It's not the easiest thing for me to say. There was a time when I would never have admitted to it. For twenty years following my deliverance from the streets, I did all I could to keep my past hidden. There was so much shame connected to it. But now, I want to share my past with others so that they will see God's grace and mercy at work in my life. I want to be straightforward about everything I've been through.

My childhood was dysfunctional and abusive. I learned it was okay for someone to physically, emotionally, and psychologically abuse me. I knew that if I wanted food on my table, I had to be the one to put it there. And when I earned money, I was conditioned to believe that it was okay for a man to take it from me.

When I was twelve, I looked eighteen. My dad constantly poked fun at my body as it developed. Then one night, he came home from the bar very drunk and got into bed with me. After that, I did everything possible to stay out of his sight. I couldn't look him in the eye because of my shame. I lived in constant, unrelenting fear that it would happen again.

I had a small battery-operated radio, a birthday gift, that allowed me to escape my reality by tuning into late-night classics on WSGW. I held the radio close to my ear so I wouldn't wake anyone, and the music calmed my mind until I fell asleep. Dad got home from work around 11:30 p.m. I could distinguish the sound of his car engine from all the other cars on the road. When I heard it, I would quickly get out of bed, close my bedroom door, and sleep sitting on the floor with my back against the door and my feet braced against the foot of the bed. This way, he couldn't get into my room.

I know my mom loved us. She's the one who raised us to follow God. Growing up, the mere thought of one of her children making a mistake terrified her. All of the church mothers felt the same way. *If one of their kids did make a mistake, how would they ever live it down? What would the church leaders and other members think if somehow their children turned out to not be perfect?*

When I told my mother about the molestation, she told our pastor. He did not believe me, and my mom whipped me until I was bloody. My body throbbed with pain, and I was made to sit on the couch for some extended time. When I was released to go to the bathroom, I stuck to the sofa and had to pull myself loose. My clothes were dried to my skin from the blood. To get them off, I had to soak in a tub of warm water. I don't hold it against my mother, as she was severely mentally ill, and at the time, she could not help herself.

On the one hand, the church was teaching me that sex without marriage was the most terrible of sins, yet I was molested in my own home. I was utterly forsaken at the age of twelve. I felt abandoned. Those feelings affected my sense of self-worth for the rest of my life. There were times when my life on the streets felt empowering when viewed in light of my childhood. At least I had some control.

My parents mostly drank and fought. Fighting always followed drinking in my family, and I became the protector of my siblings when this happened. I take great pride in the fact that I was never a drinker, and I never took drugs. Writing was my escape from reality. During the worst times, I would take my paper and pencil, curl up in a closet corner, and write. I have always had a vivid imagination, and this became my refuge.

By the time I was fourteen, I had worked in the corn and bean fields for farmers near whatever town we lived in. Payday was once at the end of every crop season. My workday started at 4 a.m. and ended at 6 p.m. Workers brought their lunch. Most days, there was nothing for me to bring. One time, I was so hungry that while everyone else was eating I walked deep into the cornfield to a spot where I was sure no one could see me, pulled an ear of corn off the stalk, and ate it. It helped. If I hadn't eaten it, I don't think I would have had the strength to work the rest of that day.

I would cash my check, tithe my money at church, and go to the grocery store to buy food for my family. I bought one outfit for school. I wanted more and could have bought more, but I couldn't let my brothers and sisters go without. I took them to the county fair. They deserved to have some fun before returning to school at the end of summer. Every season after I got paid, dad got antsy. He couldn't sit still until he took some of my money. It wasn't a little amount either. He said it was just a loan and he would give it back after his next paycheck—he never did. I didn't complain, though. It wouldn't have done any good, and I was too afraid of him. I was just grateful that he didn't take it all.

My mother's mental state continued to deteriorate. She was diagnosed with agoraphobia and got to the point where she couldn't function outside the house. Dad kept drinking away whatever money he or I would make. It seemed like we were always going to some party. These events were dubbed "picnics," but really, they were just glorified drinking gatherings. My dad used to run around with a lot of younger guys; some of his friends were only a few years older than me. They would come to me when dad wasn't looking and sometimes touch me wrong. For fear of my father, I would let them.

I was fifteen when my sister and I ran away from home. We figured that anywhere was better than where we were. Our plan was to head for upper Canada, somewhere there weren't many people, where we could get jobs and save money for a car. When we had saved enough, we would go back and rescue our mom and siblings. We decided to go to Canada via the Windsor Tunnel in Detroit, over a hundred miles away. Late one summer night, we walked west to M-15, where we hoped to hitch a ride.

A trucker headed for the Detroit area picked us up. When we arrived in Detroit at about 2 a.m., he got us a motel room and gave us a few dollars to get something to eat. He wished us luck and went on his way. He was a good man. A few hours later, my sister and I were on the tunnel bus heading to Windsor. Unbeknownst to us, an older woman on the bus somehow notified the bus driver, who informed the police. The police came, stopped the bus, and took us to the Detroit juvenile center for girls.

I had never been in or even heard of such a place. The girls there acted more like animals than humans. My sister and I were put into separate cells, and I was scared. My room had a bed, toilet, sink, and a small desk with an attached seat. Heavy metal bars covered the single window. The door to the room was heavy steel with a tiny window so high up that I couldn't even see out of it. We stayed there for two days until a juvenile officer came to take us back to Bay County. We were remanded to the juvenile detention center until we could have a hearing. After the hearing, my sister was released to our parents. When the authorities asked me why I ran away from home, I told them about my dad molesting me. I was kept in solitary confinement for nine months. I eventually returned home, but it was short-lived.

I was seventeen when I left home for good. You know it's a real knock-down fight when a kitchen table breaks and the thermostat falls off the wall! Mom and I had a fight. Mom put me out after our battle over what I *should not* wear to the bank to cash a bond. I still remember the outfit—a navy-blue sweater and pants set I had bought with my hard-earned money from working in the fields. "You need to go; pack your things before your dad gets home," she said. I found myself walking down a dirt road carrying a small, battered Stroh's beer box with all my worldly goods inside—a hairbrush, a toothbrush, and a blouse. I was a mile down the road when a neighbor saw me and offered to help. I never returned.

My neighbor knew a woman in Saginaw who needed someone to help watch her three children. The deal felt right—$200 a month, a roof over my head, and free food. This would be the beginning of a new chapter in my life! Nora, my new employer, was an odd, homely woman. It turned out she was a cheap whore, and her house was a gambling den where Black men played craps and drank. On my first night there, a man named Roosevelt would not keep his hands off me. I locked myself in a bedroom with the children, gripping a butter knife in my right hand. I can still see the shadow of Roosevelt from under the crack of the door. I cried all night, scared out of my mind.

By 6 a.m. the following day, the house appeared quiet and calm. I cautiously opened the door, stepped out into the hallway, and saw Nora, her brother, and a well-dressed Black man sitting on the couch. His name was Eddie. He was a tall, slender, handsome man who drove a baby blue-colored Cadillac. He offered to take me to the Texan Restaurant on Holland Avenue to get me something to eat because I was starving. He was very polite. No man has ever listened to or spoken to me as sweetly as Eddie did that morning. His good looks, charming compliments, and agreeable manners made me feel like I was in the presence of a real gentleman. Little did I know he would rule me for the next twenty-three years.

When we returned to the house, Nora chased me around Eddie's Cadillac with a knife much bigger than the butter knife I'd been wielding the previous night. She called me a man stealer. Eddie didn't seem bothered by any of this. He told me to get back in the car. We went to his friend's house, and he said he had a plan. When we arrived, Eddie said, "Life is not free; we need money to live." Then he said, "You will be working with a woman named Dolis, who will teach you all you need to learn." I had no idea what working with Dolis in her white Continental that night meant. Nor did I know that Eddie was, in fact, a pimp and a trafficker who was constantly watching me. At 10 p.m. that same night, I was on the "ho stroll" with Dolis for the first time. I was just a teenager—alone and scared, with no home, no money, no car, and no one to help. I was afraid for my life and driven into survival mode.

It's been forty-five years, but I still remember my first trick and the White john's face. The rooming house we used on Washington Street was $3. Dolis taught me through the act. I cried and covered my eyes with my hands the entire time. She instructed me to leave the money I made on the living room table and that Eddie would collect it later. It was $10! My first and only experience with alcohol was right after that. I drank half of a beer at the Bismarck Bar and became a crazed, drunk White girl. Eddie soon arrived and ushered me out of the bar. We got into a cab and returned to where we were currently living. It was an apartment situated on the corner of Warren and Cherry Street. Immediately, I got sassy and said to Eddie, "I am not doing your ho work anymore!" I don't remember the whole beating he gave me, but I was unrecognizable to myself the following day when I looked in the mirror.

My second night on the street was a repeat of the first. Many men showed up to the stroll nightly. After the bars closed at 2:30 a.m., hos would frequent blind pigs, which are after-hour drinking establishments—also known as "juke joints," the places you go after the bars stop serving. We could solicit and pay the owner a small fee for working out of his joint. On the third night, Dolis left me on my own. I stood on the corner of Weadock and Genesee for the better part of an hour, terrified to approach a car. Then I heard Eddie's voice command, "Make some money bitch!" I knew there was no turning back.

I truly believed that Eddie would kill me if I tried to escape. He didn't beat me as long as I brought in a minimum of $100 per night and didn't disrespect him. If he was sick for lack of dope, then I would get beaten just because. Eddie was not as hard on me as the other pimps were on their women. He didn't have to be; I did my job, and my tricks paid me well. I also didn't have a drug problem or drink alcohol to numb the pain like other women. I never slipped away to steal or get a fix.

Hos fought a lot over tricks. Usually because there were more hos than tricks. Eddie told me if I ever let another ho beat me and take my money, he would give me the beating of my life. Then he would take me back down to the ho stroll and make me fight the other woman until I finished her. "There's no way some weak junkie ho should be able to whip a strongly-built girl like you, fresh from the farm in Munger," he told me.

Other pimps degraded their women in public, but Eddie never did. Most pimps had more than one woman, and the women lived together. It was like a harem—they called it a stable, like a horse stable. There was a lead mare, and all the other horses obeyed her and followed her lead. Eddie never had a stable set-up, which I was glad of. His women had their own place to live. Because I had my own place, I honestly felt he had my best interests in mind and cared about me. Some of Eddie's other girls were not loyal, but they were highly possessive. Like Stella on Mead Street, she and I had it out over Eddie a few times. And there was this vicious one on 4th and Kirk, Vicky. She stabbed me in the back of my neck with scissors. I turned and stabbed her back near the heart with a knife which bent because it hit her rib. I knew or knew of over 200 women working on the ho stroll. White girls made money easily, but no White girl could work unless she had a pimp for protection, or to get her out of jail.

Women came and went. Most pimps who got new girls didn't bother to teach them anything. They just stuck them out on the corner and told them to work. I took a new girl under my wing and taught her. Not how to make money but how to stay alive. Strange, dangerous men came down the stroll to pick up girls. Sometimes girls would leave with a trick and never come back. Some ended up with their throats cut, or they were shot or strangled. Sometimes they were gang-raped or beaten and left for dead. I remember talking with a police officer about the terrible things that would happen to us girls on the street. The policeman replied, "Occupational hazard!"

In wintertime, when the temperatures dropped to below zero, I stood on a rusty vent on Jefferson Street that blew hot air from the furnace of the building. My clothes consisted of "hot pants" with a skimpy top, no bra, and open-toed stilettos, no matter the weather. Eddie would not buy me a winter coat, even when snow was piling high around me.

I was on the ho stroll for about six months when I became pregnant for the first time. Pregnant or not, Eddie required me to work. I miscarried a few months later, but soon I was pregnant again. I went full term and had a beautiful baby boy, Joseph. Both my sons, Joseph and James, are my precious gifts from God. I cried tears of joy, thinking how God in Heaven could have blessed a lowly person like me with such beautiful children. Child Protective Services took them from me once. That was one time too many. My love and devotion to them caused me to do whatever was necessary to ensure they would never be taken from me again.

One night, I was arrested and put in a holding tank while the sheriff's deputies finished booking the guy ahead of me. I froze and felt a wave of fear. The man being booked ahead of me was my dad. He was very drunk and didn't notice me. But the feelings that haunted my childhood flooded over me, and instinctively, I looked for a place to hide.

I ducked behind a cement column, which attracted the attention of at least one deputy. I guess this was unusual behavior for a hard-core street ho. He walked over to the cell, made a smart-aleck comment, and told me it was my turn to get booked. "Let's go!" he commanded. I didn't move. Again, he commanded me, "Come on, let's go!" I still wouldn't move. When he entered the cell to force me out, I started to cry. I begged him not to make me leave the cell, not right now.

It was clear from the look on his face that this was amusing to him. He asked me what was going on and I told him that the guy in front of me was my father and I was afraid. He paused for a moment and, to my relief, he left me in my cell until my dad was gone. My greatest fear in going to jail was usually how I would survive Eddie's fists when I got out. But the thought of being face-to-face with my dad was a million times worse. I was arrested at least twelve times during my street days—for prowling, loitering, prostitution, and weapons. Tricks were dangerous. When I wore my ecru-colored tall boots, the ones with the chocolate-covered trim, I always had my knife placed inside my right boot. When a police officer would see a girl working the street, he'd give her a warning to go home. I received many of these warnings, but what was I supposed to do? Eddie would have beaten me senseless if I had just stopped working.

On another occasion, I had been in jail for over a week when my dad's old AA sponsor recognized me. He came to my cell and asked why I was there. He knew I was sober and not a user, but I agreed to say that I was. Because of this little white lie, he was able to get me into Friendship House Rehabilitation Center the very next day. I stayed there for 40 days and had to pay a one-hundred-dollar fine.

It was hard, at first, because I was not used to living by anyone else's schedule. I enjoyed the house meetings, and the first thing I learned in the group was to admit I was powerless. I had to turn everything over to a higher power—which for me, was God. I was lucky to see my children during this time. Despite continuing to feel bound to Eddie, I knew I wanted a new life for myself and my boys. I had no idea how to make this happen, but I trusted God would show me.

JAMIE

A few months before my fortieth birthday, my doctor told me that if I wanted to see age forty-one, I needed to make some significant changes in my life. I had been experiencing excruciating pain, and it turned out that a softball-sized cyst was growing on the inside of my vagina. I later learned this resulted from infection and injury, and I was fortunate it was taken care of sooner than later. The Mt. Pleasant Housing authority offered me their last available apartment three days later. I began packing, knowing that God had heard and answered my prayers.

I left Eddie in 1994, after twenty-three years under his control. Eddie shouted as I walked out the door, "Fat ass bitch, you'll be back!" I turned and softly said, "You can kill me or let me go. Either way, I am done with you."

Before I walked out the door, I asked him, "Did you ever love me?" "No," he said. Years later, I tried to make sense of my feelings for Eddie. In my heart, I always knew that he loved Vicky, the one who stabbed me with the scissors. I feel like sometimes I saw glimpses of the man he could have been. In my heart, I believe everyone deserves redemption. I know that I have genuinely forgiven Eddie for everything. I even sang the hymn "Amazing Grace" at his funeral.

For over forty years, I was told I wasn't any good—that I'd never be loved because I was tainted. I was led to believe this was my fault, that I was just a whore. But I know now that isn't true. As a young girl, I had no control and was manipulated and forced into a life not of my choosing. I believe God can save and heal you no matter who you are or what you have done. I continue to heal with the support of the special angels God puts in my life. I am particularly thankful for one, Jeanne, my counselor from 2016 to 2020.

I had heard about sex trafficking on television, but Jeanne helped me connect it to my situation. After a few sessions together, she showed me that I was, in fact, a survivor of human trafficking. It was hard for me to grasp this reality—to look at my past in a new way. It took me about two years to be able to accept this truth. But that experience with her allowed me to celebrate my perseverance and the desire to share my experiences to help others.

I have also gone back to my writing. One day, I want my sons to hear my side of the story. I am writing a book called *Jamie's Jubilee*. God put the title into my heart and mind before I started writing it. In the book of Leviticus, God calls for a year of Jubilee. This would happen every fifty years, and anyone who had sold themselves into bondage would be set free during that Jubilee year. I see myself as that person in bondage, and through His grace and mercy, God has set me free!

CHAPTER FIFTEEN

Asha

*A*sha is a multi-faceted woman with deep spiritual beliefs—beliefs that have guided and sustained her throughout her life. She believes the divine does not speak in logic but instead speaks through the heart. She has lived her life cultivating a deep trust in herself and what she feels is true, ensuring that her life choices match her actions and that her actions are grounded by love. Asha raised all seven of her children—and many adopted children—to believe in themselves, trust their worth, respect humankind, and express love over hate. Her approach to life and mothering resulted in a life of great beauty, creativity, discovery, and connection between herself, her children, and her community.

Asha lives and works in the town of Ashland, a city nestled at the base of the Siskiyou and Cascade Mountain ranges in southern Oregon. She is the founder of Pacific Domes, *a multi-award-winning manufacturer of geodesic domes worldwide. It's a business that Asha pioneered holistically and organically while pursuing her 20-year career as a midwife—carrying for mothers and newborns, and running a midwifery school. As a woman of many facets, the irony that she creates a product of many angles is not lost on me. From growing alfalfa sprouts to hosting festivals and concerts, from traveling in gypsy caravans to her studies of Buckminster Fuller—a great American architect and systems theorist—to her commitment to living a life of love, Asha is a phenomenal inspiration not only to her family but to all who have had the honor of getting to know her. One of her favorite occupations was hosting a forum on science and consciousness for fifteen years. Listening to her life experiences, I feel as if I've witnessed just how vital the pillars of one's journey in life are—pillars that sustain and guide you through both the best of times and the worst. It is through the latter that I was introduced to Asha, first having read about the murder of her son and, now, nearly six years after this tragic event, having the opportunity to speak with her.*

Loss and grief are among the most universal human experiences, yet we shy away from talking about the pain of living and losing. For me, sharing stories has always been a step toward freedom, and so is following my heart and speaking my truth. When Asha and I spoke for the first time, she emulated those same sentiments uniquely. We both agree that loss and grief will present themselves to all of us. It's a fact. It's not something we ever look forward to, but knowing that it is inevitable has taught both of us to face it head-on, however tentatively, and listen for the lessons held. To experience some form of suffering in one's life is certain, only the degree of which is unknown.

ASHA

I came across a wise statement from Thich Nhat Hanh, an astute Buddhist monk known as the "father of mindfulness," that is incredibly compelling and relevant in thinking of loss and grief. He said, "It is not impermanence that makes us suffer. What makes us suffer is wanting things to be permanent when they are not." I found Nhat Hanh's words particularly poignant. The desire to control is natural, to do what we can to ensure safety and security, to ward off the unknown, unpleasant, or painful. The fact that things, events, and people don't last forever gives life its bittersweet quality. For me, connecting with impermanence at a young age, and experiencing the fragility of life with the loss of my father, was terrifying. However, as I matured, it became extraordinarily liberating. After Asha and I spoke, she made me feel safe in my thoughts, and I realized that my illusion in life was more of a daze. We both share the importance of deeply connecting and appreciating the moments we have. The circle of life means we are all connected. We start and end at the same spot—our lives resemble that full circle. It's the same for everyone.

From early on in her life, Asha has trusted the process of the divine. And it is this very trust that comforted and guided her through the loss of her beloved son, Taliesin, a gentle, empathic, and loving young man who came to the aid of two young women— one Muslim and the other African American—on a MAX train in Portland, Oregon, on May 26, 2017. Like his six siblings, Asha's influence was instilled early on, forging in Taliesin a profound desire to make the world a better place. He was both funny and soft-spoken, a lover of rap. In a song that Taliesin recorded, he reveals the core of who he was in this refrain, "If I got one message, it's love your life." Unafraid of challenges, even as a young child, Taliesin's act of bravery—in attempting to quell the actions of a deranged and racist man—resulted in his death. Yet, as Asha shared, while her son's physical presence is no longer with us, his divine state of being is.

    As I sat peering out the window on that particular Pacific Northwest fall afternoon, pondering the conversation I'd had with Asha and admiring the colorful changing of leaves, I was struck by the immense calm I felt in the rhythm of my breath and in witnessing nature's glorious portrayal of impermanence. The internal insights I gleaned from Asha reminded me of how our energies find alignment and how raising one's vibration can connect you to your purpose and the lessons you absorb from others. Her ability to see the divine connection with her son—their soul connection—is a powerful perspective and one she finds great solace in. Asha taught me that living is a dance between bliss and suffering; we can only choose bliss by seeing beauty in everything.

    The lessons, experiences, and relationships Asha has amassed in her life form a kaleidoscope of love that guides her journey. Her story is about courage, spirituality, and abiding love for all humankind. It's the story of a woman's resolve to shoulder the heartache of her son's death, turning to the power of love—spreading the mantra of love over hate, as her son so valiantly did in May of 2017. Love was Taliesin's message, even in his last moments.

"Tell everyone on this train I love them." These were my son's very last words.

    May 26th, 2017, is a day that will forever be etched in my mind. I had just spoken to my son Taliesin before he boarded the MAX train in Portland, OR. I was on my way to a meeting in Ashland, running late, so our call was brief; one I expected to continue later that night as Taliesin and I spoke often each day. He was in the process of buying a house and moving into it with friends; it was an exciting time in his life and a time I relished sharing with him. Instead, I received a call from my daughter, telling me what had happened.

 My son witnessed two teenage girls, a Muslim and an African American, being verbally attacked by another passenger on the train. In typical Taliesin fashion, he and one other rail passenger attempted to defend the two girls and stop the verbal abuse. The extremist on the train told one of the young women, wearing a hijab, to "go back to Saudi Arabia" to "get out of [my] country." According to those who experienced firsthand the senseless murder of my son, this extremist then started stabbing people and there was blood everywhere. My good Samaritan son is not the type of human to sit and ignore an affront or injustice transpiring in front of him. My son was fighting the frontline to avert injustice. He and one other passenger lost their lives as a result. It's unbearably tragic and, yet, I can't imagine Taliesin having done anything short of what he did.

 I learned of Taliesin's last words from a woman who had come to his aid when he was stabbed. Knowing what Taliesin said was so impactful for many that learned of his final moments, but especially for me as his mother. It was just so profound to know that even in dire circumstances, Taliesin still chose love. His desire to have *everyone* on the train know that he loved them was such an act of love in and of itself—his message was for all the passengers, including the mentally ill and psychotic man hurling insults and spewing rage.

Throughout my life, I have never thought the death penalty was something to consider; I never understood what is achieved by taking one's life for another. While I believe in seeking justice and that a price must be paid for crimes committed, I have always believed in and promoted restorative justice.

I am not a Buddhist. I am everything. I am a hippie. I grew up eclectically. I did yoga when I was young and tagged along with my eight brothers and sisters to whatever they were checking out. I grew up knowing the oneness of all religions. I brought all of this—all of who I am—to my role as a mother, instilling in all my children the wonder of discovery, the joys of spontaneity, the import of respecting all forms of life, the mantra of choosing to love over hate.

I am first generation American. My father is Dutch. My mother is an Argentinian. My father was not only innovative and inventive, but he also had five PhDs in chemistry and related sciences. My mother worked as an advocate for Mexican immigrants when the US government tried to remove Spanish from social welfare forms. She stood up and created a movement that stopped the government's efforts. She taught college for over thirty years in Tucson, Arizona. Her very first job, after completing her Master's, was at the first alternative college in the country, teaching Literature and English. My grandmother was also quite impressive. She modeled activism as Evita Peron's right-hand social worker when Eva served as the first lady of Argentina. She would take a train from Mendoza to Buenos Aires every weekend to work with Ms. Peron on women's advocacy and children's rights. They were the best of friends.

ASHA

Both my parents raised nine children in the Bay Area and eventually moved us all to Tucson, Arizona. At fifteen, I began teaching Kundalini yoga, which I started at eleven. I attended Pima College at fourteen, managing the student newspaper and many other extracurricular activities and classes. I took the first environmental studies class ever offered in a college. In addition, I took dome building from one of Buckminster Fuller's students, who also taught the math and geometry classes I was taking. I geared my regular curriculum toward my focus and passion for organic farming. Zen Buddhism and astrology were close seconds of intrigue.

Leaving home at fifteen and moving to a yoga ashram in Memphis, Tennessee, stirred new life into me; running a restaurant and working on an organic farm in the Ozark Mountains offered new understandings. Living with thirty students and practicing yoga felt right. I was a 60's girl; the three H's that served as my philosophy were healthy, happy, and holy. This was how I lived my life, and it became my motto. I was a practitioner of the meditative movement. I realized early on that I was not the "average Jane," that I experienced and exhibited an almost paranormal existence because I grew up in a family where the paranormal was accepted.

In July of 1972, I ventured to the University of Santa Cruz and was formally training as an organic farmer. Following my heart was as natural as breathing, and learning new things was exhilarating. For almost four years, I lived on a farm—under a redwood tree, in an oak tree, and in the loft of a barn in the winter. I was living very organically. We ate out of the garden and cooked on a hearth. I even ventured into making teepees. While on this farm, I met a man—the head gardener—and had my first son, Christopher. I will never forget when

Christopher was born at the farm in Santa Cruz—in a teepee! A friend and I had made a teepee village for all the farmers to live in. I was eighteen years old, surrounded by a family of farmers cheering me on, saying, "We had a boy."

We need more of these moments, just unadulterated pure joy—support for the soul. Thinking back to those days, I realize how naïve we all were.

When Christopher was two years old, I moved back to Tucson, where my family was. At that time, I started growing alfalfa sprouts for restaurants, and my business grew to forty employees within two years. My dad, a chemist, was instrumental in helping me set up our factory. My two brothers worked side by side with me and later took over the business when I moved back onto the land.

As an organic girl motivated by what I feel is correct at the moment, and paying attention to the signs the universe provides, I have lived in treehouses, teepees, and under fairy trees. Buckminster Fuller was an inspiration to me. In 1979, I sewed my first geodesic dome on an old Singer sewing machine and it became my second son Elias's home. One year later, I founded Pacific Domes due to the increasing demand for these eco-friendly, energy-efficient spaces.

I have many tales to tell, like the time I ate a mushroom, climbed a tree, and decided to join a monastery. Or when I was on Mt. Shasta and heard the angel speaking to me about the next child I was going to have. Oh, and the midwife stories! There are not enough pages here to delve into all of those, each child born being an angel in this world. I am most inspired by my children—Christopher, Elias, Indeara, Vajra, Kriya, Taliesin, and

ASHA

Aurora. Being a mother is the most fulfilling accomplishment. You may wonder about the origin of the names. They all have special meanings.

Christopher was named by a full moon circle the evening he was born. Elias was born in the first Dome I made at Madre Grande Monastery in Southern California. Indeara, who became a classical harpist, was born in a glass house her father had built on a hillside, during a lightning storm at midnight. Although I didn't know it at the time, Vajra is the title for an accomplished Buddhist meditation master, and Kriya is the title for an accomplished Vedic yogi. Aurora, who the angels announced, was named by her sisters. All of them were born at home with friend midwives attending. I loved naming my children. My name (Asha) was given to me by my yoga teacher, and my last name (Deliverance) was a chosen name from being a midwife. On the farm, we changed our names according to our trade.

Raising my children in Ashland, with its old European ambiance, was a gentle and nurturing place for them to grow up. We walked or biked everywhere, picked fruit, and tended our garden. There were no televisions or social media for my children. Instead, we rode horses and played musical instruments. Our household was communal. People were always coming and going. My approach to educating my children was nature-based, offering a more holistic approach to life, including artistic and intellectual studies. Though practical skills were incorporated, the focus was primarily on imagination and creativity. It was counter to the culture around me—shunning war, inequality, materialism, and how the government handled specific affairs. While there are many approaches to raising and educating our children, I'm proud that all of my children are selfless, nonviolent, and believe in the magic of life. I believe that this foundation has prepared them well for whatever journeys they embark on.

Taliesin was my youngest boy and the second youngest of my seven children. He was named after a sixth-century Welsh bard with excellent mental acuity, a name that proved to be exceptionally fitting as he matured. From an early age, Taliesin showed that he never feared a challenge. Defending prejudice and standing up to hate and violence was precisely who Taliesin was—a humanitarian wanting to make the world a better place. When he was three, he climbed a 30-ft tree. At five, he chose not to stay on the sidelines, confidently approaching actors performing combat moves in their chain suits as part of an Ashland-based Oregon Shakespeare festival near our home. Wielding his plastic sword, Taliesin walked up to one of the tallest actors and challenged him to a duel. I distinctly remember the guy saying, "You are no match for me." My son looked him directly in the eye and said, "Try me!"

In addition to exhibiting solid spiritual strength, Taliesin always had bravery in his heart. And, he always exuded empathy and care for others. He studied the world's religions. He took a gap year after high school and went to Thailand. His adventures involved sea gypsies and a shaman.

My son graduated from Reed College in 2016, and his life was unfolding into the next chapter. He had been working in Portland, Oregon, at The Cadmus Group, a consulting firm. He had a girlfriend and planned to move into his newly purchased home with friends. The initial shock of his death will never leave me, but I believe in his magical being. In mythology, "Taliesin" was known as the "Chief of Bards," a poet who served in the court of King Arthur with legendary stories of how he could obscure reality with his myth and magic at a young age.

I believe in angels and the messages they bring. And I feel great comfort in having experienced several occurrences that soothe my heart and provide greater clarity as I grieve and process my son's death.

The day before Taliesin died, I had given my daughter and her best friend some angel cards to inspire the self-improvement project they were engaged in. After they had pulled cards, they invited me to draw a card. I reached into the pile and pulled, "Time to Go." My daughter looked at me with deep eyes and asked, "Who, Mom?" "I don't know yet," was my reply. I can still feel the sensation of that card in my hand though I no longer possess it. I placed it on Taliesin's chest during the ceremony of his cremation. Somehow, it strengthens me to know that his departure was meant to be.

Another occurrence that has particular significance to me is what transpired during the moments leading up to Taliesin's death. As mentioned previously, I had a brief call with him. The time was 4 p.m., the day was Friday, May 26th. It was the first day of Rama's Ramadan. It might also be called Good Friday. When I answered my dear son's call, he said, "Hey, Mom!" and I said, "Hi, My Darling Dear! I am about to meet a monk who just arrived from Tibet, sent by the Dalai Lama. I will call you back." And, like so many moments in our lives, we just moved on, sure that we'd speak later. Taliesin got on the train, and I went to partake in the blessing for the children of Ashland that the Rinpoche monk was leading. (In Tibetan Buddhism, "Rinpoche" is used as an honorific term to denote an incarnate lama or highly respected religious teacher.) As I sat down with the parents of the children being blessed, as the Rinpoche monk delivered his teachings— how we must love each other from the same source—Taliesin was delivering the same message, acting out of love on that train. When I align these two moments, I feel a sense of kismet that "love" was the overarching message, despite the disparity in each setting.

      Another impactful event occurred approximately two weeks after Taliesin died. A beautiful woman I know invited me to attend a party in her garden, to enjoy the bevy of glorious irises she grows, and to have some tea. Close family friends and I were going to attend together, but first, I took a nap. Almost immediately, I was awakened by the loud chirping of birds and I could hear Taliesin's voice saying, "I have to leave now, Mom. Put on your rainbow clothes and take my ashes to the Vajrasattva stupa. I am going to disappear into a rainbow." So, I called my friends and told them what Taliesin had said in my dream. I immediately grabbed my rainbow scarves from my cupboard, and we got into the car and drove over the mountain pass to the "iris party." After enjoying the blooms, we all returned to the garden chalet. There, to my surprise, was the same monk that had attended Taliesin's cremation two weeks prior. I told the monk about my dream and asked him what the "Vajrasattva stupa" was. He said he could help me with Taliesin's request, so we all traveled back to the Buddhist Monastery, down the road, for an impromptu ceremony. An auspicious shower of rain and sun occurred as this took place. The sky opened as the rain came down, and a bright rainbow appeared. I believe that the highest accomplishment is to achieve a rainbow-light body. Taliesin is no longer bound by the physical reality that we perceive with our senses. He has gone on to a different state of consciousness and expression of a spiritual being. My son may have had to go through many lifetimes or stages to accomplish a rainbow-light body. We were all pleased to have witnessed the miracle with our own eyes, which shows that there is something beyond this reality. This is what helps me stand strong with joy in my truth. Later, I learned from a friend that the Iris flower symbolizes the connection between heaven and earth. Serendipitously, this connection was again demonstrated in something my daughter, Aurora, did months before her brother's death: she had the image of an iris tattooed over her heart.

Like the two generations of women before me, I believe in doing injustice just. I promote a movement called "We Choose Love." I support restorative justice, which brings together all sides—victims, offenders, and the community—to be heard and to outline goals of victim reparation, individual accountability, and community interests. I do believe everyone needs to be heard. It's not just about listening to other people's perspectives; being heard is healing. But I struggle with how to care for people with psychotic behavior and whether restorative justice is even possible in these cases. I believe they need a more nurturing and therapeutic setting to pull through. I believe in the goodness of humanity and I think modalities that focus on healing can make a difference in someone's life.

We need more love and unity in this world. To promote this message, I launched a website, www.wechoose.love. Here we share our commitment to stand united in love. We stand for all humanity, encouraging everyone who visits our site to download their favorite "We Choose Love" logo. I have also compiled a memorial book, *Taliesin's Rainbow,* that tells my son's story together with meaningful images.

My story will continue through my spiritual practice, an exercise that allows me to sense Taliesin's divine state of being.

We are congruent in ways I only understand in an eternal form. As life continues to astound me, I relish the time I spend with my children and grandchildren at our farm, one hour outside of Ashland. Thinking back to the days of sewing that first dome, I smile. I now have a team that welds these shelters for families, glamping sites, greenhouses, corporate events, and more. Times and trends change, and I will continue to evolve—but always in my way. I am guided by what Taliesin told everyone as he was dying—and I believe he mainly meant his words for his murderer. Taliesin's last act in life was one of love. It was an astounding gesture, a moment of divine spirituality amid such brutal and senseless hostility. I feel honored to continue living my life as Taliesin lived his—as all my children live—peacefully, as a good humanitarian, wanting to make the world better, starting with loving my family first. I, too, choose love—like Taliesin—and want everyone to know I love them.

CHAPTER SIXTEEN

Siri

After visiting Bangkok, Thailand, I became completely enamored with this Asian culture—not to mention the chicken lemongrass coconut soup and Thai tea. I found the Thai people to be extremely polite and respectful; valuing life with a non-confrontational attitude and relaxed state of being.

Creating a harmonious equilibrium between the body and mind is foundational in traditional Thai healing methodology, particularly in the modality of Thai massage—an ancient healing art established thousands of years ago. I took advantage of this therapeutic practice during my stay in Thailand and searched for an authentic replication upon my return to the States. I longed for this same sense of well-being on my home turf—as I tend to move quickly to what's ahead rather than absorbing the present moment I am in. This nature to race ahead, while likely common to many, is not a balanced state of being. And this is where Siri entered my life.

My mission within the S.H.E. community is to share lessons from various women I meet. I wish I could showcase every woman that I've come to know, as so many offer some impression or indication of how to better myself as a human. They shape how I think about my past, present, and future—adding value to my growth, which is something I hope to achieve for others with the stories that I share. When I met Siri, several years ago, I had just finished Volume One of S.H.E. Life was harried and hectic. Given my penchant for overdoing and getting ahead of myself, meeting Siri was a gift. Siri effectively calmed the chaos I was feeling, both physically and mentally. She has a naturally soothing aura, a kind and welcoming disposition that immediately puts you at ease, and an adept grasp of Thai massage. She reminded me that encountering uncertainties and new experiences are normal.

Siri believes the best journey in life is the journey back to yourself. Making a concerted effort to care for our health and happiness should not be downplayed as an indulgent "treat" but rather as a priority. Siri specializes in Thai massage, offering a full range of professional treatments at her state-of-the-art facilities in Southern California—Siri Thai Massage Clinic and Spa in Del Mar and Siri Thai Bodywork in La Jolla. The basic principles of Thai massage incorporate the therapist's elbows and knees and a gentle walk on your back using ceiling bars to reduce the therapist's weight on you.

Siri trained at the renowned Wat Po Thai Traditional Medical and Massage School in Bangkok, the School of Healing Arts in San Diego, and the Chetawan Thai Traditional Massage

School. She is a California Massage Therapist (CMT) and Holistic Health Practitioner (HHP). She also holds a Bachelor of Arts in Communication Arts in Media from Pibulsonkram Rajabhat University in Thailand. With her training in Thailand and experience in the US spa industry, Siri continues learning new methods and refining her technique. She wants her clients to enjoy a different experience that combines Thai and American massage sensibilities. If her goal is for people to leave her spa feeling relaxed, recharged, and de-stressed—with renewed vitality and energy—she has succeeded. Take a look at her reviews and ratings online. Her client satisfaction is extraordinary, with the majority indicating they feel relief, at peace, and like they are a "new person." "Siri works magic," is a common refrain. With six therapists on her payroll, this dynamo is massaging sore muscles, easing tensions, and helping people manage pain associated with serious health issues like cancer, heart disease, and stomach problems. Just during our brief first interview of 90 minutes, her phone rang a minimum of six times.

My interview with Siri took place at her Del Mar location, a tranquil setting made more so with a backdrop of soothing music and a trickling water feature. We discussed her business, her family here in the States and in Thailand, her passion for massage and, especially, this modality's drug-free, non-invasive, humanistic approach to wellness based on the body's natural ability to heal itself. We spoke of the difficulties she faces as a woman in business, the universal challenges that defy borders, and the cultural challenges that create roadblocks.

As a young girl growing up in a small village five hours from Bangkok, Siri was encouraged by her parents to pursue an education that might offer her greater opportunity in life. As farmers, making ends meet was a constant challenge. As her story *will reveal, she took her parents words and work ethic to heart. She completed her education and forged a successful career in Bangkok. Then, a chance meeting with a young American man visiting Bangkok on business led to love and a new home for Siri, far from her Thai family and culture, but the core of who she is never wavered.*

Siri is as naturally beautiful—inside and out—as the landscape that surrounded her as a child. She exudes an innate aura, grounded in her Thai culture; mindfully existing in the present. She has taught me much about inner and outer harmony. I admire her passion for freedom of expression and her committed approach to advocating for massage to release stress, soothe muscles, and alleviate pain. One of the many reasons I respect this shrewd self-starter is that she is a sophisticated businesswoman, a fantastic human, and a dedicated and loving wife and mother. Coming from a hierarchal structure, she has proven that you do not need to challenge the chain of authority to advance.

She is an incredibly grounded individual—hardworking and strong in character, but ever present and grateful for all she has. She mentioned several times in our interview how grateful she is for her husband, James, and eleven-year-old son, Jasper. She acknowledged how thankful she is for their loving support and patience; for their understanding of the demands inherent in juggling her roles as wife, mother, and business woman. And, she is especially proud of her family's ability to share the load, as best they each can. Siri's husband, James, a professor and research scientist on vaccines, has his own career demands, but is a full partner in the raising of their son. I admit I'm a little envious of both James and Jasper—they are privy to Siri's

SIRI

energy and enthusiasm daily, not to mention her mouthwatering curry chicken.

Siri's story is one of hard work and dedication; of striving to accomplish all you feel you are capable of, regardless of the seemingly unsurmountable challenges of language and culture. It's the story of home and family, both near and far, grounding you and strengthening your resolve to simply do your best; of what is right and honorable, day in and day out. It's a story of a woman remaining connected to her homeland and heritage, thousands of miles away, through her work and through her dedicated role as wife, mother, daughter, and sister.

I have had to learn to be strong.

Growing up in a third-world country—albeit known for its kind and welcoming people—presents challenges that can limit one's future, particularly for those of more modest means. But it can also prepare you to deal with harsh realities, as overcoming hardships or roadblocks have the ability to strengthen resolve. With determination, I believe one can succeed. With the support and encouragement of my family, I have worked hard my whole life to retain a positive attitude, to apply myself in all I endeavor to achieve, and to never give up.

I grew up on a farm located in a central province of Thailand, called Phetchabun. This area is situated in the very heart of Thailand, nestled in a river valley between parallel ranges of the Phetchabun Mountains, lending it a cooler climate than what most might attribute to Thailand. There are mountains, jungles, waterfalls, lakes, and national parks. We have a deep history of farming and family, and a much-beloved temple that is absolutely spectacular, called Wat Pha Sorn Kaew. While tourism is nothing like Bangkok, Phetchabun is known for its verdant valleys and majestic mountain ranges. I lived in this area until I was eighteen years old.

The village where I grew up is called Tha Phon. It is an area where many farms grow rice and vegetables, and people seldom move away. It is an area that is so peaceful and beautifully green when the rice is growing in the fields. All my relatives live in the same village—many on the same street! My brown and cream-colored childhood home, with its tapered architectural style and welcoming black gate, is still there—as is my eighty-one-year-old mother, Kumta. My Father, Vanit, passed in 2000 from cancer. He was sixty-three at the time.

My family's surname is Tritan, and my family is a family of farmers. After my paternal grandmother and grandfather passed, they bequeathed their farmland to my father. It is quite common to see extended families working and living in this area, expanding their acreage with farmland passed down through the generations. My father was a bright and hardworking man. As a landowner and farmer, he would trade goods with the neighboring country of Laos to support my siblings and me. While he was proud of our ancestry and allegiance to the land, he recognized the arduous nature of farming. It is a difficult life with little money to be made, and many hardships to overcome—physically, environmentally, and financially. He wanted more for his children; he wanted each of us to go to college, find a good job, and have a better future and life than he had. I respect my father for many things. Both he and my mother worked hard so we would have greater opportunities to carve our own futures, untethered to farming, if that was our choice.

My sister, Prontipa, and I were the first generation to complete our education. She is ten years older than me and is a teacher in our village. Sadly, we lost both a brother and a sister. Our brother, Chaiya, died in a motorcycle accident at age thirty-nine. And our sister, Bubsaba, who was born three years after Prontipa, died before I was born. I do not know how she died. All I know is she was sick. My family did not want to talk about it because my mother was so sad.

I did well enough in school to attend college in the nearby province of Phitsanulok, studying Mass Communications Media and Marketing. After completing my studies in Phitsanulok, I went on to Bangkok to study marketing. Completing my education was a highlight of my parents' lives, as it was when my sister graduated. I can still picture myself sandwiched between my mother and father, holding an oversized bouquet of pink and white flowers as cameras clicked away. My mother was wearing a red and grey printed pha sinh—a full-length, tubular skirt that wraps around the waist—paired with a beautiful brocade blouse. In her hands she held a small black purse. My father stood so proud in his brown blazer and black pants; a nonchalant smile giving away his joy. I will remember that day always. Living away from home during those years really opened my eyes to new things, as my father knew it would.

I stayed on living and working in and around Bangkok for the next fifteen years. At times, it was scary being on my own. I did not have any family there and it was common for country people, like myself, to be preyed upon. I was swindled out of money by someone I thought was a friend. Another time, I was living in a tall apartment building in Bangkok, and someone climbed into my apartment from another balcony and stole my prized camera. I learned a hard lesson. The city is very hectic and petty theft is common. Apart from having to be aware of these challenges, there was much I found to be wonderful. I can still smell the steaming food stalls, and see the flashy lights from the city. And, I do miss eating in the old Bangkok area. Honestly, I was working a lot during those years and the competition was great. There really wasn't much time to do anything but work. I left at 5 am and returned very late, so I did not really have much time to enjoy the city. My first job was working for a newspaper called Than Settakij. I was employed there for four years, working in advertising. I then went on to work as a Television Account Manager for two years, living in Chonburi—a suburb south of Bangkok. Then, I was selected to work for Siam Cement Group, a prestigious company in Bangkok that only hires gifted people—primarily men—and pushes for long hours and early starts. This company is the largest and oldest cement and building material company in Thailand and Southeast Asia. Equipped with this experience, I then joined a company to market and manufacture packaging, making and checking designs before production and delivery. It went well, affording me the opportunity to build a proper house for my mother for about $20,000. Overall, the future looked bright.

Then, in 2004, I met my soon-to-be husband, James, in a Bangkok nightclub called Bed Supper Club, shaped like an airplane fuselage. I was with my nephew and a friend, enjoying an evening out, when this young man offered a seemingly nervous "hello" as he was passing by. He eventually came over to speak with me. I remember when I told him my name, he said, "your name can't be 'Silly,' can you spell it?" When I did, he said, "Oh, Siri," which is exactly what I thought I had said, though I admit I have a thick accent. He said his name was James and that he was English, but living in California. He was in Bangkok for a Scientific Conference on HIV. We really enjoyed conversing that evening and ended up spending time together while he was still in Thailand, visiting night markets and temples. It was hard to see him go to the Don Muang airport when it was time for him to leave. I was happy he stayed in touch with me, and that he returned to visit a few times over the next year.

 Meeting and falling in love with James changed the trajectory of my life, as love has a way of doing. It was a beautiful and bittersweet time. I had finally achieved a point in my career where I was realizing the fruits of my labor, earning a good commission and all that affords. I was not sure I wanted to leave my country and my family. The thought of being so far from them, from all I knew, and all I had achieved in my career was scary. I was also concerned with the language barrier. I was only moderately proficient in English and my accent was very strong. While learning English had always been a goal of mine, it is difficult because Thailand has an entirely different alphabet, and Thai people's speech sounds are very disparate from those in English. The same word can have a variety of meanings based on the intonation—the rising and falling in voice; the variation in pitch. The word "ma" can mean dog, horse, or three other things, depending on how you say it. My husband still can't decipher between the sounds of the five meanings.

 In 2005, I left Thailand to join James in San Diego. It was a scary decision, but also invigorating. I was eager to start a life with him, but also unsure of how I would utilize my skillsets. To my good fortune, James had arranged for me to apply for a student visa to study English. Living in this big city and having the opportunity to fulfill my lifelong dream to learn English made my initial months exciting. And, I made many friends from around the world. We were married in a civil ceremony, followed by a traditional Thai ceremony in Thailand—complete with monks chanting in my mother's house at 4 a.m., and my husband proceeding through the silver and golden gates, and then continuing on through a host of various rituals that culminate in a large party to celebrate. As if all those festivities weren't enough, we went on to sing karaoke—a very traditional end to a full evening.

Marrying James allowed me to obtain a green card and citizenry in just a few years. However, this certainly didn't mean it was a smooth transition for me. I yearned for Thailand. I desperately missed my Thai family. I didn't have a job, nor children to care for. This was not how I imagined my life in my mid 30's. It had never been my wish to sit at home. Growing up in Thailand—a low-income, developing country—we are taught to work hard; a strong work ethic is a matter of survival. There are no pensions and no older adult care. Individuals and families do as much as possible to get what they need. I was not happy not working, yet finding work was not easy. While I was making progress learning the language, I still had a very strong accent. I found it hard to find work in most any consumer-facing role, whether it was working retail or pouring coffee at a café. Written and spoken communications were still quite challenging, and certainly prevented me from pursuing a career like the one I had successfully advanced to in Thailand.

Many Thai immigrants have the same challenges in language as me. As a result, Thai people generally go into one of two businesses in the US: restaurant and/or massage. I worked in several Thai restaurants, but this work presented its own set of challenges. First, the hours—my husband did not like me working late nights—and, secondly, the commitment and potential financial risk associated with opening a restaurant. So, I trained in massage at schools in the US and Thailand. Wat Po in Bangkok is a temple where they famously offer courses in Thai massage, and it is well known throughout Thailand. I also spent time at Watpo Spa in Los Angeles, where they specialize in traditional Thai massage. The therapists there created the same healing experience I was accustom to in my homeland—bringing elemental energy and harmony to create mind, body, and spiritual wholeness. I knew this was the same experience I wanted to provide in my own work.

After I completed my training, I worked briefly at Massage Envy—a nationwide wellness franchise that offers massage—and then set up my own business, starting with a simple unit in a salon building near the ocean. I ultimately opened two locations in San Diego County. Initially, my husband helped me to set things up and assist with some design and marketing, but this was always my thing, really. I understood the power of advertising from my experience working in Thailand, so I was determined to use whatever tools I could to make it work. There have certainly been hurdles to overcome, as is common in many business endeavors. Working with the public, you need to have skills beyond the service you provide. Respectful communication is key. Despite the best intentions, I've realized that there are wonderful clients and there are some not so wonderful clients, and you just have to work through the challenges. I have always strived to be professional and to offer great service at a fair price. It's definitely difficult when this isn't appreciated or is disrespected. And, like any business transaction, there is a balance to achieve between pleasing the customer and not being taken advantage of. I've learned a lot along the way, including how to deal with people who misinterpret what we do, requesting "other services." It is very upsetting to have people misinterpret our work; to dishonor the time-honored tradition of healing massage.

Through hard work and dedication, I've managed to achieve my career success in the US. It hasn't always been easy, but it has been worth it. Despite the challenges, I have met many lovely clients over the last few years, which has made me feel like I'm a part of the local community. And, engaging with clients has also helped me to improve my English. I am proud that San Diego Magazine interviewed and profiled me as the "Best Thai Massage in San Diego," in January 2022. Given the impact that COVID-19 had on businesses everywhere, I am grateful to have survived the past couple of years. Just fifteen days after I opened in 2020, we were forced to shut down due to the virus. I had to get creative in order to get through this time. I elected to close one location and renovated my massage rooms with some of the Small Business Administration (SBA) loan I received. And, the Paycheck Protection Program (PPP) money I received helped me with payroll costs and taxes. Thankfully, conditions have improved and I've been able to again have two locations in San Diego County, one in Del Mar, and the other in La Jolla.

I truly enjoy what I do, and I'm happy that I've managed to build a business that allows for some flexibility. James and I welcomed our son, Jasper, in 2011. Knowing that I really wanted to work, but also be available as a parent, I'm pleased that I am afforded both with what I do. Balancing motherhood and business forces me to be organized. Confronting challenges and conflicts is what I am learning to do as a wife, mother, and business owner. I manage many things. It is tiring, but I am happy. It makes me smile when my son Jasper is proud of me, when I overhear him telling his friends I was in a magazine, or that I own two businesses. At times, it is hard to ask for help. James is busy in his work researching infectious diseases. Some days I need a Venti-size green tea latte to reenergize. I have learned to be kind to myself and realize each day is different and requires something I may not have needed or thought about the day before. As a wife and mother, I look forward to when I can schedule time off; to share one-on-one time with my son and enjoy family time together on weekends. I will cook their favorite meals, which are very often Thai food. It warms my soul to celebrate my Thai culture and country by recreating cherished dishes. James likes my Thai hot basil chicken, and Jasper always asks for Panang curry with chicken; both meals will include jasmine rice.

Assimilating into the culture and environment of a new (and foreign) country, while still having a foot in your native land is not easy. Despite my success and happiness over the years, I miss my Thai family. Life in the village where I grew up and where my mother and sister still reside is challenging, and my ability to provide help is somewhat hindered by my distance. Over the last two years, for example, I have been fighting to protect the acreage that my Thai family owns. A lawyer from Bangkok bought the land next door to our property, moved our fencing and attempted to claim our land as their own. I feel fortunate to have hired a young lawyer who is very competent. The fact that we have a one-hundred-year history with the land allowed justice to prevail; however, this may not be the case for many of the neighbors that surround our property. So many of these residents are uneducated and of modest means, making them easy targets for unscrupulous people who prey on those less fortunate. This type of behavior really saddens me. I just don't think I will ever understand people who act this way.

As I reflect on my move to the United States of America, of my family here and my family back in Thailand, and all I have learned, I am confident that how you treat others is paramount to your success and happiness. And that wherever you come from, or wherever you go, a dedicated work ethic will sustain you through many challenges. If you work hard—showing exceptionalism and professionalism in all that you do—that you will not only find pride in yourself, but earn the respect and acceptance of others. I have shared this philosophy with many people, especially women. Whether rich or poor, don't give up on your dreams if you want to succeed. While it took time to find my way, to overcome barriers of language and culture, I am proud that the success I have achieved is intertwined with my culture. Traditional Thai massage is a time-honored practice in my country of origin. Bringing these healing techniques from my culture to my clients in the US is something that brings me great joy. Pain is so pervasive in all walks of life. Having the ability to offer a remedy is very fulfilling. While my heavy accent is still a challenge for my clients, we can work through it, just like we work through their pain—each of us patient with the process.

CHAPTER SEVENTEEN

Jen

*E*veryone *has opinions, but not every person lives their radical truth with genuine, unabashed honesty. Jen is not like everyone—others' views have not altered her truth or become her reality. She recognizes within herself a life force that can endure the unpredictable and often challenging storms of life. She has weathered many gusts and gales in her 40-plus years, none capable of dousing her spark, stealing her light, or robbing her of her love for living and giving to all those around her. On the contrary, Jen believes that all she has experienced in life has only made her stronger, wiser, and more in tune with herself.*

Jen's approach to life—one of perseverance, self-reflection, honesty, zero shame, and tenacity—was honed early on. As a young child, she weathered her father's alcoholism and struggles with mental illness. At twelve, she was diagnosed with an autoimmune disease—Dermatomyositis—where she faced her own mortality. She has survived the excruciating pain her disease can often deliver, a sexual assault, and her father's taking of his own life. Any one of these challenges would be enough to break one's spirit, but Jen has boldly met every trial, undressing the past and bathing in the present moments of what matters; of what lessons can be learned. She has cultivated a distinct internal navigation that helps guide her, something she describes as an alternate reality—creating her world with visions and intentions of what she wants to experience. Being in symbiosis with her inner wisdom—the "wise one within"—is an art Jen has mastered. Instead of recoiling, she embraces the new and the unknown; she looks for the light, but does not hide from the dark; she embraces life as an open book, believing in the freedom and connection that true "radical" honesty with oneself and others can bring you.

In her younger years, Jen loved to travel and has been to many countries, including India for five months doing tsunami relief work in villages. Then to parts of Asia—Bangkok, Thailand, and Angkor Wat in Cambodia—all of which she describes as magical. She is a seeker of knowledge. She has an innate desire to connect, to help others, to clear the windshield of life and see and experience its true, unadulterated essence. She allows her spirit to chart her course—her intuition led her to Oregon and meeting her husband. While there are many days when Jen is physically and mentally drained, her husband, Scott, has been a sturdy presence throughout their 18-year partnership. Perhaps it is their perfect balance of yin and yang—opposite but interconnected forces—that has contributed to their successful life partnership. Jen is an open book and Scott is quite private. A yin-yang connection can be a powerful combination—in marriage, friendship, or world affairs. Respecting one another's differences—idiosyncrasies, unique qualities, desires, dislikes, beliefs, etc.—is the first step to greater understanding and connection. True acceptance requires this respect; true honesty begets it.

Radical honesty is foundational not only to Jen and Scott's relationship, but also to how Jen maneuvers through life, and how she has approached motherhood. Aria is Jen and Scott's daughter, an old soul, just like her mother. Though Jen didn't necessarily see motherhood in her future, she embraced the vision and nature's course. The result was pure joy, a little girl that brings greater light, love, and life to the world.

At the same time that Jen was learning to be a mother, she was dealt another rare autoimmune disease called Autoimmune Neutropenia. This time, her white blood cells were attacked by her immune system, leaving her susceptible to persistent infection. From the age of 12, however, Jen had learned to manage pain— to move through it to find the light, to engage the power of the mind and body. The onset of this secondary disease, though equally complex, brought with it a revelation: she did not have to become a victim of her disease. Through her suffering, she envisioned a way forward. She wanted to give back, particularly to children suffering. Once she attained her master's degree in Psychophysiology (study of the mind and body connection) she was ready to teach others what she already knew: healing begins when the body and mind are treated together. With this awareness and her love of animals (especially dogs), she founded an organization, Pile of Puppies (POP), dedicated to bringing joy to chronically and terminally ill children and their families by surrounding them with a pile of puppies. When Jen sees a child suffering, she knows firsthand what it is like to feel different from the rest. She knows that looking death in the eye is scary, but also empowering.

When she is not having dance parties with Aria to the pop rock band Imagine Dragons, or upholding board member stewardship duties for Pile of Puppies, Jen helps her clients unlock their own "wells of wisdom" by assisting them to find the wisdom within their challenge—through somatic and unconscious work in her therapeutic coaching sessions and monthly wisdom weaving meetings that she holds online every third Wednesday. I was privy to attend one of these symposiums of sharing with twenty-seven people from around the world. The goal is to hold a shame-free space and learn how to build a strong life force in challenging times. In her work and soon-to-be published book, she has identified four pillars that have been a source of wisdom in her life, derived from her own experiences: Illness, Sexuality, Death, and Motherhood.

Jen is someone that absolutely knows who she is and what she is capable of. That, in and of itself, is magic—as so few can truly attest to the same. She is unabashedly authentic and open about what she thinks, feels, and desires. She lives and breathes a mantra of "no shame." She and her husband are united in their love and the raising of their child. She is a loving mother and wife, she is a free-spirit and a seeker of knowledge, and she is someone who wants to use her suffering for the betterment of other children and adults who are suffering. And, she is sexually fluid. As she will tell you, she is "attracted to people," but expresses herself as bisexual (agreeing to be only with women, with regard to her marriage commitment). Scott has always known and supported this aspect of her.

Through her own openness and honesty, Jen hopes to promote a movement of no shame. She fully embraces who she is. Perhaps when one's life is challenged, especially at such a young age as Jen's was, with the onset of her disease, you can quickly pivot to what's most important instead of fixating on a facade of who others need you to be. Sadly, it's a freedom few truly master and it really shouldn't require strife to recognize its merits. We don't need to be clones of one another—void of our own thoughts, desires, and beliefs—in order to find acceptance and joy in life. We can each be our own unique being and respectfully honor those around us doing the same, like Jen.

I am privileged to have Jen share a piece of her new project, "Radical Honesty," here in the pages of S.H.E.

Throughout my life, there have been times I feel as though I live in a fairytale and other times where I just can't imagine when the pain will end. In my 40-plus years of living, that's a lot of back and forth, a journey that has taught me that there is no light without darkness, and no darkness without light.

I am a seeker of light—where joy resides. I believe it exists even in the darkest moments. It is a philosophy that has sustained me through a great deal of pain and suffering. Realizing that light moves through transparent vessels was a profound epiphany in not only how to manage my pain, but in how I strive to conduct my life. Transparency brings illumination. When we are transparent—honest with ourselves and others—there is greater light to see truth. I call this "radical honesty"—it's raw and real. When we are radically honest with what is, the doors open and the light comes through—even in the darkest of moments. Radical honesty clears the bullshit, though it may be painful at times.

I was born into a family and a country that allowed me to show up as my true self. I felt embraced and allowed to be 100% me, which is a rare gift. I don't take this lightly. I am well aware and honor those who could be killed or harmed for living as I do. I do not take this for granted and I want to say I SEE YOU and honor you on your path.

This is my story. My hope is that it opens your heart and gives you hope that dark moments do hold space for light. I have faced my own mortality as a teenager and as a mother. I know the power that is given when we look death in the eye and say NO…NOT YET. I thank death as my catalyst to life.

I have walked my path as an "outside of the box" thinker with no interest in becoming a mother. I thought I was too wild and free to ever be one. In a blink of an eye, I learned that life surprises us with our greatest teachers. For me, my greatest teacher is my daughter. In becoming a mother, I allowed my intuition to guide me as it has always been on my side and has never failed me. The birth of my daughter is living proof of this.

Through my work, I have witnessed dying children and their families in extreme joy. It is a testament to my belief that joy can heal in the darkest of moments and that life should never be taken for granted.

I have experienced what it feels like to feel 29 again when, at the age of 42, I had an ethically, non-monogamous sensual experience with a 29-year-old doctor, who happens to be a woman.

I know what it is like to feel 100% whole in my body, mind, and spirit, while being supported in a rock-solid, radically-honest partnership with a man for 18 years.

I will take you into my life—a dance with death and illness, sexuality and motherhood. I thrive in the deep end and I am surrounded by those who believe in me. It is a gift to attract light and my hope is by the end of this even more light surrounds you. Let's begin...

Radical Honesty—Initiation Begins at 12 Years Old

When I was 12 years old, I was the fastest runner. I liked to challenge myself, to find another way of doing things, like climbing the fence around our yard and entering our home through the back door instead of just using a key to the front entrance. I liked being adventurous. I trusted my body would do what I needed it to do. Up to this point my biggest challenge was having an alcoholic father. Each time I excelled in something physical, I felt more empowered to withstand the ups and downs that alcoholism brings to a child's life. Six months into this tween age, things began to dramatically change. I started to lose the strength of my muscles. I could no longer scale the fence I once climbed over with ease. I could no longer run like I was part gazelle. My incredibly healthy body for 12 years of my life began to know disease.

I was diagnosed with a very rare disease—at the time, a one in a million statistic—called Dermatomyositis—where my immune system decided that my own muscles were to be attacked. Strange enough, I realize now that I'm an adult that I was lucky to have been gifted a troubled father who was a bipolar alcoholic, as it was this challenge of being raised by an unstable parent that gave me grit as a young girl. And, as it turned out, challenge also raised my father up. He, in fact, showed up better than he had ever shown up when I was healthy. I was also gifted with a remarkably grounded and loving mother who didn't show worry, but surrounded me with the notion that I was going to be okay and I would get through this. I also had an incredible uncle; a man who has been my mentor all my life and truly saved my life at that time, teaching me how to tap into the "wise one within" to help heal myself. And, I had a bonus dad who arrived when I was 17 and defined what a father should be—someone who is safe, who listens, and is intuitive regarding what a teenager needs.

I was on a powerful spiritual journey from the ages of 12 to 17. While most kids were just going through puberty trying to find their way, I was figuring out if I would stay on the planet. I learned that I could have an extraordinarily weak body—a body that could barely swallow or get up from a toilet by itself—and yet, at the same time, I could have a strong life force flowing through me.

Through incredible sessions with my uncle, who happened to be a renowned therapist in Los Angeles, I learned through hypnosis and guided imagery to find and understand the "wise one within." I learned how to listen to my body and how to use my mind to help heal me. I learned to accommodate for whatever limitations I had. I was determined to appear "normal." The power of the mind can breed determination.

After having profound experiences listening to the "wise one within" and having breakthrough moments that the medical world didn't understand, my strength started to come back. At 17, I started to share my radically honest story with my fellow teenagers. In doing so, I realized that my story not only inspired others, it evoked a sense of vulnerability, a transparency that allowed us to connect as humans. I found that people would tell me their deepest, darkest secrets even if we had just met one another.

Light moves through transparent vessels. We all know this to be true, but it is profound when we recognize the significance of this fact as applied to communication or connection. When we are radically honest with one another we become that transparent vessel. We drop all shame, all pretense or façade that inhibits connection; inhibits the light from moving through us. We just share a story…a human story, without barriers or restraints. I was 17 when I started to realize that we are all so much more alike than we are different. There is no shame, there is just our life story.

Facing the possibility of death catalyzed me to live. It led me to my master's in Psychophysiology, which is the study of the mind and body. The experiences I had early on, connecting with others on a deep level, served me well in my work. I learned that I had the ability to create a space for people to be 100% transparent—with no shame; a space where they could unlock old subconscious patterns of not being worthy enough. Being radically honest with myself and with others not only opened my mind and other's minds and hearts, it also sharpened my intuition.

Radical Honesty—
Into Motherhood and Mothering of a Nonprofit

My intuition led me to quit my job in San Francisco and travel to Southeast Asia for six months. I did tsunami relief work for one month, providing grief counseling to those impacted by the 2004 tsunami. I also spent 30 days practicing Tantric Yoga for six hours a day. (Tantric yoga combines several meditative and yogic practices with the goal of achieving a deeper personal understanding of oneself, including greater self-love and acceptance.) By the time I came back to the States I was a changed woman, making re-entry a bit challenging. I was depressed for the first nine months, trying to figure out where to go with my life when my intuition said the man I was going to marry was in Portland, Oregon. As an untamed woman, I never dreamed of marrying anyone, nor dreamed of being a mother. However, I did know to heed my intuition.

    Within a week of arriving in Portland, I met the man I would marry four years later. We never really talked much about having kids, but when I turned 36, I knew the window was closing and we started talking about whether we wanted kids. We were 60:40 on our thoughts about having a child—60% happy to remain childless and 40% "Well, what the hell, maybe let's be parents." After only trying for two months, I was pregnant. We were astounded and couldn't believe it as I always felt my medical conditions would impair my chances. It all just happened so quickly. It made us think "Have we just screwed up our lives?" I think it's a normal knee-jerk reaction to such a swift turn of events. I think we both went in thinking we likely wouldn't get pregnant. But my magical, brilliant, and unique child had other plans for us.

    My gut said the pregnancy would be smooth and the aftermath would be awful. It was spot on. Though my immune system started to attack itself when I was two months pregnant (with the onset of Autoimmune Neutropenia, a condition I still have 10 years later)—making it seem like I could go septic at any point—I seemed to be really stable physically. I did, however, have a nightmarish 64-hour labor where I called on my ancestral grandmothers at the 64th hour to avoid a C-section and potential hysterectomy. It was when I called on them that our Aria Shanti Trepanier was born to the song Om Shanti (which means "peace be with you"). My pregnancy and onset of a secondary autoimmune disease definitely impacted me for the next two years as I struggled not knowing if I might die due to incredible infections and breathing issues. Through all this, however, there were whispers from my "wise one within," guiding me along the way. I knew I would be okay, that there would be an even bigger purpose that came out of this suffering.

As my daughter got older, I began to teach her about how life force moves through her. I taught her about death early on. While living in Switzerland, we had a favorite little hedgehog that visited us nightly and brought us so much joy. One day he was hit by a car and we had to say goodbye to our favorite guy. Given his sudden demise, there was no opportunity to talk with Aria prior to his death, so I asked her if she wanted to go look at his body, assuring her that he was not in pain, and she said "yes." She was six years old at the time. It was a beautiful moment to acknowledge the cycle of life—from cradle to grave. We don't shy away from death in our family; we embrace life and death. This is life…. the good and the challenging, all twisted together. I have taught my daughter not to fear, but to embrace what is.

There is a deep power in embracing radical honesty with children. It allows you to sit with "what is." The power of radical honesty and joy is what led me to create my nonprofit, Pile of Puppies (POP), in 2015—a vehicle for me to give back to children who are experiencing some of what I experienced as a child, facing a dire health challenge and/or the end of life.

As my own experience demonstrates, there are really shitty moments in life and it can start at a young age. I believe it is important to acknowledge this. My approach is not to run away from this truth, but to fully acknowledge its presence in life; to show how light and dark can collide; how pain and joy can hold each other's hands.

Through my nonprofit, we surround chronically and terminally ill children with a pile of puppies. We create Joy Healings, as we call them. I have countless stories about incredible families who've had to face the end of their child's journey on this earth, and witnessed beautiful young souls who have passed on. The very first hospice POP I did was with a teenager who was writhing in pain when I arrived. I told him to let me know if he needed space or didn't want us there; that we wanted to honor his wishes and could leave at any time. He looked me dead in the eye and said, "I'm dying to see these puppies." My GOD, literally and figuratively, it was true. I remember the photos I took of his mother, radiating sheer JOY! People would have never believed her son was dying beside her because the joy she emanated was palpable. Death is final, but joyous memories and love are eternal. The last seven years have been some of the most fulfilling moments of my life, precisely because I chose to shine light in places most don't dare to venture: the death beds of children. And yet, I am here to tell you, immense joy can still arise in our last moments. Light CAN be met in the darkest of hours.

Radical Honesty – An 18-year Partnership with My Husband

Throughout my life I have not been scared away from tough subjects—death and sexuality are two of my most favorite topics. When I married my husband, Scott, he knew very well that I have been attracted to women. In fact, we'd often comment together on women we found attractive, whether it was someone we saw in a movie, or someone that caught our eye while out and about together. Neither of us are very jealous creatures and we both appreciate a woman's form.

It wasn't until we were living in Switzerland, that our story shifted in the best of ways. Ironically, when I was a teenager, I wrote in my journal that I would go to the Himalayas, the Alps, and the Grand Tetons. I had no idea how powerful all three of these places would be in my life story. I was in India when the massive 2004 tsunami struck, devastating communities all along the coastline of the Indian Ocean, killing more than 200,000 people and displacing thousands more. I was in the Alps in 2020 when we experienced the first major pandemic in our lifetime. And, I had just left Yellowstone—enroute to the Grand Tetons with my family—when it experienced a 1,000-year historical flood. I believe strongly that I was meant to be in all of these places during pivotal moments in time for a reason—to witness, to acknowledge, to lend help where possible (especially during my time in India), and to further recognize the coexistent power of light and dark. Switzerland, especially, changed the direction of my path greatly.

Two weeks after we settled on a Swiss farm/vineyard outside of Geneva, experiencing fairytale views of the Alps, my carotid artery spontaneously dissected. To top it off, my immune system decided to attack my lung. It was a surreal experience—unreal pain and unreal beauty all at once! I felt like I was living a nightmare intertwined with an extraordinary dream-like landscape in one of the most pristine locales I had ever known.

When my carotid artery dissected and my immune system assaulted my lung function, I knew it wasn't a death sentence, but it certainly offered me a reminder of just how short life is and that we need to f****** live it to our fullest. One night I looked over at my husband and said, "You know, I haven't been with a woman in 14 years! What do you think about me popping on Tinder?" Scott and I had only experienced a monogamous marriage and it felt right for 14 years. The truth of the matter was I was living in a dream-like landscape, with a terribly unpredictable body. Sixty percent of people who experience a dissected artery have a stroke. I was in the lucky 40 percentile. I never took my luck for granted. I have always lived each and every day fully, and have never shied away from taking calculated risks. I knew I felt a tidal change within me. I wanted to remember what it was like to be with a woman again—plain and simple.

To my surprise, without a hint of hesitation, my husband said, "Go for it! Go date women!" WHATTT??? OMG, this was so exciting. I immediately looked at a YouTube tutorial on how Tinder worked and instantly put up a profile. I felt like I was HIGH on life. I'm not on this planet to regret anything and THIS was probably the most thrilling idea I had had since jumping out of a plane. Prior to being a mom or a wife, I was wild and free. Luckily, I never really became "tamed" because my man married me for who I am and never tried to change me. He believed in my CRAZY, unheard-of idea for a nonprofit and, in this moment, he gave his blessing to reawaken the bisexual side of me that I had not acted upon in 14-plus years! I had no idea that this crazy idea would unlock a side of me that I never knew before. The journey was extraordinary. I felt SO DAMN COMPLETE. I felt ALIVE and untamed, yet so unlike when I was in my 20's. This time around, I had the grounding of maturity—20 years of experience and wisdom to guide me. I was in a stable, long-term, radically honest partnership. I was blessed to be a mother.

Though I may have been dealing with medical conditions, I was also sourcing the strongest life force I had ever felt before. Most of the women I met simply for connection, to have a tea and talk—to learn what it was like to be a lesbian or bisexual woman living in Europe. Honestly, one aspect I loved was that so many of these women put their top three songs on their Tinder profile. So, while I might not even connect with them, I collected an entire hundred–plus song library from music-loving women around the world. The Geneva population, at that time, was 60% expats—so truly the whole world was at my fingertips.

I was learning what it was like to be a millennial in the dating world. I learned that I didn't necessarily have a type anymore—I just loved women. Back in my twenties I tended to be attracted to women that had something I didn't have, like larger breasts or a tinier waist. In my 40s, I was seeing the beauty in all types of women.

Mind you, all of this happened in 2019 so the exploration had to end quickly once 2020 reared its ugly head and human connection was swiftly curtailed. What I learned most during this experience was that having a partner that deeply trusts you strengthens your bond. You are able to honestly communicate, set boundaries that work for both of you (lines that you don't cross), and establish a level of comfort that you both know will not adversely affect your relationship.

When I made love to a 29-year-old woman who happened to be a doctor, I never felt more alive than that moment. When I looked into her eyes and saw her youthful face, I was 29 again. When I see old men dating younger women, or visa versa, I kind of understand why because I had that moment; that moment where you genuinely feel young again—carefree and wildly curious. Whether it was the 29-year-old doctor, or the other younger women that I just spoke with, they all seemed a bit surprised by me—someone who was honest, in a relationship with a man, and having an ethically, non-monogamous experience. I got the sense I gave them hope that there could be other ways of looking at marriage, especially when you're a bisexual/sexually fluid woman.

The sex life Scott and I experienced—which was always fiery and fun—went to another level! I now had real life fantasies I could play out in my mind while making love with my husband. In him allowing me to be "fully expressed" and radically honest, he received ALL of me…the WHOLE JT. I even saw a different side of myself. Yes, I had been with women in my 20's, but I hadn't been in a solid, devoted relationship with a whole lifetime of experience backing me. This time I was fully expressed, fully seen in the most profound way.

I have no regrets. Regrets rob you of joy. You have one life to live and I believe we are meant to write our own story—and the way we want to live it. Stepping into radical honesty might be scary as fuck for some, it's a vulnerable space, but I have not feared it because I learned early on that it can light a fire in you that will glow so bright that it will outshine the darkness that might try to creep in. Your life is a gift. The more present you are to the "wise one within" that whispers to you—that voice of intuition, of knowing, of wisdom, of self-compassion—the more you will be set on your path.

JEN

I am forever grateful for all the painful and beautiful experiences I have had as they have created a life worth living! So much so that I have written an entire book on the four pillars in life, firstly for my daughter and secondly for you!

CHAPTER EIGHTEEN

Marina

*M*exico *is a large country, about one-fifth the size of the United States, and has a lot more to offer than margaritas under a beach umbrella. One of the country's hidden gems can be found in its interior, about a four-hour drive northwest of the capital, Mexico City. The town is called San Miguel de Allende, located in the Central Highlands region, nestled among the Sierra Madres Mountains in the state of Guanajuato—an active expat community with welcoming locals, charming cultural traditions, and a focus on the arts.*

My interest in the local cuisine and the possibility of taking a cooking class is how I found my circuitous route to Marina in the city of San Miguel de Allende. I arrived with my husband, hand in hand, ready to learn Spanish and the cooking ways of this patient, kind, and soulful woman. On the day we met, we explored this captivating city on foot. I was immediately immersed in Marina's world, walking the cobbled streets, taking in the vibrantly hued passageways, baroque architecture, and charming cadence of life. Every corner we turned in this colonial-era city, there were plazas and parks filled with shady trees and benches. It's a place that begs one to walk and to explore, to take in its beauty, and then sit for a spell and simply enjoy its captivating, old-world ambiance—one free of traffic lights, billboards, and neon signs. Our first stop was the Mercado (market), where Marina would not let us pay for the avocados or chiles she selected. Learning that my husband is an avocado and lemon farmer in California, the conversation quickly turned to the importance of fresh produce. After we made our selection of vegetables from the bustling, open-air market and purchased chicken from Marina's favorite local vendor, we perched ourselves on a bench in the center of town and happily took in the hive of activity that surrounded us—food vendors selling an array of treats and treasures, children playing and cavorting in the sunshine, and folks milling about, chatting on benches and in cafes. It was a delightful way to take it all in, to be among the tourists, residents, and passersby that seemed to effortlessly and joyfully go about their daily lives. San Miguel de Allende exudes an ease, one equally matched by Marina.

I quickly learned that this engaging woman came from very modest means, pulling herself up from a hardworking, rural upbringing in an arid patch of the Mexican countryside to become an educator. She specializes in teaching what she knows well—the Spanish language and cooking. With little to no education, no electricity or running water, and little to no money, Marina's early years taught her grit. And it is this strength of hers that allowed her to visualize a way of life that would offer greater abundance and joy; a grit that sustained her through challenging times, allowing her to successfully negotiate the obstacles in her path, to envision opportunity. Her life has been a tender act of turning herself inside out, discovering who is she and what she is capable of achieving—despite the limited schooling and resources that availed her, and the prejudices that intertwined therein.

Through several Spanish translators, Marina was willing to share how she lived forward, not always knowing if her path would lead to something better. What initially drew me to Marina was her love of life and learning, not to mention that mischievous smile. There are things we all bury and never bring out to the open. There can be a sense of fragility in storytelling, in exposing ourselves. The reward in storyteller, however, is that it can also bring one greater freedom, insight, and peace.

While I connected with Marina with the intent to learn more about some of the local cuisines common to this part of Mexico, I gained so much more than cooking skills during my time with her.

In addition to knowing her way around a kitchen, Marina is an expert in Spanish home immersion, a method of language learning when a person is immersed in the Spanish language in a domestic and school environment. Home immersion aims to provide a natural and authentic learning experience, allowing learners to acquire the language and improve their fluency quickly. It can be a good option for those who have a solid base of the language, but want to improve their conversation; and for those who have limited time to study, but want to achieve fluency. Prior to devoting her energies to both cooking instruction and in-home Spanish immersion, Marina taught at Habla Hispana Spanish Language School, a locally situated school offering an intensive language instruction program. How Marina came to *become an educator—in both cooking and Spanish—is truly remarkable, given that she had minimal schooling growing up and little to no experience cooking or working in a kitchen. As she says, she "worked like a man" during her youth, doing the multitude of chores a working ranch requires. Yet, it is this very upbringing that instilled in her a work ethic that propelled her forward, finding opportunity despite disadvantage.*

Once we arrived at Marina's home, we got straight to business in her cocina (kitchen), prepping the components for our afternoon almuerzo (lunch). I blistered verde (green) chili peppers over an open flame on the small white oven burner. As I worked, I could not help but admire the tangible display of Marina's faith in humanity: a collage of crosses arranged on the wall near the table where my husband was detaching chicken off the bone. As we all chopped, prepped, and mixed away, Marina encouraged me to practice the many words I know in Spanish and string them together while we created her culinary masterpieces. When our meal was ready to serve, Ernesto, her husband, joined us for lunch. He saved the day when he left unexpectedly to purchase the coldest cerveza (beer) in a can that I have ever had—Modelo to be precise. It was lovely being together in Marina's home, where she and Ernesto have raised their four children amid the warm memories of Ernesto's own upbringing. Returning to San Miguel de Allende to settle in her husband's childhood home brings added significance to the saying "the best journey brings you home."

With Marina, I not only learned how to cook chili rellenos, sopa, and flan, but also experienced the beauty that food offers beyond sustenance. A shared meal, thoughtfully prepared, brings people together in an intimate and loving way, fostering community and connection. Marina, again, orchestrates this beautifully. It is a talent that I believe is her superpower—that ability to make those in your home feel welcome, at ease, and cared for. It is something that goes beyond the act of feeding others, it's nourishment of both body and soul. She's perfected this skill in the Spanish home immersion work she crafted as a means to connect with others and help provide for her family. No one knows this better than the friend of mine, Elisabet, that initially connected me with Marina. Elisabet graciously shared a few meaningful moments of her time living with Marina and Ernesto for one month. "From the moment Marina opened her front door and sat down with her children and grandchildren, to the last day we ate one of my favorite 'Marina meals' of chiles en nogada, she made her home feel like my home," Elisabet shared. She then went on to add, "Marina is a woman of deep faith, friendly and fun—not to mention hardworking. The Spanish immersion program, both academically and while living at her home, became far more than a beginner Spanish class. Together we shared our lives, tears, and hugs—something special we need more of as women." I don't think I could have expressed Marina's gift any better than Elisabet!

Human connection for Marina is the theme of her storyline. Her social interactions have greatly influenced her growth, both spiritually and mentally. She has touched the lives of endless people of all ages and fostered interpersonal relationships with everyone who enters her home and classroom. Teachers play a vital role in society by educating and shaping the minds of future generations. They are unsung SHEROs (superheroes) due to their dedication and perseverance to make teaching and learning possible for everyone at any age.

Marina is a true teacher in every facet of her life. Barriers that challenged her youth—hard physical labor, limited resources, lack of educational opportunity, isolation, sexism, etc.—were overcome by perseverance and grit. The day I spent with Marina showed me that learning about oneself is healing and empowering. It is a process of gaining knowledge and growing that knowledge into opportunity. Understanding one's thoughts, feelings, behaviors, and motivations is a form of self-exploration. Marina and her life story emulate an understanding of one's culture and personal history, exploring her values and knowing her strengths and weaknesses. For all of us, it's an ongoing process that can be challenging but, as you will read, an enlightening one.*

I am a wife, a mother of four, and an educator. When I look back to where I began my life on an arid ranch in rural Mexico, devoid of running water and electricity, my life today is one that I might have only dreamed of.

I was born the third daughter of nine children, three girls and six boys. Antonio (Toño) was the eldest and the one that I spent the most time with. Toño's vision was impaired from birth and by the time he was 18, and I was 12, he had completely lost his sight. From that moment on, we were a team. It didn't take long to figure out our way together. He'd put his right hand on my left shoulder, and off we'd go to complete our chores. He knew a lot, including how to read and write, and I knew the way. I'd guide us physically from one task to another

In the ranch house where we lived, there was no electricity or drinking water, but there was a spring from which we would draw water with the help of a donkey. We also loaded boats and cut wood to cook and heat our home. When we went out to cut firewood, I did the gathering and Toño carried the logs. Because of our limited resources, we needed to be industrious. To provide us with some light, my father made candles using the wax from some beehives we had. He'd gather the wax and then Toño would help him mold the candles. We also had a few cows that provided us with milk and cheese, and some chickens that supplied us with eggs. One summer, I remember we planted corn and beans. What we had, we largely created for ourselves.

While Toño and my other male siblings all learned to read and write, my father didn't consider these to be important skills for me or my sisters to learn. His belief was that it was more important that his daughters learn to perform household responsibilities correctly. While my older sister was good at helping my mother with these duties, I didn't favor them. However, being the second eldest daughter, I fell in line. I did eventually learn to read and write, but I remember my dad kicking me many times when I didn't understand something simply because I didn't know what the words meant. My mother just cried and never complained.

Eventually, a school was built on the ranch and the teacher that helped me learn to read and write taught there. All the children from the ranch attended, but Toño and I initially stayed back to help our father with the cows. Eventually, we also went to the school. I will never forget when my brother and I arrived. As soon as we sat down, one of our classmates went directly to the teacher to report that I had brought in cow lice. As a result, the teacher put a lot of salt on the patio as a preventative measure. I took it as a punishment, suggesting that I was not clean. This school experience brought me shame and sadness. I was only nine years old and definitely impressionable. I did not want to go back after that, but my father told me I had to.

MARINA

My father continued to purchase additional cows. He was a farmer and, on occasion, he found minerals that he sold. With that money, he bought a ranch for the cows, but it was two hours away on horseback. We had cows that would stay six months with us and then six months at the new ranch. When I was fifteen, I wanted to take responsibility for the other ranch. I was very sure of myself. Father finally gave me the opportunity. He saw that I was ready and eager. Each day, we left at four in the morning. I accepted all the circumstances around me without problems for six months and then I had to return to our home ranch to tend to duties my father felt were a better use of my time. And, Toño had hit a rough spot. He began to drink a lot of wine. He had been tending the cows, making candles, and preparing food during the time I helped my father with the other ranch, but he got bored with his routine. As a result, I had to stay back and help with his duties. Up to this point I had spent much of my life working outside, milking cows, riding horsing, gathering firewood, and doing various field chores. I thought I might get some credit for all the good work I did, but I did not. I returned to working with my sisters. I made one hundred cheeses a day, and my sisters did the housework. The three of us worked all day, every day. I would motivate myself by saying, "this is how strong people are made."

When I reached the age of twenty, I told my father I did not know how to cook like my sisters, nor did I know almost anything about household duties because I had "worked like a man" most of my life. I recalled that my father had some compadres (friends) who lived on another ranch 15 kilometers from our house. They worked for a mining unit of the ranch. And there was a dining room that serviced all the workers. The daughter of one of my dad's compadres was the dining room manager so I approached her for work, hoping to learn the skills

I was lacking. I think my father thought I was completely wild, but said he would permit me to go live and work at this facility for a short time—until I learned how to cook and clean. I had never lived away from home, so I left with both pleasure and fear. Everything was new. Suddenly, I had a shower to bathe in, clean clothes to wear, neatly combed hair, and great food! While Gloria, the manager, indicated that my dad had commissioned her to teach me to cook, I asked to first learn how to clean.

      I lived and worked with other girls and interacted daily with the many engineers and personnel that were employed by the mining unit. Within two months, I locked eyes with one of the engineers, Ernesto, and we developed a friendship. I was completely naïve to having a relationship. We spent our free time together, getting to know one another. Then, about a year and a half later, things got a bit more serious. Ernesto indicated that he wanted to be intimate. I knew this what not something my parents would approve of, and certainly not something I could consider while living at home. I was so inexperienced. I initially told Ernesto that it wasn't going to be possible, but that was not how I really felt. I wanted to be with Ernesto and ultimately decided that since we were both far from home, this was something we could experience and not have our families know. The second time we were together, I became pregnant. This was not something that I thought would happen. Again, I was so naïve. Growing up, my mother never told us anything other than kissing a boy was bad and if we did kiss someone that she would know. I remember once being kissed on the cheek by a boy when I was sixteen and I washed my face before I got home. I think I felt so guilty that I lowered my eyes and hung my head in a way that my mom suspected I had done something wrong and she ended up spanking me with a switch. I knew I couldn't face my parents, stained by the sin of impurity. After a brief period of unrest, unable to come to terms with my condition, or know how to approach

Ernesto, my pregnancy couldn't be hidden any longer. Ernesto wanted to approach my parents, to ask for my hand in marriage. I gave him detailed directions to our ranch, knowing that it would be hard to walk to since it was very rural. He went with his brothers to tell my parents that he wanted to marry me. That was in January of 1977. We were married the following month in San Luis Potosi. I thought happiness was all mine, and I was five months pregnant. Ernesto continued working at the mining company and they lent us a semi-furnished house. We were missing pots and pans to cook, and dishes to serve food on—which we ultimately acquired. Now that I had learned to cook, I relished the opportunity. I began to recall the meals my grandparents prepared. My grandmother on my dad's side was a very good cook. My mom, unfortunately, did not know how to cook. However, my grandmother cooked delicious meals and desserts, like rice pudding, flan, and many more.

In 1980, we moved to San Miguel de Allende, Guanajuato, the birthplace of my husband. We stayed for two and a half years or so. Times were difficult, however, because Ernesto earned too little money in his work, and we already had two children. Not able to make ends meet, we decided to return to the same mining company we had worked for previously. We lived there for a short time before again returning back to San Miguel de Allende. We have now been in San Miguel de Allende for over thirty years. When we returned, we returned with four children. Ernesto was still earning a lower income, so I thought about how I could help support my family. This little town was already beginning to be more touristy and there were schools emerging to teach Spanish to the many expats and visitors. Ernesto's sister knew the secretary of the Academia Hispano Americana, the first Spanish language school to open in the city in 1959. With her help, I approached the school to propose offering immersion instruction in my home. After three months, they sent me my first student, someone interested in living with a Mexican family and putting their Spanish into practice. And so it began to be, I had the beginnings of an educational program. I spent the following years receiving foreigners every month, and they all became members of my crazy Mexican family.

Our first student left such a fabulous experience in my memory, primarily because we thought she would be very different from us—we truly didn't know what to expect—but no, she was very much like us. And then Susan came for instruction and she, too, was very nice. I remember my children were very young. I also remember telling my children not to talk much, unsure of how Susan would accept the antics of our young ones. But in less than two minutes, she was already laughing with them. They fit perfectly together and talked quite a bit.

Then I remember having another student from Las Vegas who gave us a fan, the first in our lives. Then, of course, there was the student from the United States that bought us a turkey, as it was during the Thanksgiving holiday. It was a delicacy that lasted three days! This connection with students went on, with several other students giving us thoughtful gifts, and each one leaving a lasting and positive impression. Over the years, we have had students from Japan, China, Germany, Switzerland, Brazil, France, and Canada, but most were from the United States. For my family and me, these are times that we will never forget, and we never thought we would have such extraordinary experiences. For me, it has been the best. I thank them for enriching my life and my work. I also give thanks to my husband, Ernesto, for championing my efforts and for supporting our children. I am so proud that we were able to send all of our children to study at a university. For me, someone who barely received a proper education, this feeling is very moving and memorable. It is truly a great miracle of life and God that we have been so fortunate.

All of my students have become family to me. One husband and wife attended classes at Habla Hispana for four weeks in 2022. They loved San Miguel. One time the wife came without her husband and took advantage of my homestay opportunity through the school. I remember her saying many times how fabulous it was for her and how much the experience enhanced her exposure to the Spanish language. My accommodations are adequate, with a very comfortable bed in a private room, a designated bathroom, and a beautiful street view. Ernesto and I try to be good hosts and take the time to interact with all our homestay students. All ages come and stay with us, some even older like me and retired. My students often get to meet many of my family members and friends. We converse together while they are staying with us. I enjoy cooking meals for them and sometimes they help me. My cooking has improved over the years, and it is a delight to have everyone around the table together. This is quite an accomplishment for a girl that never really knew her way around a kitchen until she reached adulthood. I enjoy making chicken tortilla soup for lunch, and poached fish, chili rellenos, or chicken mole for dinner. It really depends on what I can find fresh at the market. I like to think I am the best restaurant in San Miguel!! Having great company and conversation makes me smile. Sometimes, I like to take long walks around the area with my students when they are not attending school, usually during the morning hours.

To me, there was no better place on the planet to teach than in San Miguel de Allende. The schools I have taught at are excellent at accommodating the learning needs of all people without a problem. While I no longer teach in that capacity, I very much enjoy playing house mom now. Having students stay in our home, live and feel the culture of our community and heritage, learn our language, and enjoy our food, feeds my soul. When I did teach outside the home, I enjoyed mixing instruction with experience. Tours of the city not only exposed students to our way of life and culture, but also allowed them to experience our language in practice. Habla Hispana was the last school I worked with. Located in a lovely oasis near the center of town, it has a notable reputation, serving countless students over the years. And, while many students chose my homestay option, the residence at the school is also very accommodating.

    I am so grateful for the life I have, for the family that Ernesto and I have created, for the fortitude it took for us to maintain a home and provide for our family. Hardship was a mainstay of my youth. It was something that I sometimes cursed, but later realized gave me the strength to create the life I wanted—to persevere, despite the overwhelming challenges we sometimes faced. We all have potential. The key is to realize this. I knew I enjoyed engagement with others. I knew my language well. I knew I had acquired the necessary skills I needed to cook for my family and others. And I believed that staying with the Lopez-Flores family, would not only offer exposure to the language, but an opportunity to experience our culture and the warmth of our family. My maternal sense is to take care of my family and students. I like to work hard, but I am never pressured to be someone I am not. I learned this the hard way when I was young at the ranch with my father and brother Toño.

CHAPTER NINETEEN

Jane

*M*y life, as an avid seeker of knowledge and connection, has rewarded me with amazing journeys, experiences, and encounters—so many beautiful moments of meeting remarkable people and establishing kinships, without knowing precisely why. And then, having the added honor of being invited into those individuals' lives—their sorrows and their triumphs; all of which have added greater depth and understanding to my own life.

I feel fortunate to have met Jane several years ago at a private dinner at Tattersalls in Newmarket, England. Tattersalls is a leading bloodstock auctioneer in Europe that has been in operation since 1766. Jane's husband, Jimmy—quite a cheeky and clever man—serves as Director of this notable facility, overseeing the sale of 10,000 horses annually. Our husbands have known each other for years, having met through their mutual love and involvement in horse racing. My husband, Tim, annually attends several sales at Tattersalls. On this particular occasion, I happened to tag along with Tim and opted to stay for the dinner, as guests of Jimmy and the auction house. I was happy I did.

Upon meeting Jane, I quickly discovered that there is nothing ordinary about this charming woman. Her British essence instantly drew me in, not to mention her valor and vulnerability in openly discussing the obstacles she had overcome in her life, with an unusual degree of wit and wisdom. Though our initial encounter was short-lived, as dinners are, I was left wanting more. Her unique journey—her upbringing, her marriage story, her journey to motherhood—captivated me. She has a rich, multi-dimensional personality and a fascinating family history—one deeply entrenched in the equine world. I remember feeling aligned with Jane on many levels, and elated when she agreed to my interview request two years later.

Logistics were tricky, as can often be the case when you are communicating between two continents and several time zones. At one point, I happened to be in Italy, vacationing with four generations of my family. I attempted to set up a time and place for the interview, as Jane and her family were heading home from a holiday in Sotogrande, Spain. We managed to find a window of time and it happened to be on a Group 1 racing day in Newmarket, for the Darley July Cup, which will make sense and was only natural once you delve deeper into Jane's story. Prior to the races and our scheduled interview, Jane's brother William and his charming wife, Lynda, hosted me for lunch in their garden at Phantom House, which happened to be William and Jane's childhood home. French rosé flowed, accompanying an avocado mousse with fresh, unshelled shrimp—a lovely

JANE

lunch, to say the least, and a meaningful introduction to the place where Jane grew up.

Following my lunch with William and Lynda, I visited Jane at her stately English home—the Reydon Lodge, a magnificent manor set upon a gently rolling lawn, nestled in a grove of trees. A formal, architectural garden, with geometric patterns and exquisitely pruned plantings, only proved to add to the beauty and awe of this captivating estate. After brief pleasantries, Jane and I proceeded on to her sunroom to chat. We settled into high back chairs in front of an open door that led to yet another enchanting garden. As the birds chirped in the background, Pinny, their composed black lab, and Jimmy's crafty Siamese cat, Monty, joined us. Jane is excellent at just being herself—she exudes an effortlessness that immediately draws you in; a natural charisma that welcomes connection. Her life has been a balancing act—straddling the generational pull of her family's deep roots in the world of horse training and horse racing, with her own life's journey and the challenges she faced and overcame with grace and grit.

She is a prime example of how our past does not have to be a predictor of the future, but often influences our choices; how a strong role model can buoy you in times of need; and how privilege—though respectfully honored—does not protect you from life's trials. Jane has intelligently used her experiences to inform herself and those around her about how to move forward in life with awareness, not limitations. We recreate what gives us pleasure, Jane believes. And this, I believe, is the overarching mantra that has served her so well in persevering through adversity—a difficult first marriage; a challenging journey to motherhood; and the demands of maintaining and honoring a family lineage in education and business, while retaining her own sense of self and purpose.

I boarded the plane that day reflecting on the valuable lessons we can all learn from our past, but only if we are willing to look at them objectively. Our life experiences are often filed away, with little honor given to the value they might serve in charting our future. There is much to be gleaned from past experiences, from history, from the generations that came before us if we are only willing to receive, to inquire, to learn. I have always found the antiquity and formality of England to be captivating—a sense of the past that is rich in lessons, heritage, and the legacy of family that is not equaled in the United States, simply due to our youth as a nation.

Jane's story is one of a woman whose identity is deeply woven into the rich and intricate fabric of a racing dynasty that spans generations; a story of a woman who embraced and honored her family's history—following in the footsteps of her parents and grandparents—to honor both their lineage and their homestead; and a woman who, despite her privilege, faced challenges head-on and was not deterred in building the life she always imagined.

The passing of Queen Elizabeth II made me think of my mother, Jean. It has been thirty-eight years since Mum's death. Both she and the Queen Mother were extraordinary women—serving until their very last breath. Both managed marriage, children, and grandchildren while standing at the center of their families through numerous upheavals—solid and sturdy. These two brilliant women were strong, private women in completely

JANE

different roles—one overseeing a Monarchy and very much in the public eye; and one in the private domain, keeping a watchful eye on her small community. I read how Queen Elizabeth II was a "constant in a sea of chaos." My mother, Jean, who I aspire to emulate in many ways, also had that same sense of steadiness and continuity—minus the title and crown. My mother was such a strong, capable, and compassionate woman—an amazing role model—whose presence in my life has both propelled me in good times and buoyed me in difficult ones. Holding her in the same regard as the Queen Mother seems fitting to me.

People shape us, and events ultimately shape us as well. It is the history of one's life experience—generations that set our path, people that influence our character and mindset, events that occur both in and out of our control—that guides us to the person we want to be; to create what gives us pleasure.

I was born on February 25th, 1962, at Addenbrokes, part of Cambridge University Hospital, sometime in the late evening. I grew up in Newmarket, Suffolk—an English town west of Bury St Edmunds and northeast of Cambridge—considered the birthplace and global center of thoroughbred horse racing. I had a happy childhood with two loving parents who were devoted to each other. They did not fuss over much and trained horses and the family as a team. Our lives, from as far back as I can remember, was governed by the racing calendar and horses. One of my fondest memories is of my mother feeding carrots to her favorite horses at the end of each day.

Horses have always played a pivotal role in my life, and continue to be a focal point today. Most of my extended family was involved in horse racing. The sport was that of kings when I was growing up. My great grandfather on my father's side was a racehorse trainer in Newmarket. My grandfather, Willie Jarvis, was a private trainer to King George V, and was very successful with classic winners. His wife, Isobel (nee Butters), was arguably from an even more famous racing family. She had two brothers, my great uncles Fred and Frank Butters, who were enormously successful. In addition to Isobel's family lineage, Willie also had two brothers—Jack and Basil—who were quite successful in their own right. In fact, Jack was knighted due to his success as a trainer.

My Grandfather Willie had two children, my father, Ryan, and my Aunt Bridget. My Aunt Bridget married a jockey named Bill Rickaby, continuing the family's horse-centric lineage. Sadly, my Uncle Bill was injured in a terrible car accident, not only ending his horse racing career but confining him to the care of my aunt for 17 years. My Aunt Bridget not only took wonderful care of my uncle but she became a second mother to me. As for my father, he started in the military—part of the tank regime—before segueing to horses and ultimately becoming a top-flight trainer, overseeing the careers of many fine horses. As for the lineage of the Jarvis family, neither of Willie's brothers had children. Willie's son Ryan, my father, had a son who now also has a son, so my brother and nephew continue the Jarvis lineage.

On my mum's side, the Hall family was also deeply entrenched in the horse world. They were well-known racehorse trainers (all on the flat) in Yorkshire—her father, Tom (who died young at 42, but was successful), her brother Charlie (a very well known National Hunt trainer), and the most youthful Sam (a great character and very talented trainer). My mother also had two sisters. The youngest, Sally Hall, still lives in Middleham at the family training/stud property, Brecongill, a stunning 200-

acre place right in the middle of the Yorkshire Dales. Sally only retired as a trainer three years ago, at the age of 79. She also had a successful career as an amateur jockey, prior to becoming a trainer. My brother William is sixty-two and he, too, became a horse trainer. Would he have, I often wonder, be something other than that? I somehow think not. Horses are, and have always been, the way of my family, going back generations. It's hard to imagine taking another path.

Also featured prominently in most English families, including my own, is boarding school. When I was young, it was customary for middle/upper class families to send their boys to "prep" school, at the age of eight, where they boarded during the term and had a half-term holiday and three weekends at home each term. Girls generally did not go off to boarding school as young as that, but most of my friends went around the ages of 10 or 11, often to the Junior School attached to their subsequent public school. At thirteen, children moved on to their final school until the age of eighteen. These schools are called "public" schools in England, though they are actually private and exclusive.

Personally, I loved my three years at boarding school, and my now-adult son, Rupert, adored his prep and public schools. My husband, Jimmy, and his brother, William, also enjoyed their boarding school experiences, but it is not the same for everyone. I have many male friends who absolutely hated boarding schools. I think the choice of school was often the issue. For fifty years, fathers have sent their sons to the same schools as they attended, irrespective of whether it would suit their child. My brother William went to boarding school and stayed. He did not have the additional time and influence of family as I had all those years at home, having attended a day boarding school. Things, however, have changed considerably since I was a young girl. Now parents are way more discerning. Most prefer to have their children at home (I certainly did), and there is very much a trend for weekly boarding only, as well as day schools. Cost, of course, is now a huge factor. It is approximately £35,000 for a year's term (more than $38,000); a hefty fee for most families. Our state school system, which is free of charge, provides some excellent education, but on the whole has problems. So, private instruction is still preferred for those who are lucky enough to afford it.

    Boarding schools are certainly a very time-honored English tradition, yet I am happy that the custom is evolving with the times—with more family-friendly arrangements. While it's important to honor tradition, it's also good to evolve with the times while still preserving the foundations that serve you. This is true with a lot of life experiences; having the ability to modify and reorient ways of doing things allows us to grow. It doesn't mean that we abandon our time-honored traditions, it simply means we progress them.

    Family estates, community, and time-honored traditions were all part of my growing up. A family estate—property held over generations—is held in high esteem in my family. As said earlier, it is often a family's main asset. My childhood home, Phantom House, was passed on from my parents, to be split equally between my brother and I. This was a bit unusual, as primogeniture still exists among the aristocratic families in England, to prevent the family estates from being broken up among siblings. My parents were unique in leaving Phantom House equally to my brother and I, obviously confident that we would do the right thing in keeping the estate whole. It was, after all, our family's prime holding. As William had already started his training career when my mother died (dad died seven years later), they knew his career as a trainer was already a given. While my parents certainly didn't know where my interests would land, I am proud to say that William and I have never had a cross word about any of this, and I am delighted that he is still able to train in the family yard.

Community was always important in my family. My mum was a mother to all my friends. My childhood home and the stable yard where my father trained horses—and where now my brother trains—was known as the "face of many strays and sideways." There were sons of trainers, and loads of neighborhood children that routinely visited and were always welcome in our home. My mum created continuity in the lives of many. Her openness to humanity is something she passed on to me. The value of having a proper friend— one you can tell everything—was instilled in me at a very young age. My childhood mate, George, who is literally a week younger than me, lived next door to us for thirty-five years. George's father, also a racehorse trainer, trained at a newer yard (Kremlin Stables) next to where I lived growing up. And, community in the form of the family unit was equally honored. My father could come across as gruff, but he was truly a teddy bear, and valued family above all. Despite the long hours and physical work required in training horses, our family meals were always taken together, even lunchtime—one p.m. sharp, in the dining room.

While both my parents were very instrumental in my life, my mum was the one that truly shaped many of my adult priorities. In hindsight, she was instrumental in getting me to obtain my secretarial certification, during which time I lived in Cambridge and had a great time. After the course, I got a temporary job at the International Racing Bureau (IRB). On one particular weekend, I had the choice of attending the Prix de l'Arc de Triomphe, a Group 1 flat horse race, or starting university. I opted for the race, which began my career at IRB—at the forefront of international thoroughbred racing. For over forty years, the business has provided valuable services and amenities to racing organizations, racecourses, trainers, owners, breeders, and media outlets. This decision officially marked the beginning of my own career in the horse arena!

Life often takes one in different directions—no need to repeat the past, only to understand it, I say. At twenty-four—after only knowing one another for three months—I married a top-class jockey who had a way with words. My family was not very happy about my choice. At thirty-six years old, Tony was not only charismatic, he was also deeply flawed. Initially, I discounted his flaws as I was fascinated with the lifestyle. I simply pretended not to notice, until the situation was just too apparent to continue pretending. I dealt with Tony's alcoholism for eight years, which then manifested into clinical depression. My mum had passed two years after I married Tony, which was a tremendous blow to me as she was truly my rock. It was hard to fathom not having her guidance and wisdom at one of the most difficult times in my life. My dad's sister, Aunt Bridget, was instrumental in helping me heal. Aunt Bridget and her mature, emotional wisdom helped me get along. I learned to flow with the contrast of life's storm instead of fighting against it. Both Aunt Bridget and Mum were powerful emblems for my advancement. They each achieved this intricate interplay of being soft and strong. Mum was precisely the same size and height as me—and I am told I look like her. However, she had darker hair than me and brown eyes. She was very much a people's person and was very well-liked. When she died, there were 500 people at her funeral, from all parts of her life, which was pretty special.

I detail all this simply to convey how instrumental these women were in getting me through this time. I managed to continue my career aspirations, ultimately being made Director at the IRB, at the age of twenty-eight. (I now own a third of the business.) Things with Tony, however, did not improve and we ultimately divorced. He had been on a self-destructive mission and was unraveling when we moved to Hong Kong for a short stint while he was still racing. I remember him dovetailing and drinking brandy at 11 a.m. before he had to ride. These were hard times. The resilience of youth, and the strength I took from my mother and Aunt Bridget, helped me cope with the mental abuse I endured. Sadly, Tony took his life just six months after his own brother had committed suicide.

My life began anew when I married Jimmy, who I met through my dear friend Lizzie. She is, to this day, bonkers and I adore her. I can't stand pompous people. And Lizzie, like all my friends, is cheerful and kind. We are people that can laugh at our own foibles. I wanted these same characteristics in a husband, a life partner, and I found them in Jimmy. I was initially unsure if I wanted children, until I thought about my mother and her influence on my life. Jimmy and I were not that worried about starting a family, believing that children would just naturally come along. After five years of marriage and no pregnancies, we decided to get some help. We opted for one round of in vitro fertilization (IVF), a 12-week period of daily injections. And one round was all it took. I'd like to believe that our initial luck was because we were so relaxed about the outcome. I will never forget when Jimmy and I were at a party and I was pretty tipsy on champagne, but I still managed to give myself the timely injection…in a porta john! Whatever the reason for our good fortune, we were thrilled.

Becoming a mum requires you to learn strengths you do not know you have, and deal with fears you do not know exist. First of all, I have twins—Rupert and Charlotte, now ages twenty-four. They are known as the "George Twins" (with George being their surname). *Double the giggles, double the grins, double the trouble if you are being blessed with twins.* They are the apple of my eye, and I cherish them. The stamina it takes to raise children, however, can leave one knackered. Children need a great deal of our attention. While I never voiced this to my mum, or even entirely to myself, the task of motherhood is daunting.

When the children were young, I returned to work straight after the six-week maternity leave. I did find that once they turned four, communicating with them was much more manageable. As soon as they started school in Newmarket, I very much wanted to be more of a stay-at-home mother—to take them to school every morning and do the pickups. Plus, all the endless arrangements that occur with young children—Charlotte with her wretched ponies, attending a plethora of shows; and Rupert playing tennis. I truly loved it all! In order to be home more, I started to work part-time with the International Racing Bureau, where I am still employed. Working part-time during those early years definitely benefitted everyone and has given me a wonderfully close relationship with the children. Today, Charlotte works for a horse racing media group, and Rupert is a horse trader for a bookmaker. So, the horse hysteria and traditions continue in our bloodlines.

Like my dear mum, I enjoy entertaining; giving supper or lunch parties hold no fear for me, primarily because I was brought up helping my mum entertain. The table she set was beautifully laid with gleaming silver and flowers. She was brilliant at Yorkshire puddings and roast beef with all the trimmings. All those memories still have such profound meaning to me; to remember not only the good times, but those that were difficult as well. For it's the memories of the ones that came before—the strength they instilled—that guide and sustain me. And it was sustenance I needed when, at the age of fifty-one, I detected a throbbing in my breast and opted to have the soreness looked at with an ultrasound, mammogram, and biopsy to follow. I remember sitting in the garden with my childhood friend and horse trainer, Edward Freeman, when the hospital called. They asked that I immediately come in, which was odd due to the late hour of the day. They diagnosed me with the exact same breast cancer my mum had; we had both taken the same "wonderdrug," Tamoxifen. As I said earlier, my mum died when I was twenty-two. I was just seventeen when she was first diagnosed with cancer. While such a difficult time, I am fortunate to say that I have been cancer-free for eight years now.

As traditions continue, five years into our marriage, Jimmy and I ended up buying Reydon Lodge, a house and garden similar in size to Phantom House, my childhood home where William lives and trains. (That home is one of the oldest training establishments in Newmarket, with seventy-five boxes/stables and a great deal more land.) Where I live now is in a quieter area of Newmarket, and oddly enough it is literally next door to my oldest and dearest childhood friend, George. His family home is Mesnil Warren, a home his grandparents had lived in. He has been my closest male friend for over fifty-six years. After University, he became a stockbroker, and later in life he became a trained psychotherapist. And now he serves as our Mayor. He has a son the same age as Rupert and they are terrific friends. And so, the pattern and traditions continue.

S.H.E.—SHARE HEAL EMPOWER

I feel fortunate for my health, for persevering through a difficult marriage, for finding my life partner, for my children, for the beauty and hard work our family has found in the "business" and love of horses, for the traditions carried down in our family through generations, and for the strength and resilience I am so fortunate to have had modeled by my mum. I am proud that my own family remains steeped in the Newmarket family fabric of horses—a tradition that has held strong for over 200 years. And I'm proud we continue that tradition… each in our own unique way.

CHAPTER TWENTY

Virginia

I met Virginia while touring the city of Madrid, in Spain. At the time, she worked for Tuk Tuk Madrid, an Eco tour company that provides tours to every corner of the city in 100% electric tuk-tuks. I set out that day, with Virginia as my guide, excited to discover more of this renowned European capital city. I was pleasantly surprised by my good fortune as I was immediately impressed by Virginia's breadth of knowledge, enthusiastic energy, and contagious intensity for life and the planet we inhabit. We cruised to many emblematic places on our route, a journey through centuries of antiquity, art, and culture. At each location, Virginia was beyond conversant. She took the information to a level of interest that not many can. I left wanting to learn more from the Royal Palace to the Prado Museum and Fountain of Neptune, which hardly happens on tours.

Along with sharing intimate details of this magnificent city, Virginia also shared her impressions of her birthplace and how her life is evolving as she maneuvers the push and pull of familial tradition, culture, and her desire for discovery and a sense of self. Her openness in discussing how we evolve and transform as individuals spoke to me, evaporating the formalities that might exist in meeting someone for the first time. It reinforced the notion that we are more alike than different, that we share many of the same fears and questions about life—about finding purpose—than the miles between us may imply.

Following the tour, Virginia insisted we visit a favorite neighborhood tavern to sample some of their many tapas—Spanish appetizers this locale is known for—and to sip their specialty vermouth—a fortified wine with gin dust—out of an old-fashioned perfume bottle. In keeping with her expertise in touring the city, Virginia was on point with this recommendation, from the giant butter bucket to the oxtail empanadas and the neon green aperitif served with gumdrops.

Virginia and I talked about how often we compare ourselves to what others are doing and why we feel it's even necessary to follow a prescribed format. This perspective is not unique to us, as I believe most people would attest. Yet, Virginia's willingness to accept the unknown as simply a part of the process of evolvement reminded me of just how important it is to authenticate yourself even if the answers are unavailable and the journey is often bumpy. Virginia shared that she is still discovering herself.

Meeting and spending time with Virginia drove home just how similar we all are in questioning our purpose in life, in examining what others expect from us or what we believe society *expects from us. Our discussion illuminated the significance of "unearthing" ourselves and being patient and kind with our journeys. That "not having the answers" to our questions is okay. This is the story of one young woman who shares the universal challenge we all face: who am I, and what is my purpose? It's a story of not having all the answers and not being sidelined by that unknown. It's about staying in the game of life, seeking answers to your questions of purpose, and adapting to what you uncover. It's about allowing yourself to acknowledge the pressures of family, culture, and society; to respect their place in your life while still striving to discover your journey, wherever it takes you.*

I am 27 years old and feel very fortunate to have amassed a number experiences that have helped to mold and shape who I am. Yet, I continue on a journey of self-discovery—one I believe most people travel, though each with our own timeline. For me, it is a journey that continues; an unearthing of self, of meaning, of value, of joy. It's a journey in search of a life that enriches my soul and grounds me in purpose.

It would be neat and tidy to have a specific set of goals you achieve at pivotal points in your life, culminating with a career, lifestyle, and locale you always dreamed of. Some people certainly carve that path, yet not all are pleased once they arrive. This realization is so profound to me; it has fueled my quest to discover who I am and what I want out of life. I don't want to fall prey to what others expect me to do or be influenced too heavily by heritage or culture, as I believe you can take those parts of you with you and should not step into a prescribed box simply because it is there.

Pivotal stages in my life have helped shape and guide me, providing insight into who I am. I believe everyone gets these nuggets along the way, and they simply have to be open to recognizing them and gathering them even when they don't feel helpful in the moment. I believe that, in time, they build upon one another, directing your journey and your sense of self.

I was born in the south of Madrid on a rainy Sunday morning, the 17th of September 1995. I am a member of the third generation in my family—my parents and both sets of grandparents having preceded me—to be born in Madrid. As such, I'm considered a "Gato," a true madrileño, a true inhabitant of Madrid. In my home city, there are many legends and stories offered to explain our history and heritage. While "Gato" translates to "cat," in English, it is a name long used to denote this third-generational distinction. There are various legends to explain the term "Gato," all slightly different, some dating back to the eleventh century, but all having to do with some story of feline-like agility—whether it was a brave soldier in the Middle Ages who adeptly climbed the fortress walls of the city with the help of only a dagger, or how the proximity of city buildings promoted agile jumping from rooftop to rooftop. All the stories conveyed a cat-like agility that birthed the term "Gato" as a fitting honorific to the extended generations of true madrileños.

While there is some disagreement as to the number of generations required to assume this title, it is commonly argued that it must be at least three generations—you, both parents, and all four grandparents born in Madrid—to be deemed a Gato. Given our globalized world, it's somewhat unusual to have multiple generations born and raised in the same city. In my family, being a Gato is significant. Perhaps it's simply the rarity of having multiple generations evolve from the same place. And given that rarity, its significance can take on a life of its own. There is a pressure to preserve identity and integrity that I feel is passed down, perhaps unwittingly—a pressure for a continuity of heritage that does not necessarily align with the natural progression of life and discovery. It is something I feel both honored and constrained by. My standing as a true madrileño is as much a factor of my identity as my upbringing, education, and life experience. I continue to assess how much each of these identity factors impacts how I chart my path in life.

Growing up, there was one public school in our neighborhood, so we were a mix of cultures, nationalities, and social positions. We lived in a small apartment which offered us everything we needed, except perhaps the space to have a pet. My parents decided it was wrong to have a dog in a place with little room to roam. Maybe this influenced my passion for discovering new places and having different experiences—the opportunity to stretch my wings a little bit more, to roam. My school offered a bit of this opportunity to discover, as each year we went on an excursion to an educational farm. I always looked forward to those trips as they were a way to escape from the day-to-day routine and co-live with our friends and colleagues in another way. Being from the city, they also allowed us to connect with nature and "manchar las manos" for a few days— get our hands dirty. I clearly remember that even at that young age, I didn't want to return home. I relished the freedom I felt in those days; clearly something that has stayed with me—that desire to get out of the routine and experience new things.

The Internet entered my life when I was around 14 years old. I started using social media to be able to connect and share different interests. I realized very quickly that learning

English would be essential to me. While I had never been passionate about grammar or particular expressions, I loved understanding, communicating, and learning from people from other parts of the world. I learned English not because I liked it, but because I needed it. While I had the privilege of going to English academies after school, what really helped me absorb the language was watching TV— series like *Lost* or *Gossip Girl*. Doing so allowed me to feel the language and see how it was expressed. That's how my passion for languages started. It was really my introduction to the Internet and the ability to connect with others—to broaden my boundaries—that I realized how beneficial being multi-lingual could be. This realization opened the door to my ability to experience other cultures, people, food, and places on a level I hadn't before experienced, but always felt I longed for.

Like so many other young people, I continued with my formal education in a fairly rote manner. Though I liked school—mainly Math, English, and History—going through the motions was really just the way to move on to the university level (something I was not excited about, but it was the path that society created for me). In Spain, the last two years of school are focused on passing a test to enter university. As the most prestigious universities are public, you need to get a specific qualification, so you must truly dedicate your efforts. I chose Media Communications as my focus, but, like many students nowadays, I felt unfulfilled. Something was missing. While I progressed well in my studies, there was a void. As a result, I decided to do a university exchange during my last year. I spent several months studying in Portugal. While I experienced many emotional phases during that short period, I always had a deep connection with myself, which I lacked while in Spain. As challenging as this experience was, I was exactly where I needed to be. It was illuminating to know that I could thrive and feel at home in this new environment. It was a nugget of insight!

Once I returned to Spain, having completed my education, I again began to experience that feeling of emptiness, of not knowing what to do in my life. There were many opportunities, but none of them seemed right for me. I didn't want to stay in an office or be economically exploited just because I was young or without experience. And then, suddenly, the opportunity of working for a tourism agency presented itself, and I started traveling around Europe. This job opened my eyes in a way I can't describe. At this point in my life, I had truly embraced a love for language and could speak four fluently—Spanish, English, Portuguese, and Italian. Being multi-lingual was especially helpful in my travels. I was often referred to as a polyglot. While I am proud and grateful to communicate in several languages, I'm not particularly fond of that term.

Passing from one country to another in Europe is relatively easy, given our close borders. As such, the opportunity to learn multiple languages is available to most Europeans. Being multi-lingual just seemed like such a natural path for me, so I don't see it as significant, but I understand how some who aren't exposed to different languages might. Language simply broadened my horizons, so to speak—to step outside of Madrid, out of Spain, and see and experience other ways of life. In my travels, I was meeting new people and visiting other countries while continuing to improve my language skills. I was challenging myself with new adventures and different ways of functioning. I felt so good—much akin to how I felt in Portugal. Only now, I was gainfully employed. It felt like I was living a dream that came true. I couldn't believe my good fortune.

Yet, like so much that challenges you to grow and to stretch, there were still fears and situations that were difficult to handle. Recognizing this was happening during my work travels, I tried to take the concerns and reframe them as having the power to provide greater insight. While it wasn't always easy, confronting and dealing with different situations allowed me to grow by leaps and bounds. I found that I was able to make adjustments as circumstances necessitated. My insecurities aided my ability to adjust as they had crafted in me an ability to read conditions and people; they heightened my power of observation. I felt I could make whatever adjustments might be required to make people feel comfortable. I truly enjoyed my job, and I know my success was due in part to my ability to adapt. Traveling requires adaptation, especially if you are dealing with clients. That's one of the greatest things about travel. It requires you to be flexible and to think on your feet. As a result, you are constantly growing, changing, improving yourself, and discovering things about yourself that you didn't know. It doesn't mean you still don't have questions. Questions about who I am and where I belong still fill my mind. But each time I pivot, adapt to a situation, solve a problem, or have a new experience, I evolve and add greater insight.

Being in the tourism industry has taught me a lot about myself and people. I am both an introvert and an extrovert—a mix of both. Sometimes I'm an extrovert, as I love talking and meeting people, but I can't keep that mood all the time. I also need time to recharge all the energy I spend. My sun sign is Virgo. It is said that the people of this sign are perfectionists and critical, but love to care for one another and focus on wellness. Perhaps my desire to connect with others honed my ability to adapt. That desire to engage with others—to form a connection—requires a give and take; a flexibility to conform or adjust to facilitate communication. It sometimes makes me feel a bit like a chameleon, in a good way. I see this trait as an asset, knowing that the core of who I am (my essence) is solid within me. An amphibian changes his skin depending on the landscape he is in. But even if he changes his color, he retains his essence. This was another insight: knowing how I enjoy engaging with others and how I need to recharge to maintain my energy.

The opportunity to travel as part of my work has indeed been magical and transformative. While continually posing questions, I'm not disillusioned with not having all the answers. I am hopeful that I will be able to formulate questions to ponder, to help me find my way. I do admit, however, that being unable to describe myself in a world full of tags can sometimes be overwhelming. Despite this, I give myself some latitude. Like scientists or researchers, posing questions helps you validate or dispel various notions to form conclusions and find answers that guide your direction and actions.

As I gained more confidence in my work and the path I was forging, COVID-19 hit. Travel was curtailed. This forced me to take a step back, stop and sit with myself, and assess my next moves. *What should I do now?* Travel had become a significant part of my life, a way of living that provided great insight into who I am and how I flourish. Because that was no longer possible, I embraced a "forced" gap year and went to Italy to live and volunteer on a sustainable farm. At the time, I expected to make some poignant discoveries about myself—epiphanies that I had yet to unearth. But no such unearthing materialized. While I loved my time in Italy, much like I enjoyed the educational farm excursions of my youth, my intuition told me that my time there was done. After a full year of intense work, I returned to Madrid and started from zero again.

I believe I had to have the experience of living and working on that farm in Italy to understand that I don't need to "find" anything because everything I need is already inside me; that essence I spoke of earlier. I learned the necessity of trusting my gut, having faith in my intuition, and not losing my energy in something that is not meant for me. It's okay to pivot. It's okay to realize that you have many interests. While attending university, I came across the term "polyvalence," which means versatility. In the business world, it describes a person who has multiple skills or can work in different areas. The term resonated with me—I love so many things that I can't choose just one. However, the word I prefer to describe a person who can develop themselves in entirely different fields is "multipotential." While I see this quality as a positive, I can also appreciate how some may find it a bit more challenging to accept, given how our world favors neat boxes. It may translate as more fickle than fabulous. Not having a neat definition of who you are or what you do is hard for many to accept.

There are familial, cultural, and/or societal pressures to define yourself—to fit into a particular slot, if not only for the purpose of giving others a context to relate to you. As a society, I think we rely too heavily on titles (lawyer, mother, wife, doctor, etc.) to define someone when the terms are truly too generic to offer any real essence of the person. The monikers simply offer an ease of classification without nuance; a simplicity of introduction, without effort or depth. While I truly understand the comfort some feel with neat and tidy boxes, for many people—myself among them—there are a world of options to discover that may or may not result in a perfect descriptor for the masses. And while I am open to my journey of self-discovery, it is definitely laden with this competing pressure to specify, to settle, to claim an identity that is universally relatable and permanent.

The idea of conforming to a particular construct—whether spoken or unspoken—is, perhaps, more difficult for my generation and those that come after me, simply due to progression. Progress—advances in technology, in transportation, etc.—opens the world to us; it beckons us to explore and discover; it propels us to seek growth and understanding of ourselves and the world around us. There are so many opportunities, and neat little boxes are rarely a fit for those who crave variety and have multiple interests.

Again, while some people pick a lane and follow it without falter or question, I genuinely believe that for many people this is not a norm. Perhaps my quest is driven by my desire not to regret seeking. *What if the path that I'm looking for is the one I am already taking? What if I only need to follow that low voice that speaks to me daily? What if I allow that voice to guide me, in its own time, in its way, without force or impatience, without outside pressure?* I try to think and act like the trees in Autumn. They lose their leaves, but they retain their structure, their true essence—the trunk that holds them to blossom later in the spring. It's okay to feel bare sometimes, to feel vulnerable or unknowing. Instead of fearing this, I see it as a season.

There are many seasons in life, many cycles. In recognizing this, I also acknowledge that while my curiosity may contribute to my not settling into something permanent, it's also who I am. And with that comes some instability, and that's okay. In Euskera (a primitive language from the north of Spain), curiosity means jakin-mina. The exact translation of this term is "the pain of knowing." That's exactly how I feel.

I have a tremendous curiosity to discover; an overwhelming thirst for knowledge. I have accepted this as something that will go along with me for the rest of my life, and that it may be painful at times.

As I continue to work to learn more about myself and what I want, I grapple less with the need to explain myself. We continue to grow and discover ourselves until we leave this world. "Knowing who we are" is a lifelong quest. I will be on this earth for a short time and don't need to do something extraordinarily remarkable to be valued. I just want to feel alive while I'm here. I will listen to Rumi, the poet, and "be like a tree and let the dead leaves drop." If I don't let the leaves drop, the new ones will not appear.

Life teaches me to let go and keep exploring who I am outside my family and community, not swayed by what others are doing—to focus on my path. I do trust life. Transformation or transition is unavoidable. I don't have it all figured out. I know that travel feeds my soul; connecting with people, speaking their language, and learning their culture, energizes me; and having multiple interests is a superpower. My family constructs are valued but will not deter me from being me. Though I tend to overthink things, I am confident in knowing that I need to keep moving forward and connecting with people who add sunshine and wisdom. My advice to my future self is to be brave and bold. I know I am loved and worthy—and the answers I seek are within me.

CHAPTER TWENTY-ONE

Charline

I met Charline, an amazing wanderlust woman with an insatiable curiosity and zest for discovery, through a mutual friend. Though nearly six years have passed since our first encounter, I still vividly recall the immediate connection I felt with her as we chatted about our visits to India and our mutual passions for learning and traveling. Charline, as I quickly discovered, was a kindred soul—adventurous and inquisitive. I was immediately taken by her commitment and perseverance in following her North Star; of not letting fear or risk of failure deter her. She welcomes the discomfort of the unknown, fully knowing that the transitions that accompany that discomfort can be illuminating and life changing.

Transitions are part of the process of living. I often forget how many we make each and every day—some so miniscule that they largely go unnoticed, and others that can give us a bit of a run for our money. Yet, transitions are what challenge us to grow, to learn, to improve—to not be static. I am definitely an advocate of transition! And so is Charline. I found that we each recognize that discovering and nurturing who we are is pivotal to our personal growth and happiness; that there is beauty and exhilaration in venturing to the unknown, with the knowledge that you will return home a transformed person. That travel, and the abundance of experiences and knowledge you return with, enhances your place of home. "Home" being the deepest level of knowing who we are as people. That welcoming transitions in our lives provides us with a better understanding of the world around us, and of ourselves.

From a relatively young age, Charline has felt the pull of faraway lands, the yearning to discover new cultures, and the desire to learn new languages. She is a seeker of knowledge, both through her travels and through formal education. Raised in Brussels, Belgium, Charline was surrounded by a love-fueled family. Her parents and grandparents instilled cultural intelligence early in her life, and in the lives of her siblings. Powerful and essential to her sense of identity, exposure to the world has illuminated her understanding of people and culture, and impacted how she interacts with all those she meets. Spending time with her again, I found that she exudes a calm and patient presence, a seemingly intrinsic quality to authentically connect with people, and a clear curiosity to learn. She sees people for who they are and what they represent—a kinship we share.

Charline and I reconnected at her home in Brussels, a charming 1910 art nouveau-style home that once served as a horse stable. It is a home she shares with her fiancé, Guillaume, their cat, Johnny, and their two chickens, Poelvoord and Pouligan—their names derived from the French word poule

CHARLINE

(chicken). It is a home filled with love, where chickens roam free in the garden and each day is welcomed with wonder. It's a beautiful setting, equally as glorious as the neighborhood we walked through to dinner, next to a wooded park and the stunning La Cambre Abbey, founded around 1196. Being in the center of Brussels with Charline filled me with clarity of why history and cultural intelligence matter, and of how education and travel can expand our minds and hearts in such a profound and meaningful manner.

Charline's commitment to learning and discovery has led her to advance her formal education and to explore as many parts of the world as possible. She pushes herself in ways that sometimes feel uncomfortable and challenging. She welcomes the unknown for she has experienced the other side of that journey, always coming out having expanded her outlook on the world, its people, and herself. Discovery is the end goal. It is the gift you receive by widening your lens on the world.

Charline is a fiancé, a daughter, a sister, a friend, an educated businesswoman, an artist, a traveler, and a mother of chickens and a cat. All these things are essential to who Charline is—titles for the various and meaningful roles she holds in her life—but it is her quest for discovery that truly defines her. Through education she has expanded her knowledge in the areas of interest that give her life meaning, and through her travels she continues to learn and to grow. Charline's penchant for discovery—through education and travel—not only moves her forward, but also helps move humanity forward due to her keen and sensitive awareness and acumen for people of all cultures. She makes every encounter matter, not only for herself, but for others as well. It is a skill she has mastered simply by virtue of having interacted with and experienced so many cultures—cultivating a deep empathy and interest in how others live.

 This is a story about one woman's love of learning and travel, and how those passions have instilled in her the beauty and importance of discovery. How discovery opens us up to a better understanding of the world and the people in it, whether you travel afar or whether you venture within your own community. There is so much to see, to learn, to draw in. So much that can enhance our lives by simply being open to it—by listening, by witnessing, by participating. The connections that are possible are limitless, the opportunities for growth and purpose are vast.

 You have to be open-minded when traveling. Getting past the fear of what we don't know is not easy. Traveling to different countries where communication may be difficult and customs are not familiar can be challenging and discomforting. As a result, travel may not be for everyone. While I certainly feel uneasy at times, I welcome that unsettled feeling for I know that the benefit I receive always outweighs that temporary sense of disquietude.

 Thus far, the journeys I have experienced are very much linked to the things I love—nature, animals, and, of course, the sun. I move around on holidays. Sitting on the beach is something I enjoy but cannot do for very long. I always feel a pull to explore. In my thirty-one years, I have been fortunate to have visited over forty countries, but there are still so many places I want to go (and places I want to go back to and see more of because I enjoyed them so much). The lure of travel is very real for me; a passion that threads throughout my family and one

I believe rooted in me at a very early age—beginning with an appreciation for language and extending to a desire to discover places, people, and cultures around the world.

With everything in life, my parent's best advice has been to *dare to do it*. I definitely took their advice to heart.

From a very early age, my parents expressed the importance of both language—the world is multilingual after all—and education. Belgium is not a large country. To offer some perspective, it is about the size of the state of Maryland in the US, or about one-third the size of the country of Portugal. Even a short excursion of several hours will land you in a different country, with a different language, and different customs. So, the logistics of where we lived definitely influenced the value that my parents placed on being multilingual. In Belgium itself, we have three national languages, so hearing multiple languages in my country is quite common. My parents insisted that we first learn to speak Dutch and English. They believed these languages were essential to securing a good job in Belgium.

In addition to the importance of being multilingual, my parents also believed in the value of a good education and took a keen interest in my studies and progress. I attended the same school in Waterloo for the first 12 years of my education, completing both my primary and secondary levels. I took the "language" option and had English, Dutch, and German classes. My parents also gave my two brothers and me as many opportunities as needed to grow up in a multilingual environment; opportunities that would assist in honing our communications in these languages—from summer camps, to travels, to extracurricular classes. In addition to annual summer camps where my brothers and I would spend two weeks immersed in either Dutch or English, I spent one semester during my 5th grade year living in the northern part of the Netherlands, in an area called Friesland. I attended a school there, in the small town of Buitenpost (6000 inhabitants), to study Dutch.

While language and education were always front and center growing up, my parents also impressed upon us the value of travel. Though often viewed as a luxury by many, my parents really promoted travel as another component of our education. It was important to them that we appreciate how other parts of the world lived—customs, rituals, living environments, etc. Having the ability to communicate multilingually was definitely viewed as being advantageous to seeking employment as we grew up, but it also served as an entrée to the world—facilitating communication and greater ease in traveling. Recognizing the import that language has to assimilating in different environments was pivotal to my interest in linguistics. My love for traveling and learning new cultures made me go the extra mile to be able to communicate when traveling, making each trip so much more impactful.

From the time that I was a small child, I have been going to Portugal on holidays with my parents. This experience provided me with a different perspective on how people outside of my sphere lived. I recall one year, early on, when my mom decided to start studying Portuguese in an effort to better communicate. I then decided to join her in her classes and, although she is far more versed in the language, my mix of Spanish and Portuguese (called Portugnol) served me well and enhanced my ability to soak in Portugal on an entirely different level. As a direct result of my experience traveling to Portugal as a child, I chose to study translation after completing my secondary education. This field of study offers a great mix of learning languages, general culture, and local cultures.

By the time I finished school in Waterloo, at age seventeen, I had learned four languages—a gift that continues to give. Instead of moving directly on to my university studies, I opted to take one year off, spending five months in California, with family and friends, to attend a local community college where I took art and architecture classes in English and Spanish. I then traveled to Guatemala as part of the World Education Program (WEP), a student exchange program dedicated to making a difference in helping young people of different cultures gain an understanding of other countries' ways of life. The WEP promotes education as a powerful tool to improve the quality of life and increase economic opportunities for people worldwide, offering social development programs. During my time in Guatemala, I spent two months immersed in a Spanish course, followed by a month of personal travel, and two months of volunteering in a school for children of the street where I taught five-year-old children in Spanish at a school called Niño Obrero, which translated means "working kids." This was a free school for kids of working parents. During my one month of personal travel, I opted for Spanish-speaking countries to continue to practice what I was learning, visiting both Belize and Costa Rica.

Living with other families during my time in Guatemala made me realize how lucky I am to have grown up with a family who provided me with everything I needed—from a secure and safe home, to education, to travel. In Guatemala, eight of us shared one bathroom, located outside with an open roof. Evening meals consisted of sliced tomatoes and one piece of flattened chicken. And, breakfasts consisted of frijoles, beans in Spanish—unfortunately, not my favorite food. I remember my host family offering me bread and strawberry jam in an effort to make me feel more at home. I still, to this day, recall how generous it was for them to make efforts to appeal to my ways as I was there to appeal to theirs. While in Guatemala, I also was involved with ARCAS, a non-profit wildlife animal protection organization addressing the causes of illegal wildlife trafficking and environmental problems. These experiences were life-changing.

I then returned to Belgium from my year away, contemplating whether to pursue Architecture or Translation at university and, ultimately, chose the latter. During my third year of obtaining my bachelor's and master's degrees in Translation and European Institutions, in English and Spanish, at the Institut Libre de Marie Haps, I did an exchange program in southern Spain. The program, called Erasmus in Europe, was in Malaga at the Universidad de Malaga. It was an exchange program for translation. Having the ability to speak Spanish certainly added an extra sparkle to the experience. I also had the opportunity to participate in a three-month internship program at Omega Pharma in Bellerose, Australia, learning about market analysis, advertising campaigns, translation, and customer service. I relished the sunshine, as the weather in Belgium can get gloomy.

My globetrotting continued after I finished my degree in June of that year. I traveled to Indonesia for the summer, and then back to California with a friend who was starting school at the University of California, Berkeley. While in the Golden State, I shared time with our family friends, the Jensen's, and left with an offer from Don Jensen to come work at his engineering firm. I was thankful for the offer but asked to postpone the opportunity for one year, as I had just registered for a master's in Business Management. As it turned out, starting my master's program in Oxford was not my cup of English tea so I returned to Belgium to complete the same degree at ICHEC–Brussels Management School where I received a Complementary Master's in Economics and Management in one year. Upon completion of my studies, I contacted Don to check if the offer to work for him was still on and, in January 2016, began the process of obtaining a US working visa. As fate would have it, this is the same time that Guillaume entered my life. I had met Guillaume at a friend's party. He is pure kindness. I always appreciated how easygoing he was; how witty and wise. Truth be told, I found him infectious and welcomed our connection.

Being with Guillaume felt natural. His support and encouragement in my decision to work in the US for one year was wonderful. While he was not overly keen when I initially told him I was heading to the United States to work, he completely understood my desire to further my development. I absorbed many things working for Jensen Design and Engineering. It was definitely out of my comfort zone, but it was super interesting! I handled all their website management and creation, marketing support, communication with sales agencies/County offices/ architects, basic plan drafting with Autocad, logo creation, project management, and proposal writing for project submissions.

After my visa expired, I returned to Belgium and to Guillaume. I started looking for a new job and ultimately took a position with Ladbrokes, a betting and casino operator. I evolved into a brand manager and implemented above-the-line campaigns, developed websites and apps, worked in team and project management, and managed sponsorships. The company offered me two additional degrees while working, and I could not turn down the opportunity to take them. I have completed the Executive Master in Digital Marketing and Communication at SOLVAY-Brussels School of Economics and Management, together with the achievement of a Sworn Translator Certificate from UCL-Université Catholique de Louvain.

Traveling and experiencing other ways of living at such young ages really made me appreciate my own family in ways that I might not have otherwise. It is so common to take our families for granted. Yet, missing my family and witnessing other families during my travels made me take note of how fortunate I am to have my parents and my brothers. Julien is my older brother, by two years. Given our proximity in age, we grew up extremely close to one another and also very protective of each other. We always played together, even at school. Yet, we were quite different. I am bad at being alone and consider myself a people person. Julien, on the other hand, used to be super shy growing up. We were so close that when our parents announced that we would be welcoming another sibling, we weren't enthralled with the idea. Nevertheless, Felix joined our family. He was literally a live doll for my eight-year-old self. He would always be around us and was everybody's favorite when they came home. Due to our gap in age, Felix was around older people most of his life. He was also very outgoing—a trait we shared—and the smarter of the three of us. Both of my brothers are just amazing. Julien wishes he was a comic book writer, but in the meantime he is a salesperson for an IT company; and Felix is working IT in artificial intelligence (AI).

I have such fond memories of our sibling antics and family customs—customs I believe I hold in even higher regard as a result of having been fortunate to have experienced so many beautiful customs in my travels. St. Nicholas Day is especially memorable. In all houses in Belgium, on the evening of the 5th of December, children make a list of gifts they would like to receive—often pasting together collage images from children's shop magazines—and they write a letter to St. Nicholas (also referred to as Sinterklaas), saying they have been good kids and had good grades. St Nicholas is a very Belgian tradition, and traditional as well in the Netherlands and Luxembourg. My brothers and I would put our "lists" next to the fireplace, adding a beer for St. Nicholas and a carrot for his donkey. Once we were fast asleep, our parents—as all other parents were also doing—would eat the carrot (our parents leaving remnants of it everywhere) and drink the beer. Then, they would place a few gifts, chocolates, and tangerines by the fireplace—all in evidence that St. Nicholas had come and gone, leaving us with his offerings to acknowledge that we had, in deed, been good children and made good grades.

I have been lucky that we celebrate Christmas with the family skiing in the Alps every year—a little over seven hours from Brussels, by car. Even now, we still go. The five of us skiing in the Alps for a week fills me with such joy and appreciation. On most occasions, our grandparents join us, staying in the flat next door. So, every year, we have at least one week all together. My parents, Sophie and Thierry, have been married for thirty-three years and together for thirty-five. They were, and continue to be, very present in my life. Each have brought their strengths and co-parented seamlessly. They each have their activities, yet they work on projects and business together—an extraordinary alchemy. My parents have been the best support and example I could have ever hoped for.

My maternal grandparents, Marc and Hilde, will be married for sixty years. They are eighty-five years young and exemplify how I want to be at their age—robust, open-minded, and young in spirit. When I was twelve, they took the whole family to Kenya, an experience that imprinted upon me the immense diversity of culture and lifestyle that exists around the world. My grandparents were always so supportive, visiting me in the numerous countries I went to study, and encouraging me to immerse myself in translation and further my education. Travel genes have clearly been passed down several generations.

The support of my family and the experiences I gained through travel covertly instilled in me resilience and adaptability. Things happen when a situation goes awry—like flight delays, lost luggage, accommodation mix-ups, logistical snafus, and travel bugs. I've learned how you handle these challenges is key to overcoming them. I try to channel this energy into enthusiasm, instead of falling into thoughts of what can go wrong…and panic. Traveling is supposed to be fun, but it can also be taxing. I try to approach each situation calmly.

Every time I travel, I ask myself, "Is that a good idea?" I, too, have fear like everyone else. Getting out of my comfort zone is scary, but worth it given the new people I meet and experiences I acquire. Part of my personality is governed by not wanting to go back on what I say. If I say I am going to do something, I will do it! I choose to work past my fear at that moment. I do not believe that succumbing to fear helps you make shrewd and sensible decisions. This approach has worked for me. At the same time, I recognize that fear is a natural and primitive human emotion. I just don't want it to hinder my growth.

Being open to discovery, working to remain calm when difficult situations arise, and turning fear into finding solutions, have allowed me to experience so many beautiful countries, people, and cultures. The opportunity to immerse yourself in another culture gives you such valuable insight; insight that helps remove barriers that divide; insight that expands your knowledge; insight that dissolves simplistic stereotypes.

The most noteworthy country I have visited would probably be Guatemala. It was my first real trip far away to a country so different from my own. I did not know anyone there. It was also the trip where I learned the most. Culturally, Guatemala is quite different from Belgium. Yet being immersed in a culture so diverse from one's own is incredibly illuminating. I came away not only with a profound respect and appreciation for the people and practices of Guatemala, but also for my own—for the many opportunities and daily amenities we often take for granted, like running water and inside bathrooms!

I feel I'm lucky to travel and have accumulated many memorable experiences. The most recent trip that really impacted me was one I took to Yellowstone National Park. We traveled to Yellowstone right after the storms in June of 2022 that took out roads in the northern part of the park. We wondered before leaving if we had to change plans and go elsewhere, but we stuck to our strategy, making just a few changes due to certain areas not being accessible. As it turned out, a lot of travelers cancelled their plans so we were largely alone in the park, which was such an excellent and rare experience. It definitely paid off to be flexible and open to a change in plans. Seeing Yellowstone in such quiet solitude was magical.

Even traveling during less-than-optimal conditions can result in a wonderful experience. My trip to India is a perfect example. I visited during their summer, which had temperatures that hovered around 45°C (about 113°F). Given that we were backpacking through the country, the heat was extreme. It definitely made for an uncomfortable trek in an already complex country to travel. However, despite the conditions, the places we visited in India were just unique and unforgettable!

The most important lesson I have learned in my travels is that avoiding stressful situations only avoids the stress. And, avoiding stress usually means that you also avoid the experience. If I were to give into my fear, or the potential panic of a problem, I would have missed out on a lot of living. I enjoy the thrill of travel and expanding my knowledge base. I cannot begin to tell you how often my heart has pounded, my palms sweated, and my brain has gone into mental overdrive due to being faced with uncomfortable situations. When I face my fears, however, the intensity of discomfort that I experience is less than I thought it would be. The silver lining is there, whether I fail or falter. What I have learned along the way is that, in the end, the experience is going to be interesting and exciting—it always is.

There is a constant trade-off between feeling fear and allowing it to consume me. I think my way through it. Often it is the unknown that actually motivates me to move forward. I am the type of person who likes to face things head on, consider the circumstances, address the issue, and find a resolution. Plus, I am stubborn. When I decide to do something, I don't go back on what I say I am going to do. Though I have never really taken the time to think cognitively about what drives my need to discover, I believe I seek out challenges to increase my sense of well-being and improve my understanding of the world.

Pushing past my fear is a theme. So is spontaneity. I am the type who will go deep and not look back, like when I obtained my open water certification for diving. My thirst to discover is driven by an almost insatiable curiosity to take in and experience as much as life offers; something I believe is available to all of us. The opportunity to discover holds no exact form—it's simply borne of interest; that little seed of wonder that propels you. I believe the only hindrance is denying, negating, or shying away from what you feel.

I don't say this out loud, but I am artistic. I have loved drawing, experimenting, and creating since I was a kid. Traveling to unknown places and creating art is strangely satisfying. I also enjoy puttering in the garden, and just recently took up sewing. I made turquoise curtains and cushions for my fiancé's 1987 Volkswagen van! I am a strong proponent of doing, not just thinking about doing.

Two years ago, I was given the opportunity to have my artwork exhibited at a pop-up exhibition in Belgium. I was terrified to put my work on display, uncomfortable with having to establish a value for each piece, and worried about whether it would sell. I had thoughts of the shame I'd feel of having to return the artwork to my car and bring it all back home. Fortunately, a surfboard with my graphic images sold in a few hours and my sense of unease abated a bit. I then participated in a few other exhibitions, but it still remains quite a stressful experience. Art is so personal—you are judged by your work, no one else is involved in the process. That sense of exposure really opens you up to being vulnerable. Calling myself an artist is a big word as this is currently more of a hobby. Yet, it is a creative endeavor that I truly enjoy, and I am willing to sit with whatever discomfort I might feel in exposing my work because of the joy it gives me. It's so important to allow the joy you feel in something to override whatever discomfort you may feel pursuing that joy. Growing and growth are always about going beyond the uncomfortable bit to be bigger, better, and brighter than before.

 I love learning and believe it's not worth contesting the unknown. Transitions in life and how you view the world are part of the process, which I savor. As the future unfolds, I look forward to marrying my best friend on April 22, 2023, surrounded by family and friends. We will have a traditional ceremony here in Brussels and another reception the following month near Faro, Portugal, a couple of hours south of Lisbon. Ten years from now, I would love to have a family of my own and continue to nurture the next generation in both the love of travel and knowledge. Guillaume and I dream about having a small farm in Belgium. But I also wish to leave for a sunnier place by the sea. I embrace the unknown with open arms and I welcome the transitions that lay before us, knowing that the journey we share will be one we approach with a wide lens and open hearts.

 In the wise words of my parents: *dare to do it*. The gift of discovery will be your reward.

CHAPTER TWENTY-TWO

Ohafian Women Warriors

*M*y *affinity for intergenerational influence will never wane. What fascinates me is the interplay of how our familial interactions—together with learned behaviors cross-culturally—shape our lives. This last chapter highlights a remarkable group of women deeply connected to their Ohafia heritage. Specifically, it is a narrative about one particular woman, Chief Miennaya, born amongst the people of Ohafia—an Igbo town in Abia State, Nigeria—and her daughters and granddaughters. It is a story that illustrates the extraordinary impact of a solid matrilineal heritage passed down through generations, and the empowering role that education played within that lineage.*

In most African nations, it has been observed that people are highly conscious of their past. Ancestral rituals and shrines, historical epics, and extensive detailed cultural knowledge of their lineage are customary. Despite the parallel discourse that exists regarding the struggles for social mobility and economic and political power between men and women in the history of Nigeria, historians—largely dependent on oral translations—continue to enlighten us on the significance and high standing of Igbo women. According to a paper presented in the Ohio University Press, "for women, the subjective meanings of history are enshrouded in how Ohafia became matrilineal, how women determined the dominant kinship affiliation between Ohafia and its multiethnic neighbors, and how the age-grade system of the bilateral Ibibio [coastal people of southern Nigeria] enabled Ohafia women to establish powerful courts, and ancestral matriarchs."[1]

Prior to the colonial period, the ancestors of the Ohafia people were renowned as mighty warriors; its women were seen as proud, fearless, industrious protectors and stateswomen—an aspect of history that remains fundamental to the identities of Ohafia women through to the present day. And it is precisely this identity that has been foundational in Chief Miennaya's life and in how she raised her daughters—Ogbonne, Dr. Nnezi, and Chinyere—and, in turn, how these three women have raised their daughters—Dr. Ekene, Grace, and Cecilia. Each of these women has been blessed to understand the impact and power of their intergenerational identity and why it matters; each is an avid defender of the core, fierce, feminine values of their Ohafia heritage.

Chief Miennaya, also known as the educational diva, is the matriarch of this family. As I traced the kinship of the matrilineal connection within the Umu Olugu family line, I learned Chief Miennaya is the eldest in her family, which made *her the head of all Umu Olugu families in Akanu, a village in Ohafia. You may wonder how I met this tribe of warrior women.*

Several years ago, I randomly walked into Tribute Coffee Shop in the Los Angeles area, searching for an Americano. As I contemplated my order, I chatted with a woman there and discovered that she was the co-owner of the establishment. Her name is Ogbonne and I immediately found her to be extremely hospitable and friendly. We exchanged trivial talk and, within minutes, were swapping book recommendations. Though initially somewhat reserved, Ogbonne was self-assured and quick to share that she was a proud Ohafia woman, deeply connected to her heritage from Nigeria in West Africa. Our mutual excitement and energy for the wonderment of the world collided. She gave me her book <u>Be Still</u>, a collection of personal reflections. Inside were pages and pages of poetic writings, along with beautiful photographic images captured by her son, Ugochukwu. Her poetic words spoke to me, as did the delicious drink she recommended—her homemade ginger ale, tinged with a touch of spice and sweetener; as refreshing and expressive as her personality and gratefulness to God.

After encountering Ogbonne, I later recalled her saying, "all the women in my family tend to be domineering—unfortunately, or fortunately, very strong women." I remember instantly smiling at that moment as she was speaking my love language. I immediately knew that I had to learn more, that this dynamic family of women could provide a wealth of knowledge. Four years later, I gathered this assemblage of women on a lively and vibrant exchange on Zoom with the matriarch, Chief Miennaya, front and center on my screen. The bantering and sisterly love radiated—Dr. Nnezi, the second sister, played favorites and shared her sisters' strengths through storytelling.

The lighthearted interactions between this spirited group of women were nothing short of phenomenal. I felt fortunate to have been included and coveted their intimacy.

In African ancestry, truth matters—a belief I have come to accept after sharing time and interviewing each of these women. I learned that being oriented toward our past often gives us more profound gratitude and reverence for our ancestry, and a greater understanding of how crucial our heritage is to the formation of our character. Each of the women in this family considers herself a "freedom fighter," raised to be definitive and forthright, each acutely aware of her cultural inheritance and the empowerment of education. And each mindful and extremely thankful for the influence and guidance of her family.

The ancestors of Chief Miennaya's family were fighters, feared (rightfully so), and respected. The overall family formula of the Igbo tribe from Ohafia is simple: honor and do whatever it takes to complete a mission to earn respect within your tribe. As history attests, an Ohafia man was not deemed a "man" until he came home from battle with a bleeding head. Upon completion of this act, a symbolic red hat was awarded to signify his accomplishment. In recent years, these red, white, and black striped caps have been given to people (women included) in recognition of having accomplished incredible feats. For example, in honor of her becoming one of the first female professors of the Akanu Ohafia people, this hat was presented to Dr. Nnezi and Ogbonne's daughter, Dr. Ekene, who was the first in her extended family to become a medical doctor. I also learned that the mother of Chief Miennaya, Mrs. Ezi Kalu, received her red hat posthumously, and that the red hat now symbolizes the Igbo people at large, not just Ohafia people.

OHAFIAN WOMEN WARRIORS

The social identities of all three of Chief Miennaya's daughters were formed by watching their mother interact with their highly visible father, the late Chief Ochea Uduma Ikpa. As Nigerian ambassador to Sudan, Spain, and Equatorial Guinea, the Chief's work took the family to many locales, resulting in all three of his daughters being born in different places, as were their three male siblings. Despite his elevated stance in the community and his representation as Ambassador, Chief Ochea Uduma Ikpa supported his wife and her dedicated efforts toward greater and greater advancement in education; a stance counter to that of most men of his standing and their views regarding the responsibilities that women had to their families and homes. Going against cultural norms and traditions, the Chief transcended gender and bias in a culture with prescribed rules and roles.

As a reader, you will find the insights of this collective group of third-generation warrior women embedded in each section, adding to their mother's and grandmother's short story accounts. Dr. Ekene, Grace, and Cecilia's individual and collective personalities will highlight the importance of intergenerational relations and their role in families. Let it be known there is no attempt at cross-generational comparison, but rather a showcasing of interpersonal dynamics that have occurred unconsciously through lived and loved experiences.

Our identities are always in the making, with an undeniable familial influence. As a group, we felt it powerful to have Chinyere's son, Uduma, introduce his grandmother, mother, aunties, sister and cousins; and to have him close their stories. This poised young man impressed me with his verbal expressions, radiating a deep appreciation for his relatives with the desire to commemorate them. I believe the women represented below are examples of what it means to crave connection with people who genuinely respect and have your best interests at heart—representative of the sisterhood kinship so prominent in their heritage.

The intersecting factors that shape and embody each of us are integral to our educational, emotional, and social aspirations. The cultural bridges we build bring understanding and stand sturdy for years to come—across generational and gender lines.

Theirs is a story of deep familial connection, a solid cultural foundation, and the proven empowerment of women through education and role modeling.

AN INTRODUCTION FROM UDUMA
Grandson of Chief Miennaya & son of Chinyere

Allow me, as her proud grandson, to introduce an incredible teacher, my grandmother, Chief Miennaya. She is a remarkable woman who taught me so much in my life and the lives of all her children and grandchildren—from giving us the gift of the English language and the value of education, to understanding the protocol and etiquette required in addressing royals in different countries. She raised three incredible daughters: a business mogul and author (Ogbonne), a renowned architect and professor (Dr. Nnezi), and an accomplished lawyer and accountant (Chinyere). Each of Chief Miennaya's daughters has, in turn, raised three outstanding women: Dr. Ekene, Grace, and Cecelia. Three generations of greatness directly result from Chief Miennaya's strength, dedication, and love.

CHIEF MRS MIENNAYA IKPA
Matriarch

Born more than eight decades ago in the quiet, sleepy village of Akanu, Ohafia, I, Chief Mrs. Miennaya Ikpa, was labeled as a soft, seemingly unassuming young lady who excelled in the new culture of schooling the colonialists had just introduced to Nigerian rural aspects. My parents were peasants who did not go to school, but were beginning to value education like the rest of the country at that time.

Known then as Miennaya Mgbeke Egbichi, I was identified in my village as personable, friendly, and homely—not given to wild ways or partying as some of my mates were. I loved school and concentrated on getting good grades. Unfortunately, my father died quite early and the possibility of continuing my education was momentarily threatened. However, a much-beloved uncle, Udo Kalu Aja, came to my rescue. My uncle was a policeman at the time, living in the city, and very much aware of the importance of education. Udo was the half-educated younger brother of my mum and, given my father's passing, was foundational in ensuring my continued studies.

At about the same time, a suave, upwardly rising young man, Mr. Ochea Uduma Ikpa, came into my family's orbit. He had just completed his education at one of our nation's pioneer universities—a rare thing at that time! Mr. Ochea Uduma Ikpa was a man of good standing and repute. He knew members of my family, and also knew he wanted a bride! He approached my aunt, Mrs. Okpaku Imo, indicating his desire to marry me. At the time, my aunt was adamant in her objection. Like my Uncle Udo Kalu Aja, she did not want anything to deter my educational path. However, my aunt's husband, Mr. Ikeogu Imo, was a significant community leader and Mr. Ochea Uduma Ikpa's mentor and senior friend at that time. As such, Ochea had a bit of influence on both husband and wife and, before long, both began to put immense pressure on their ward (me!) to accept the marriage proposal from Ochea, considered by many to be a superb prospect. As my father had passed, Ochea "carried wine" to my Uncle Udo Kalu Aja, indicating his desire to marry me. My uncle listened carefully but told young Ochea that he intended to see me, his "highly intelligent niece," complete her studies at the university level, which was not the norm then. My uncle sent Ochea away, asking him to return once I had completed my studies. Though Ochea respected my uncle's wishes and went away disappointed, he surely didn't give up.

Ochea soon joined the diplomatic service of his newly independent country of Nigeria. He was assigned a posting for consular service outside of the country, thus reigniting his desire to marry before leaving. As such, he returned once more to ask for my hand in marriage. At this time, it was evident to all that Ochea was a great catch and had a bright future, so my Uncle Udo Kalu Aja accepted the wine for me, but only after exacting a significant promise from Ochea that I must go to university, despite my marriage to him. And, as he had assured my uncle he would, Ochea fulfilled this promise years later. After the arrival of our sixth child, our family was complete, and I was fortunate to attend the University of Nottingham to continue my education.

Thus, years later, I began my impactful walk with education! Apart from raising six graduates, whom I am incredibly proud of, my educational experience leaves me feeling very fortunate. This is unparalleled in many cases of women in Africa. As a young bride, I followed my husband to his consular posting in an Islamic country where women were not allowed much freedom in education. I volunteered to teach English to the wives of the embassy staff, marking a more informal start to my educational journey—though nonetheless gratifying and impactful. I taught many women over the years; the end of our instruction came only when their husbands were posted to other countries at the end of their sojourn in Sudan.

On a more formal stance, starting from the basics of teaching primary school children, I went on to become a very effective, highly sought-after lesson teacher for various ages. I accelerated from Assistant Headmistress to Headmistress—a position I held in multiple cities, as Ochea and I continued to raise our six children.

As a proud Ohafia woman with a deep understanding and reverence for the history of my sisterhood, the education of my daughters and granddaughters has always been paramount in my life—a commitment to the continuance of the "fierce" standing of Ohafia women, always. As a result of my work and dedication to education, I was acknowledged for my achievements in Aba, Abia State, Nigeria, and appointed to the position of Secretary of Education. In this role, I worked diligently to reorganize the chaotic education system and bring order, equity, and excellence to the system, until I retired several years later. Even today, I continue to teach and train my children and grandchildren; education begets empowerment! This is no more evident than in the lives of all my children and grandchildren, for the education they have all managed to achieve has empowered all of them to attain a place in life that has given them each immense joy, satisfaction, and purpose; and also buoyed them in times of challenge.

OGBONNE
Firstborn daughter

Ogbonne is an author, accomplished accountant, sought-after mentor, successful entrepreneur, and well-known consultant. She is a successful businesswoman with compassion for God and people. Though she has garnered a lifetime's worth of achievements, it is her children—whom she considers her legacy—that she takes her greatest pride in, and into whom she has poured her heart.

Two months after I turned seventeen, I was sent to school in America because I had failed to secure a place in a Nigerian university, despite being a top ten scholar out of hundreds of students every year in my secondary school.

In those days, coming to America had a bit of a stigma. One of my life lessons is that failure has its rewards. I ended up attending one of the world's most-recognized universities, the University of California, Los Angeles (UCLA) and graduated with a degree in Economics. I continued my post-graduate studies, earning my Master of Business Administration (MBA) and an accountancy license to become a Certified Public Accountant. I am a businesswoman, an investor, and an author. While incredibly proud of these achievements, being a mother and a child of God are the two things I most cherish in life.

My greatest influencers were my father and mother, who instilled an appreciation for education and excellence, sent me to the best schools, and modeled love and discipline. I believe, like my mother, that with education comes empowerment and freedom.

In my life, "being a single parent" has never been at the forefront of my mind. It was just simply how I lived. I woke up at four o'clock in the morning, prepared my children for school, dropped them off, drove 40 miles to work, did my full-time job, picked them up, prepared dinner, did homework, and repeated the same the following day. I loved and needed my children as much as they needed me.

As a parent, you discipline, praise, listen, teach, and comfort; you attend doctor visits, teacher conferences, school games, and activities. Through all of that, you must be present. You must negotiate the fine line between cuddling and discipline, all the while expressing love. I am so grateful God was present at every step in my journey. I did have moments of loneliness, uncertainties, doubts, anger, resentment, blaming, and "why me" questions. Yet, I pushed them all aside and focused on the tasks at hand. Nothing else I have done in my life has been as rewarding as raising my children. Nothing!

I have exceptional children and tell them at every opportunity I get that they are my gifts. Throughout my journey—in both obtaining the education I have, and in being the matriarch of my nuclear family—I have learned that failure is essential to growth. Whether it was failed relationships, challenging career moves, moments of uncertainty, or goals unrealized, all those experiences contributed to my life. As painful, humbling, and sometimes shameful as it might be, failure always has underlying benefits. As Nathaniel Hill said, "every adversity carries with it the seed of an equivalent or greater benefit." I always aim to find the benefit or blessing.

Many years ago, after a failed relationship that devastated me, I chose an affirmation that has served me long past the event: *I am enough*. It sounds simple but trust me, it works. Still, I did not do it alone. My brothers, their wives, and my friends were tremendous support, as was the bulk of my family in Nigeria. The ties that bind us—namely, my extended family and the foundational support threaded deeply through each generation—are pivotal to the success I have achieved in my life. My thought continually is not about surviving, but about thriving. If one focuses on surviving, that is all they get. Therefore, thrive!

DR. NNEZI
Second born daughter

Nnezi Uduma-Oluğu is a renowned architect, professor, and wonderful mentor. She has served as a role model to numerous women seeking careers in architecture and academia. Despite her own personal successes, she has always made room for her children to choose their paths. While she served as an example and role model on her own path to success, she never forced her children to adhere to her way, but instead to chart their own individual courses forward.

Despite growing up as a young girl in a middle-income family of achievers—with parents that believed in hard work, success, and excellence with no patience for gender inequality—I never thought of myself as a phenomenal woman.

With three sons and three daughters in our family, the competition amongst us siblings could be unbearable at times. This was especially the case with my two sisters, as I was sandwiched between these super brilliant girls. Ogbonne is the oldest sister, always mature beyond her years, exceptionally sharp, and a treasured mentor of mine; Chinyere is the youngest sister, somewhat impudent and super intelligent. In my younger years, I'd often refer to her as a "brat," as she was always sure to give a witty answer before I could fully form my question, often belittling me as having a "slow mind." While Chinyere may have perceived me as slow, I was really just "slower" to act, more thoughtful in my decisions, quiet, and shy. I typically would give up on things before I began them.

However, my dad, the late Ambassador Ochea Uduma Ikpa, would have none of that "quitting" business. He continually engrained in all three of us girls the importance of thinking like men. He told us there was nothing we set our minds to that we could not achieve. He was our greatest cheerleader, cheering us on and telling us that being female is not a disadvantage at all. If anything, he told us, we can outdo our male colleagues if we put our minds to it. This is something that stayed with me through adolescence, and certainly wasn't the norm in terms of how most men or fathers perceived women. Even as I approach middle age, the strength of my father's words—and those of my mother, who has always been an avid cheerleader and mentor in her own right—has given me a profound sense of empowerment. My parents' emphasis on education continues to resound in my ears, even at this stage of my life.

Getting to know God is truly what finally stripped me of my adolescent insecurities—my lack of self-esteem and feelings of being intellectually inadequate. My connection to God opened me up to greater insight and understanding of myself, leading swiftly to a series of many serendipitous landmarks in my life: achieving a First Class in Architecture; receiving a Gold Medal in Landscape Architecture during a commonwealth scholarship in Canada; being happily married with two children; achieving my dream of practicing both as an architect and landscape architect. I have also been fortunate to have lectured at a prestigious university and written two books— one on marriage, *To Leave and To Cleave,* and the other on landscape, entitled *Idyllic, Historic Landscape.* In addition, I was made a Fellow of Landscape Architecture at Society of Landscape Architects of Nigeria (SLAN) and, as of this writing, am serving a two-year post as Head of the Department of Architecture (CAA Accredited) at the University of Lagos!!! All this while enjoying countless trips to different countries for conferences and tourism!

A fun fact about me is that I love to travel, to see other countries, and to meet new people. Also, I love fashion—I like to dress and look beautiful! So much for that shy, quiet little girl. I feel incredibly fortunate to be economically sound, to have achieved a level of success that overrides any lingering sense of insecurity I had as a child. It also gladdens my heart to know I have mentored several people to be better persons—spiritually, professionally, or intellectually. I really love my children and am deeply grateful to God for finding me worthy to be their mum. Motherhood has taught me to be so much more appreciative of my own mum, in particular. I was not so close to her while growing up. Now, it is obvious that her strength and fortitude greatly influenced me in becoming the strong woman that I am today. Her influence on my children is particularly spectacular, and second to none.

None of this would have been possible without the express help of the Holy Spirit of God. He has helped me develop a close relationship with God, enabling me to live by His principles and achieve much more than I could have achieved alone. Consequently, I am surrounded by so much peace, love, and unmerited favor. I could never have achieved so much without God and my parents on my side. My parents' foundational structure—instilling the importance of our heritage and education—has been monumental in my life. Phenomenal is what my life has been like, and I am truly grateful.

CHINYERE
Third born daughter

Chinyere Okpo has spent most of her life in service to other people. Her list of accolades is endless; however, what she is admired and appreciated for most is her sense of selflessness. She is a widow who, despite her grief, raised four remarkable children. And she is a leader who has dedicated much of her time to helping her community not just grow, but flourish. To honestly, generously, and lovingly give of oneself is honorable, but nearly impossible to execute. Chinyere, however, has always had a way of making the impossible possible.

Growing up, my father taught me that being a woman gave me an advantage over everyone else. I was taught that women are focused, resilient, disciplined, full of wisdom, and can achieve whatever they set their minds to.

Well, life has given me plenty of opportunities to prove those teachings.

I grew up at a time when parents wanted their children to study only courses like medicine, law, and engineering—you get the picture. My first love, however, was education. Undoubtedly because my mom was an educator. My second love was accountancy, though I did also truly enjoy public speaking. That being said, I studied law at the behest of my parents because they believed that a foundation in law would offer me the greatest versatility. With law as my foundation, I went on to pursue an accounting degree. This is, ironically, where a bit of that versatility paid off as I was able to practice enough law to pay for my accountancy education. And today, I'm not just a proud accountant, I am also a Fellow of the Institute of Chartered Accountants of Nigeria.

Despite my academic success, life took an unfortunate turn and I was widowed before I turned thirty-five—leaving me with three rambunctious boys and a precocious girl, all between the ages of 15 months and 12 years. I had to do a mental reset about my long-held beliefs. Re-learning things I thought I knew about family and friends, work-life balance, and being the sole bread-winner. I was a father, a mother, and a friend to my children. I was also the sole disciplinarian and, for a season, had to cope with being the enemy.

Overcoming the culture of silence, I spoke with my boys (without being awkward) about the birds and the bees. And by the grace of God, my children have received the education they wanted—following their own paths in life, unhindered. They have all achieved their own goals and confidently pursued their own dreams.

In days gone by, there were times when getting up from bed was half the battle for the day. I know that I am more fortunate than most because I had a mom who moved in with me. My experience, however, propelled me to seek out and help other widows. I devoted time to working with widows, encouraging and supporting them—especially through bereavement—and assisting them to get the help they needed to get back on their feet and move on with their lives. I traveled around the country, speaking with groups and providing encouragement.

In the past five years, my focus has shifted predominantly to Lagos, where I live. It saddens me to say, however, that my work with widows did not stop life from being very unkind. I live in a country where sexual harassment is considered a joke; therefore, I have had to choose which battles to fight. I've worked in consultancy, banking, the oil industry, and I'm now back to consultancy. I lost my job at the multinational company I worked for because I was not "one of the boys." That being said, my unique qualifications in law and accountancy have held me in good stead—despite having experienced an initial period of loss and depression.

Today, my time belongs to me and I spend it not just working with widows, but with severely deprived young people—especially female children in challenging circumstances, struggling to find themselves and shake off the chains of poverty. It is gratifying to know that through this work I continue to reinforce the foundations of strength and empowerment so pivotal to the culture of the women of Ohafia.

DR. EKENECHUKWU
Granddaughter of Chief Miennaya & daughter of Ogbonne

Dr. Ekene Akabike graduated from the University of San Diego School of Medicine. She is the first medical doctor in her family, a great inspiration, and a friend. Despite her outstanding academic achievements, she is very grounded, with a heart driven to make an impactful change in her field and the will to accomplish it.

Head high, headstrong, head forward. These are words that come to mind when I think of my heritage as a descendant of Ohafia warriors. It brings a sense of pride and accomplishment to be reminded that their blood runs through mine. Their blood is the bond that binds together the generational traits of strength and resilience that I've seen throughout our family, especially in our matriarchal lineage that includes my mom, my aunts, and my grandmother.

In my personal experience, there have been many times when I have been in awe of how these generational traits reflect in the quiet dignity, perseverance, and inner peace my mom has revealed over the years, raising my brother and me by herself.

These traits she carries are now traits that my brother and I seek to emulate, imitate, and formulate in our daily lives. In this way, the blood, spirit, and character traits of a warrior tribe are passed along from generation to generation, deepening the unseen bonds that pass through our family.

GRACE
Granddaughter of Chief Miennaya & daughter of Dr. Nnezi

Grace Uduma-Oluğu continuously defines what type of woman she wants to be and what kind of lawyer she aspires to become. She believes it starts with getting to know yourself. She subscribes to taking life as it comes at you, celebrating your successes, and learning from your mistakes—essentially, to strive creatively and to define your life rather than to let your experiences define you.

I'm proud of my heritage and my bond with my grandmother, aunties, and mother. My grandmother continually inspires me to be the best version of myself. Her achievements constantly astound me, and she is always supportive.

My aunties are excellent cheerleaders, and I look up to them as they are also achievers in their chosen fields. My mom is beautiful on the inside and out and always tells me I can do more. She lovingly encourages me, and I'm so proud of her achievements. She has taught me to be bold and to speak up for myself. She is my best friend and confidant. She is the person I'm closest to, and I always want to fight with anyone who makes her the slightest bit unhappy. I'm forever grateful for all her sacrifices and selfless love. My mother is my rock, and I can't wait for her to enjoy the fruits of her labors. Someday I hope to take her on a world tour. I am so blessed to be connected to these wonderful, strong women.

CECILIA
Granddaughter of Chief Miennaya & daughter of Chinyere

Cecilia is a natural fighter, like a tigress groomed in the jungle. As such, the field of law always seemed like the most realistic career path for her. However, taking on what is expected of you is not always an easy road; it often takes a great deal of courage and strength to carry the weight of that responsibility and all it entails. Courage and strength are two traits that accurately define the "apex predator" that is this feminine dynamo.

> "a lion which is strongest among beasts,
> and turneth not away for any"[2]

Envy is often carelessly flung in the direction of my relationship with my mom. I have been a citizen of our world for twenty-six years, or maybe twenty-seven years (hey, who's counting), but I have only started to understand why in recent years. We have a dynamic that movies sell you.

Our relationship was not always la vie en rose. I raised hell in ways only one you love can, and my mother handled me in ways that I can only pray I will have the strength to conjure if I am in those same shoes. I am a mommy's girl in every sense of the phrase (don't tell me your secret, I'll let her know). More than anything, I respect and strive for the strength and capacity she has shown over the years. I have three siblings, and we can all argue with facts that we are each her favorite child. I have friends with mothers who raise their hands in conversations and declare my mother the undefeated champion of role models for mothers.

    The dictionary may disagree, but I know that the warrior is not the most experienced or the bravest; the warrior instead is one who continuously faces the battles of life when they do not feel brave and do not know if they have the strength. I see the warrior I am growing into and genuinely know that "daughters become their mothers."

    You should meet my mother. Your life will change by knowing who she is, where she comes from, and all she still gives.

    You should meet my grandmother, she raised my mom, and they have a relationship just like my mom and I do.

    Ours is a matrilineal heritage of strength, commitment to one another, and reverence for our history.

    Chief Miennaya has raised two generations of uncompromising warriors. We are proud grandchildren of Chief Miennaya and the daughters of Ogbonne, Chinyere, and Dr. Nnezi. We are women warriors with a heart of flesh, a love for people, and a passion for fighting for our beliefs—each striving to be a living legacy in our grandmother's and own mother's images.

UDUMA
Grandson of Chief Miennaya & son of Chinyere

In conclusion, it is professed in our family that to understand the daughter, one must look at the mother. And, to understand the mother, one must look at the grandmother. Three generations of greatness are what Chief Miennaya, her daughters, and her granddaughters represent. Three generations of triumph, strength, and the unquenchable resolve to carve their paths to greatness. I am tremendously proud of the women in my family. All of whom beautifully exemplify the matrilineal strength of Ohafia women, imparted by the matriarch of our family, my grandmother, Chief Miennaya.

It is difficult to replicate success, even less so to create champions repeatedly. The success that each of the women in our family has achieved is defined by her passions, her commitment to family, and the sacrifices she has made (and continues to make). The wonders that are these women are the very leaders we strive and pray for as mentors. They are the ones that tell us not the rose-colored truth, but the reality of how to create the life we want, regardless of circumstances. They continue to inspire, instill educational values, and model the importance of familial connection and cultural heritage.

They are the strong women of Ohafia!

---

[1] https://www.ohioswallow.com/extras/9780821423899_Introduction.pdf, page 22.
[2] King James Bible; an excerpt from Proverb 30:30.

ARTIST GALLERY
~Introduction~

In compiling these stories, I engaged twenty-four artists to share their work, representing the women featured in this volume. Each of twenty-three artists (including one granddaughter partnered with her grandmother's artist) were paired with a specific SHERO and asked to create a stylistic piece to visually represent the uniqueness of both the woman and her story. The work of the "twenty-fourth" artist appears on the back cover, incorporating the totality of all the SHEROs that are showcased.

Each artist's representation that follows displays a range of creative expression, emotion, and experience. The artists selected and defined their forms of visual illustration—from photography to traditional acrylic painting, to graphite pencil, digital art techniques, and more. I continue to marvel at their surprising insights and perceptions.

I applaud and celebrate these altruistic artists of all ages and abilities. Without financial compensation, each one took time out of his/her busy schedule to be a formidable part of the S.H.E. community. I extend my deepest gratitude to all the audacious participants as their artistry is a critical component in the overall impact of this book. Thank you one and all.

~ Shannon Hogan Cohen

ARTIST GALLERY

CHAPTER ONE
Rylee Hooper
~Danielle & Olivia~

The Mother-Daughter Dyad

Olivia and Danielle's story really touched me as I, too, have experienced a delicate and fragile relationship with my mother. As I was growing up, we both endured heartache and traumas beyond comprehension. At one point in time, however, I realized my mother was learning just as much as I was (if not more) about how to navigate our pains and burdens—similar to Danielle and Olivia. This realization allowed for us to come back together stronger and more compassionate than ever!

CHAPTER TWO
Michele Loftus
~Linda~

She Will Weather the Weather

After reading Linda's amazing story, I knew instantly what I wanted to create in honor of her. I painted a dancer, dancing in what could be perceived as the rain—her head back, her body strong—ready to take on whatever comes her way. This imagery resonated with me. She is a woman that has persevered through great challenge. The arch in her back, with her arms extended long over her head, is a triumphant pose; victorious and graceful.

ARTIST GALLERY

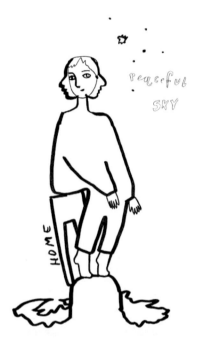

CHAPTER THREE
Alevtina Kakhidze
~Yuliya~

Peaceful Sky

Working with Yuliya's story, I visualized words as my inspiration, as words are always instrumental in my process of creating an image or piece of art. I envisioned the words "not forgetting," "not leaving," "home," and "peaceful sky." These words illustrate the emotions and hardship she faced in leaving her family and homeland, in time of war, in search of safety for her son. I've illustrated this piece in black and white, reflecting the directness and honesty of Yuliya's story—a real-life look at the impact of war.

CHAPTER FOUR
Tayla Domini Akins
~Brittany~

Tears of the Sincere and Meek

Brittany's story truly resonated with me. Her words and expressions are deeper than paper, ink, paint, and canvas. It is mourning over racial battles, bloodshed, non-reconciliation, and isolation from belonging—a type of mourning that delves into the depths of longing for correction from something higher. Thus, this illustration reveals the centuries-deep sadness felt, its connection with a higher force, and the power of sincerity.

ARTIST GALLERY

CHAPTER FIVE
Ashley Slonek
~Alix~

A Work in Progress

Alix's story brought up a lot of emotions as I have had similar struggles with addiction, mental health issues, body image, and body dysmorphia—with loving myself. Alix's truth inspired me to create this piece, as the torso represents the core of life—embodying the womb from which we are birthed, and the seat of our instincts and feelings. It is a fitting representation of the core strength she has continually tapped into in finding her way forward.

CHAPTER SIX
Bailey Gibson
~Bailey~

Pathway Into the Mind

I chose to create this work for my own story to represent the mental pathway to growing. There are many doors and pathways that trauma and your past can lead you down, and at times it can be tricky and scary to navigate. It can be hard to feel lost in your own mind, but there is always a better future ahead.

ARTIST GALLERY

CHAPTER SEVEN
Mariette Carrillo
~Sharon~

Living is an Act of Courage

Sharon's story touched my soul as it illustrates just how unpredictable life can be—sometimes beautiful and sometimes heartbreaking. Her story reinforces just how important it is to truly appreciate every moment and to value our family, friends, and surroundings. For this piece I resonated with the heart as a symbol representing pain, void, love, and the passion to feel strong emotions.

CHAPTER EIGHT
Martha Brumbaugh
~Dr. Debby~

The Franklin Square House

Debby's many leaps of faith speak to a multitude of women, myself included. Sometimes we must close our eyes and remember how to fly. In many ways, doing this artwork—after a long period of creative drought—allowed me to follow my SHERO as I leapt from my comfort zone of collage art and sculpture to return to pen and ink, a medium that I had dabbled in thirty years ago. This piece became a collaborative effort with Debby and her granddaughter—a joining of creative forces.

ARTIST GALLERY

CHAPTER EIGHT
Regina Thrash
~Dr. Debby~

In Full Bloom

I was inspired to illustrate a daisy to represent my grandmother's growth in her education, which has inspired me to work harder and know that I can achieve anything I put my mind to.

CHAPTER NINE
Brigitte Edery
~Izza~

My Buddhaful Izza

I experience my Aunt Izza as a dynamo, uplifting whatever situation she finds herself in. I chose to paint her at the center of a group of Moroccan Berber women, singing and playing tambourines (in her happy place). In her expression, there is an undeniable pleasure as she claps and dances to the music, her red dress billowing all about her. This is the Izza I love so much. She brings the party wherever she goes...and then she films and documents it!

ARTIST GALLERY

CHAPTER TEN
Peyton Zirretta
~Mia~

Perspective

I was inspired to paint this piece of Mia, as her generation represents a unique milestone—the first raised entirely in a digital world! As a young teen navigating a social media infused culture, I want the reader to get a glimpse of this world through Mia's lens. The carefree style portrays her hopeful and youthful perspective. Mia has learned that followers and views don't define who she is. She is able to focus on the "tools of her trade" and simply focus on creating content authentically.

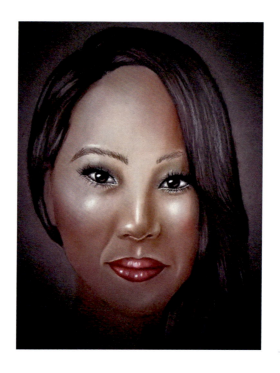

CHAPTER ELEVEN
Elise Marnell
~Tomoko~

Growing up in rural Japan, Tomoko's love of singing and early exposure to other parts of the world gave her hope that greater opportunity existed beyond her small village. This talented singer took control of her day-to-day life, and with the combination of wonder, ambition, grit, and a natural born gift, she achieved her goals. My portrait of Tomoko is intentionally simple—the focus is on her, as she drove her success. Regardless of the various obstacles she faced, she continued to take steps toward her own self-fulfillment.

ARTIST GALLERY

CHAPTER TWELVE
Charlie Comber
~Monay~

Monay is an absolute gem and an important part of my life. Beyond her captivating smile and generous heart, she is filled with laughter. Her story is very inspiring to me and I have loved watching her beautiful soul grow throughout the years. Creating this piece of art was a real honor. It was quite difficult to find the right medium because I wanted to show her colorful and bold inner beauty combined with her playful, almost shy, outer-self. I ended up completing this piece in layers—drawing in graphite, then pen, then Prismacolor marker, and then the final layers and color in Adobe Photoshop.

CHAPTER THIRTEEN
Monique Feil
~Ania~

This pose showcases the beauty of a woman's strength within, and the dedication to love yourself every day.

Self-love is a daily stand to respect our mental, physical, and spiritual well-being.

ARTIST GALLERY

CHAPTER FOURTEEN
Kayla Peake-Trautner
~Jamie~

  Upon reading Jamie's story, the first thing that came to mind was how resilient she is. It was inspiring to read about her truth—something she struggled to share for so long. I admire the level of vulnerability that comes with that. I was also impressed by Jamie's faith. As such, I felt it was important to showcase those two elements in my illustration of her.

CHAPTER FIFTEEN
Adriana Nani Kamphius
~Asha~

Mother May

My inspiration to paint comes easy with Asha, as I have known her for years. The painting depicted here is one of the pieces of art I created for a book we collaborated on, entitled *Mother May*. I feel this artwork best represents Asha's continued humanitarian efforts. The goddess image represents Asha as the guardian, and the fox represents family. She is a mother to many. Her house and heart are always open. My medium is a watercolor process, unique to me and my own style.

ARTIST GALLERY

CHAPTER SIXTEEN
Jill Baughman
~Siri~

The Walk of Life

Remaining strong and positive amid the struggles life may present is something I truly admire in people and seek in my own life as well. I felt inspired to create an image worthy of Siri's journey—one that fell into place in my mind like stepping stones. I depicted this as a lily pad pathway through a water garden; the "stepping stones" representing the two countries and cultures she loves. We can only see part of her journey because she has so much more to witness in her life, but what a beautiful life thus far.

S.H.E. SHARE HEAL EMPOWER

CHAPTER SEVENTEEN
Carson Pickett
~Jen~

The Starseed Portrait of a SHERO

Jen and I met serendipitously and immediately bonded over our shared histories of overcoming the hardships of chronic disease. The light, love, and energy she has cultivated within herself is palpable and inspiring. She embodies a strong, passionate enthusiasm for life. That is exactly the feeling I tried to capture in her Starseed Portrait. Every symbol and marking in her portrait are unique to her personal story—including her hopes, dreams, and passions in life.

ARTIST GALLERY

CHAPTER EIGHTEEN
Lula Cajigas Garcia
~Marina~

The Heart of San Miguel de Allende

Señora Marina came into my life as a result of my traveling to San Miguel de Allende to further my study of art. Staying in her home, meeting her family, and enjoying meals together made my time away from my own home and family so much easier. Her kind and welcoming nature truly radiates from her very being and that is what inspired my art. Her smile is the warmest of all!

CHAPTER NINETEEN
Barbara Smith
~Jane~

Reydon Lodge

Reading through Jane's story, my inspirational subject changed from an equestrian focus—given her family's history of horse trainers—to illustrating a woman who is joyous in having had a second chance at happiness, after the challenges she faced earlier in her life. I decided to do a graphite pencil silhouette of her gazing at her home, Reydon Lodge—reminiscent of her beloved childhood home—where she and her husband, Jimmy, have happily brought up their twins, Charlotte and Rupert.

ARTIST GALLERY

CHAPTER TWENTY
Clara Papandrea
~Virginia~

Pathway to Self-Discovery

Virginia's story really spoke to me in the way that we are all on our own journey, wondering if we're on the right path. I believe that everything in life happens for a reason and that, in time, we all end up where we are meant to be. The piece I created for Virginia's story illustrates her personal journey—one that will culminate in her finding her true calling and place; hence the light at the end of her path.

CHAPTER TWENTY-ONE
Brook Aragona
~Charline~

Like Water

After reading Charline's story, I became influenced by her life views of "going deep" and daring to be fully encapsulated by the things we hold interest in; to always pursue our dreams and goals without inhibitions. Drawing a parallel between her life views and her love of the sea—and her own ocean-themed artwork—I chose to illustrate Charline in a water setting, organically ebbing and flowing with where life takes her.

ARTIST GALLERY

CHAPTER TWENTY-TWO
Michelle Babich
~Umu Olugu Tribe~

Legacy

The power of legacy spoke to me in the Umu Olugu story. The uncle made a promise that young Miennaya would receive a proper education. And that promise was kept and passed on. While reading, I envisioned Chief Miennaya leading her daughters and granddaughters. I imagined her as the earth itself, solid beneath their feet. Her wisdom crowned upon them like the sky.

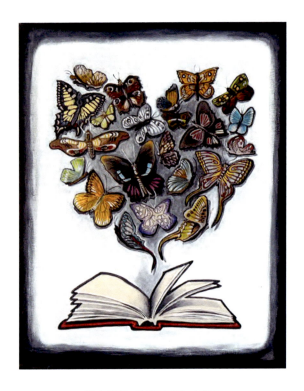

BACK COVER ART
Gretchen Belcher
~SHEROs~

The back-cover art was a meeting of the minds between Shannon and myself along a whimsical trail of happenstance. The butterflies represent the stories of twenty-two brave women who shed their souls to make this book happen.

The "butterfly effect" theory swirled in my head as I painted this piece—the idea that the flapping of butterfly wings has the ability to create a vibration so powerful that its effect can be felt without measure around the world.

ARTIST BIOGRAPHIES

Rylee Hooper
CHAPTER ONE
~Danielle & Olivia~

I was born and raised in a little suburb outside of Los Angeles, California, called Thousand Oaks. It is a place that will always be home to me, yet I've always known that I would need something more; a place that would allow me greater opportunity to spread my wings.

I grew up under a lot of chaos and hardship. In an effort to find peace, purpose, and clarity, I turned to art at an early age. It was my salvation from all the noise around me. Drawing was my biggest outlet and my greatest strength. It didn't take me long to realize that I would become an artist in one form or another. I knew I could never settle for the typical nine-to-five job. When I was twenty, I discovered the art of tattooing and ultimately went to work for a tattoo and piercing shop in Los Angeles. This experience has expanded me far beyond anything I could imagine for myself, and for that I am grateful. Never did I think I would actually end up living my dream so soon. I find that through the art of tattooing I am able to establish a unique bond with people—the process itself demands that I earn the trust of my clientele. Tattooing offers me a beautiful connection between art and humanity. All I wish to do is touch people with love and allow their visions to come to fruition.

Instagram: @ryleehooper @roseistance.tattoos

Michele Loftus
CHAPTER TWO
~Linda~

I have had a crayon, paintbrush, or pen in my hand since I was a very young girl. Growing up, I liked to create handmade gift cards for my parents' friends. There was something about creating an original piece of art, even something so small as a card, that gave me a feeling of peace, satisfaction, and accomplishment. As I grew older, I continued creating art. I went to a school that was focused on art and music. There, I played the piano and painted my days away. Today, I paint every chance I get. My children—now grown—are very good artists. When I was pregnant, I knew I would immediately introduce arts and crafts to them.

I feel very lucky to have my painting as a "filler" in my life. I rarely have moments of despair because if I start feeling out of sorts or uneasy, I will force myself to paint, sketch, or create some art. At this stage in my life, I love to create pet portraits for people because they just make people HAPPY. I also love to create large abstracts and an extensive array of other subjects. Heavy-bodied acrylics are my choice. I also love where I am today with my art because I understand the definition of subjective opinion. Painting is a part of me, hopefully forever.

Facebook: Paintings By Michele Loftus
Instagram: @artistfromsocal

ARTIST BIOGRAPHIES

Alevtina Kakhidze
CHAPTER THREE
~Yuliya~

I am a multidisciplinary artist whose practice encompasses performance, drawing, time-based media, curation, and collaborative works. My art investigates complex issues from consumerism to plant culture, and feminism to life in conflict zones. I am based in Muzychi, Ukraine, twenty-six kilometers from the city capital of Kyiv. Having grown up in the Donetsk region of Ukraine, known for coal mining, I have experienced Ukraine's abrupt and chaotic changes from the days of the USSR to the imbalanced environment after, including the undeclared war between Russia and Ukraine that is going on today.

I attended the National Academy of Fine Art and Architecture in Kyiv (1999-2004) and the Jan van Eyck Academy in the Netherlands (2004-2006). I was named the Kazimir Malevich Artist Award winner in 2008, and was the first prize winner of the Competition for Young Curators and Artists at The Center for Contemporary Art at NaUKMA in 2002, in Kyiv. I have also worked with the United Nations Tolerance Envoy in Ukraine since 2018.

Website: www.alevtinakakhidze.com
Instagram: @truealevtina

Tayla Domini Akins
CHAPTER FOUR
~Brittany~

Art seems to be a natural talent of mine, so I discontinued majoring in art while attending California State University, Fresno. Instead, I pursued a major in psychology and a minor in music. However, I loved participating in the oil, ceramic, and print block classes that I did take.

My medium of focus is oil, in which I experiment with different canvas textures. I enjoy painting on wood as was done in the Renaissance era, where I derive much inspiration. The Renaissance era is fascinating in the realm of art and in the realm of the highest potential. Many great Renaissance painters and sculptors were also philosophers, scientists, musicians, and architects. Thus, I consider myself a modern Renaissance woman, exploring my skills in art, music, psychology, language, science, and math.

Instagram: @TayAnnoDomini

ARTIST BIOGRAPHIES

Ashley Slonek
CHAPTER FIVE
~Alix~

I am very passionate about art and always have been. It's one of the main ways I have of expressing myself. Art is my happy place. I love sitting with a pencil and paper and letting my imagination take me. Charcoal or pencil sketching (on cartridge paper, which is best for dry drawing) is my preferred medium. I'm 21 years old and currently attend school at the Academy of Art University in San Francisco, majoring in visual development, hoping to one day work as a character designer. From about the ages of 16 to 20, I struggled with addiction and finding my way without depending on a substance. I am genuinely grateful for where I am today and happy to be alive and more than two years sober! I never thought I would make it to this point.

Instagram: @ashley_slonek

Bailey Gibson
CHAPTER SIX
~Bailey~

Art drew me in initially as an outlet from my life and mind. I could always focus on the latest piece and express my feelings visually. I started with mostly pencil drawings and in high school fell in love with relief printmaking. I preferred black and white works up until college and then started to experiment with paint. Art has always been a safe outlet for me and allowed me to express things that can be hard to put into words at times. While it is still a hobby for me, I try to make new pieces monthly. I have a wide range of past works, but most recently have concentrated on paintings or pencil drawings.

Email: baileygibson01@gmail.com

Mariette Carrillo
CHAPTER SEVEN
~Sharon~

I'm a binational (Tijuana/San Diego) artist with an interest in expressionism and gothic/dark art. My passion is to create art based on emotions, personal experience, and day-to-day inspiration. I'm currently a fine art student in San Diego, focusing on museum studies. I'm a fanatic of music and enjoy listening to indie, techno, and house genres.

Website: https://mariettecarrillo.myportfolio.com
Instagram: @phunktheory @phunkreature

Martha Brumbaugh
CHAPTER EIGHT
~Dr. Debby~

As an educator, writer, artist, and shaman, who has been practicing Cross-Cultural Shamanism and Earth-based Spirituality for more than five decades, I enjoy being a coach, and mentor, working with thesis and dissertation students focusing on the juncture of writing and spirit. I received my doctorate in Transformative Learning and Change from the California Institute of Integral Studies in San Francisco, California, in 2006. My doctoral dissertation, *Out of the Mists: An Organic*

ARTIST BIOGRAPHIES

Inquiry into Sacred Ways of Knowing and the Shaping of Reality, focused on the impact of cross-cultural Shamanic practices on middle-aged, middle-class women of Celtic descent. More recently, I have published articles on my own lived experience of shamanic states of consciousness. I am currently exploring the deep feminine as it connects to consciousness, and I continue to teach in the private sector and present at conferences with Debby Flickinger, Ph.D.

Regina Thrash
CHAPTER EIGHT
~Dr. Debby~

I am a thirteen-year-old artist. Choreography and photography are activities that I enjoy; in addition to loving avocados, and baking cookies and peach cobbler. I am a competitive dancer and love performing in live theater. I also enjoy drawing, which I do daily.

Brigitte Edery
CHAPTER NINE
~Izza~

People have called me an artist and a painter for a long time now. Even after all these years at my easel, I still feel that when a painting works it's not my doing. When that happens, I don't feel as if I'm really there at all. It's as if some mysterious magic has taken over.

I've painted, drawn and sculpted since I was a little girl. Now, at the age of 66, I still feel a bit awed by a white canvas.

I like to paint brand new paintings over old ones to try to give them a new chance at life. Also, I often turn the painting upside down or sideways to see it with fresh eyes. This helps me get out of my head and more into the moment.

    I grew up in New York and studied architecture and painting at Cornell and The New York Studio School, before earning my MFA from Parsons in 1984. I've exhibited at Woodstock, in New York City, and in Austin, where I currently reside. I paint almost exclusively with oil on canvas.

Instagram: @brigitteederyart

Peyton Zirretta
CHAPTER TEN
~Mia~

As a college freshman at Baylor University in Waco, Texas, I'm pursuing a BA in psychology and minoring in art—areas of study that I hope will allow me to fulfill my desire to better understand and support people. I find creating art offers such a unique way to connect with and speak to people. It is also a way in which I can offer support to those less fortunate. At present, I am donating the proceeds from my art to help support an eight-year-old girl in Indonesia, and a nine-year-old girl in Ghana. I'm tired of turning a blind eye to people in pain and want to instead run towards them in any way I can. I'm hoping I can do more as the future unfolds, perhaps allowing my buyers to select a cause of their choice to direct my proceeds to in donation.

ARTIST BIOGRAPHIES

I've always been fascinated by the world we live in. Growing up in Southern California, the breaking waves of the Pacific Ocean always captivated my attention, leaving me in wonder and search of their creator. This is when I first encountered true joy and purpose, which inspired me to begin painting. Most often I paint out of the overflow of that joy, using uplifting colors in a soft, loose, carefree style. I find art to be a healthy outlet to express all types of emotions that words often struggle to define.

Esty Store: girlinthecurlart.etsy.com
Instagram: @peytonzirretta & @girlinthecurlart

Elise Marnell
CHAPTER ELEVEN
~Tomoko~

I am an undergraduate student at Brandeis University. With my appreciation for art history, I decided to major in international studies and minor in fine art. Over the next few years, I hope to study the art that has built our modern-day civilizations. Art has always been an outlet for me in times of uncertainty. The opportunity to engulf my mind in a canvas or a piece of paper is an absolute blessing. My favorite genre is painting portraits of women. The wide spectrum of emotions that accompany living in a female body are often silenced and ignored. I hope to unmask the painful and hidden dialogue that most women endure daily as a result of men, media, etc. I cannot wait to explore the possibilities this passion of mine can bring.

Website: www.wildlyvivid.org
Instagram: @wildlyvivid & @elisemarnellart

Charles Comber
CHAPTER TWELVE
~Monay~

Ever since I can remember, I have held a deep passion for art in every form—fine art, graphic and web design, body art, plant art, music, and performing arts…. I love it all! When it comes to fine art, I'm drawn to all different mediums, with my top five being a combination of graphite, pen, marker, acrylic painting, and tattooing. My wife and I own a shop called Pinups & Needles—combining tattoos, piercings, beauty salon, fine art, apothecary, and custom apparel. We especially love spending our time in the apothecary making herbal remedies and creating new workings to assist others in their weaknesses, growth, and endeavors.

Art has given me a purpose to share with others the talents that I've been blessed with. I've been tattooing full-time for almost 17 years now and am grateful for every day that I get to go to work. My wife and I also run a burlesque troupe called The Bayside Bombshells, who we consider our chosen family. We are all LGBTQ activists and do everything we can to empower others to be their true selves.

I also have a little side business that I have run for the past 18 years, doing websites and graphic design for businesses, and a newer launch called The Ganny Project, in memory of my grandma and her mission to grow plants for others looking to venture into the gardening world. Through this project, I teach different growing and propagation methods, continuing the legacy of Ganny through love and wisdom within the plant realm.

ARTIST BIOGRAPHIES

Website: www.CharlesMemphis.com
Instagram: @charles_memphis
Facebook: @thememphisapproach
Twitter: @charles_memphis
Tumblr: charles-memphis
TikTok: Charles_memphis
Snapchat: @pinupsneedles
YouTube: @CharlesComber

Monique Feil
CHAPTER THIRTEEN
~Ania~

I have a love for natural beauty that emanates through the camera. This relationship results in images that are not just pictures, but contain emotion. I like to create a comfortable atmosphere of trust with my clients, allowing them to relax and enjoy being themselves. My passion and creativity result in unique and contemporary photography.

I have been published in many bridal and professional photography magazines and have received many international awards, such as the Kodak Award of Excellence and the WPPI Grand Award (Wedding Portrait Photography International).

Website: www.moniquefeilphotography.com

Kayla Peake-Trautner
CHAPTER FOURTEEN
~Jamie~

I own a mural and sign painting business called KP Originals, based in Saginaw, Michigan. My motto is "have fun, be weird, stand out," and it's something I try to convey in my work as a reminder to others to take a step back and honor yourself as an individual. My background is in graphic design, but after a few years of working in the industry I knew I needed to get back to a physical medium, and painting has been that outlet for me. My work is inspired by many vintage paraphernalia, such as traditional American tattoos and mid-century typography, and tends to have a feminine spin. Growing up the youngest girl with two older brothers, I think I told myself that "girly" things were wrong. At 27 years old, I am still trying to kick that ideology to the curb with my work, one canvas at a time.

Instagram: @kaylapeake_
Facebook: kaylapeakee
Website: kaylapeake.com

Adriana Nani Kamphius
CHAPTER FIFTEEN
~Asha~

I moved from my hometown in the Netherlands to America in the '60s to study alternative child rearing in communes. I raised my children in communities striving for sustainability and nonviolence. As the founder of The Waldorf School of Natural Living, I have spent my entire life (I am eighty years young!) dedicated to providing children with space in nature, where it is safe for them to play and experience the natural environment as a loving and fun part of their developmental process. My work has taken me to many places—Mt. Shasta, California; Haiti; Ashland, Oregon; Australia; and Mexico, to name a few.

For me, a natural lifestyle and a connection to Mother Earth are imperative for future generations. I am many things, but I pride myself as an artist, teacher, activist, and painter. I have many stories to share, from herding sheep on Navaho reservations to being known as the medicine woman and fairy godmother to many. I like to live my life by example. You can find me in a ten-by-ten-foot tiny home called the Moon Lodge, located completely off the grid between a beautiful golden meadow and a cedar forest.

Jill Baughman
CHAPTER SIXTEEN
~Siri~

My love of art grew as a surprise to me. From the time I was a child, I have been enthralled by music. Throughout grade school, I was in band class, playing my little heart away on the trumpet. While I intended to continue this interest of mine in high school, the music program was only being offered as an after-school class due to budget cuts. Because I needed to be home after school to help the family, I wasn't able to continue taking music. With an open period during the day that had to be filled, I signed up for beginning art with Mrs. M. She and my mom are who I thank for fostering the love I have for art today. I instantly knew I had found my passion in life and put my whole soul into it, often staying up late to paint something new to show my teacher the next day.

 I got accepted into California State University, Channel Islands, and spent the next five years learning all I could from my professors and peers. Soon after I received my Bachelors of Fine Arts degree, I began working for one of the local elementary schools where I get to teach art and other fun lessons to my class. It can be difficult, but also so rewarding working with children. Today, life can sometimes keep me from my passion, but I always come back to it with fondness whenever there is time. I hope there will be copious time for art in my future!

Website: www.jillianbaughmanart.com
Instagram: @theartistjill

Carson Pickett
CHAPTER SEVENTEEN
~Jen~

I was born and raised in a small farm town on Chicken Dinner Road. Yep, welcome to Idaho. Growing up, my passions included sports, art, and nature.

 I believe everyone is innately creative, especially as children, but not everyone continues to use it. This was certainly the case for me in college as I pursued sports and a degree in health science. Pushing myself harder than my body could handle, I developed an auto-immune condition that forced me to medically retire from college sports one year early. With that extra time on my hands, I discovered Bob Ross and headed to the craft store on a whim to purchase my first set of paints. I felt an immediate connection to painting and was grateful for the peace it offered me. As I began to embrace my creativity again, my condition began to heal. Fast forward to four years later, I am healthy, and my art has blossomed into a multi-medium career (thanks, Bob).

The creation of art is a mystical process that I believe will never be fully understood. I have learned that art is a portal of connection between the Divine and human life. What an amazing thing it is to create something that evokes different emotions in different people. The emotions I witness in reaction to my art give me even more motivation to continue connecting with this gift of creation.

I am currently pursuing my Doctorate in Naturopathic Medicine and Acupuncture, while creating art in my free time. I give credit for my health to art and natural medicine. I eventually plan to integrate the two and empower others to embrace their own creative nature. There is so much healing and self-discovery to be found in creativity. Thank you for supporting mine.

Website: www.carsonpaints.net
Instagram: @carson.paints

Lula Cajigas Garcia
CHAPTER EIGHTEEN
~Marina~

I was born and raised in Hermosillo, Mexico, located in the northwestern state of Sonora, to Manuel and Lourdes Cajigas. I was born on 01/01/01! Not surprisingly, my favorite number is one! I am the second oldest of six children, five girls and one boy—Julieta, (me,) Victoria, Isabella, Natalia, and Manuelito—ranging in age from 23 to 10. In addition to my siblings, all of whom I am very close with, I have a large extended family and feel especially fortunate to still have both sets of grandparents in my life.

From as early as elementary school, I have been drawn to nature and creativity. I have always had a strong imagination and calling to express myself through art. In 2019, I began my studies in Architecture. In an effort to broaden my exposure and knowledge of art—specifically, painting—I traveled to San Miguel de Allende in 2021, staying with Señora Marina. My time in this art community was especially gratifying and inspirational. I am so thankful to have had the opportunity to meet and stay with Señora Marina, who made me feel right at home in her home. I returned to Hermosillo excited to continue my studies and my journey in art. I feel my time in San Miguel de Allende gave me a new perspective on life. I realized that the only thing that I have for sure is the moment that I am living in—this precise moment—and that is why I want to give my best. I want to feel my work. I have found happiness in it.

Instagram: @lulagaleria @lulacajigas

Barbara Smith
CHAPTER NINETEEN
~Jane~

I have loved doing art ever since I could pick up a crayon…and, later on, a paintbrush! I have a Bachelor of Fine Arts degree that emphasizes art history, architecture, and design.... among all the other classes that a degree requires. Beyond university, I have experience creating various art forms, including ceramics, sculpture, weaving, oil painting, printmaking, and papermaking (where I started with Japanese grasses). When I travel, I now tend to zero in on contemporary art galleries—having seen the art and sculpture of antiquity for years.

Clara Papandrea
CHAPTER TWENTY
~Virginia~

Art and self-expression have always been priorities in my life. I've always loved using art to exaggerate the beauty I already see in the world. I love to use color and unique shapes, creating things I've never seen before. My favorite mediums are acrylic and crochet, but I love mixing and exploring. I'm a 20-year-old student at the University of San Francisco, working toward obtaining my teaching credentials with the ultimate goal of nurturing students' creativity!

Instagram: @claripapa

Brook Aragona
CHAPTER TWENTY-ONE
~Charline~

I am a 28-year-old, multi-disciplinary artist from San Diego, California. Art and all things crafty and creative have always been heavily prevalent in my life, but I only began seriously creating and finding my own style in 2014 while attending an art education program at San Diego State University.

I am endlessly drawing inspiration from and finding beauty in everything life has to offer. I am intrigued by all walks of life in the art world and strive to dabble in as many different crafts as this world allows. I have taken influence from having worked with painting, drawing, 3D design, ceramics, tie dying, silk screening, silver casting, jewelry making, glass fusing, multimedia, mosaic and even a little participation in theater, performing, and orchestral arts. I am constantly itching to try and work with new and different media! My work embodies my love of color and fascination with Greek mythology. But a common theme that is most prevalent in my work is the visual representation of drawing the connection between plant life, nature, and the female figure. The organic shapes and lines in nature emulate those of the female body. In my work, the soft curves of flowers and fruits mimic and complement the soft curves of the bodies of my female references. Both women and plant life provide and create life, as well as sustain growth. Marrying these two concepts with the fluidity of acrylic paint is the ultimate end goal in the work that I create.

Instagram: @brookaragona

Michelle Babich
CHAPTER TWENTY-TWO
~Umu Olugu Women~

I was a woman in my forties with an unfulfilled dream to paint. Rather than let more years go by, I simply decided to dive in. Over the past four years, I have spent countless hours in my bedroom—making messes, making many mistakes, and making some beautiful art. I am self-taught, and I work solely with oil paint on canvas. I have shown my work at Parklane Gallery in Kirkland, Washington, and I won "Best in Show" at their Winter 2022 Miniature Contest. To create makes me feel right with the world. I may have found the paintbrush a little late, but I don't plan to put it down. Follow along and watch my passion unfold.

Instagram: @paintedbybabich

Gretchen Belcher
S.H.E. BACK COVER ART
~All Twenty-Two SHEROs~

Hanging in my apartment is a still life of avocados that my father painted. I absolutely cherish that painting. His dream was to live on an avocado orchard, to have an endless supply of them to eat. And so, he did…and, we did! While I didn't eat avocados myself, growing up in his dream world was magical for me, too. Those memories and the still life he created keep me connected to what is important—to do what makes us happy.

Painting for me, I suppose, is much the same—bringing something to life. I find it most interesting when I understand the true impetus or origin of my paintings only after they're completed—sometimes even years later. Perhaps it is similar to keeping a journal and documenting thoughts. You express yourself in the moment, organically, only to look back later to grasp the true meaning and emotions that spurred your creation. Like my father manifesting an endless supply of avocados, I will manifest my visions, dreams, and emotions through my work which, along with my father's, can be found on my Instagram page.

Instagram: @bgggretchen

ACKNOWLEDGMENTS

I am humbled and honored to be sharing this second volume of *S.H.E Share Heal Empower*—a continuation of community conversation about change and personal perseverance from women tucked in different pockets of the globe; women who embody unimaginable vulnerability and courage to be fully themselves. I appreciate everyone involved (those who took part in this book and those who will read it) for coming on this journey with me. I have many people to thank, so please bear with me on round two of crowd-pandering.

Thankful, blessed, and infinitely indebted to Lorie—my fairy godmother with a sturdy magic wand—who spent countless hours working alongside me as this book took shape. With twenty-two narratives and twenty-four artists, she was an invaluable sounding board with a remarkable ability to address my incessant information sharing. Her ability to shape my words, providing thoughtful insight along the way, added profound dimension to these pages. Lorie, I will forever be grateful to you for saying YES! You are forever my girl guru! Your creative genius and support are unmatched—I hope to return the favor someday.

To my SHE conduits instrumental in connecting me with some of the SHEROs and their artists in this volume… I am so appreciative of your efforts. Special thanks to Edward, Bri, Audrey, Brittany, Paige, Sam, Gina, Jenine, Linear, Joni, Amy, Kathryn, Reagan, Karen, Cody, Esmeralda, Elise, Elisabet, Shelby, and Alexis.

I am eternally grateful to my husband, Tim, for listening to my verbal vomit—whether book-related or otherwise. You are a phenomenal partner and an equally phenomenal human! Because of you, I don't have to change who I am—a gift that continues to give and grow, just like you.

Equally grateful for my two adult sons, who both make the world a better place, and me a better mom. Ever the agents of change, you never cease to amaze me. Cody, as my front-of-the-house supporter (wearing the SHE necklace daily!), you are a naturally gifted networker. And you, Cole, managing the behind-the-scenes action on the website, are a steady and adept force in all things business-related. And perhaps best of all, the wry comicality you both possess keeps all of us giggling. I am beyond blessed to be your mother, men.

I appreciate the generous friendship and loving encouragement from my mother, Joni, who has supported me every step of the way. I am inspired by your rock-solid resilience, Mom. You are a shining example to all the SHEROs in my life—a woman who courageously shared her story, helping heal yourself and others. I respect and admire you more each and every day.

A special shout-out to my mother's husband, Richard (living proof that the third time's a charm), who eats fruity pebbles, puts chocolate on my pillow at "turndown," locates wood to ensure I have a rip-roaring fire every time I visit, is always up for a lengthy conversation while chauffeuring me around town, and truly is the most undeniably great girls' basketball coach known to man!

ACKNOWLEDGMENTS

To my two sissies, Shelby and Brittany Jo, without your sister support, shenanigans, and silly text threads, I would not be as stress-free—cheers to Far Niente wine, Sergei's fireside massages, and late-night double cheeseburgers.

I am enormously thankful to everyone I meet who helps me decode the language of life and loving, and brings new perspectives to my world. Many women and men have been deeply inspirational to my growth. While some may appear in future pages, all hold a special place in my heart.

The SHERos presented to you in this book—forty-six to be exact, comprised of twenty-two storytellers and twenty-four artists—selflessly shared their time and talents, and tolerated my badgering in making this *Volume Two* possible. I am humbled and blessed by their openness and generosity in sharing their stories and expressive art, furthering the S.H.E. Foundation's mission to share, heal, and empower themselves and others. My deepest hope is that I have honored them on these pages.

~Shannon Hogan Cohen

S.H.E.

Share • Heal • Empower™
FOUNDATION

The Share Heal Empower Foundation is dedicated to the empowerment of women of all ages and cultures. We will contribute our resources to promote positive change in the lives of women through education, and support through sponsorship. In partnership, we hope to improve the health and well-being of its recipients.

You can make a contribution online through PayPal by using the "Donate" button on the S.H.E. website:
www.sharehealempower.com

or send a check to:
Share Heal Empower Foundation
1155 Camino Del Mar, Suite 116
Del Mar, California USA 92014.

100% of all donations received will be invested in supporting women's potential, power, and possibilities.

The S.H.E. Foundation is a 501c3 nonprofit foundation. Thank you for your support!

ABOUT THE AUTHOR

Shannon Hogan Cohen has always had a special place in her heart for storytelling—from biographies and writings of life, to memoirs and obituaries. Her love of sharing stories has provided her a safe place to listen, learn, and laugh. As a freelance writer, she has been published in various media outlets—covering community and grassroots advocacy, travel literature, and personal narrative.

In addition to motherhood and marriage, two of Shannon's most gratifying endeavors included serving on the Women's Legacy Fund at the Ventura Community Foundation and starting Living Legacies Ventura County. She also worked with Camarillo Hospice for ten years.

Shannon is an advocate of women supporting women and believes stories change the world. This is her second volume of *S.H.E. Share Heal Empower.*

She lives in Del Mar, California, with her family.

Every story matters, including yours.